CLASSICAL ARCHAEOLOGY
OF GREECE

EXPERIENCE OF ARCHAEOLOGY
Series Editor: Andrew Wheatcroft

The Archaeology of the Arabian Gulf
Michael Rice

The Near East
Archaeology in the cradle of civilization
Charles Keith Maisels

CLASSICAL ARCHAEOLOGY OF GREECE

Experiences of the discipline

Michael Shanks

London and New York

First published 1996
by Routledge
11 New Fetter Lane, London EC4P 4EE

Simultaneously published in the USA and Canada
by Routledge
29 West 35th Street, New York, NY 10001

First published in paperback 1997

Typeset in Adobe Garamond by
Keystroke, Jacaranda Lodge, Wolverhampton

Printed and bound in Great Britain by
T.J. International Ltd, Padstow, Cornwall

British Library Cataloguing in Publication Data
A catalogue record for this book is available from the British Library

Library of Congress Cataloguing in Publication Data
Shanks, Michael.
Classical archaeology of Greece: experiences of the discipline / Michael Shanks.
p. cm. — (The experience of archaeology)
Includes bibliographical references and index.
1. Excavations (Archaeology)—Greece—History. 2. Greece—
Civilization—To 146 BC 3. Greece—Antiquities. 4. Archaeology—
Greece—Methodology. I. Title. II. Series.
DF78.S534 1996
938—dc20 95–9085

ISBN 0–415–08521–7 (hbk)
ISBN 0–415–17205–5 (pbk)

CONTENTS

CONTENTS

CONTENTS

LIST OF FIGURES

ACKNOWLEDGEMENTS

Peterhouse, Cambridge was an intellectual base and a home for me during the time that much of the work was done for this book. It was written when I was a member of the Centre d'Archéologie Classique, Sorbonne, and afterwards when I had moved to the Department of Archaeology, University of Wales Lampeter. Some short passages have been published in articles already. I attended an inspiring summer school at the British School at Athens in 1978; the staff and students have been supportive on the few occasions I have visited since then.

I thank the Museum of Classical Archaeology, Cambridge, for allowing me access to its photographic darkroom, and for permission to reproduce some photographs in its collection (acknowledgement is also given separately with each item). Funding is gratefully acknowledged from Routledge, the British Academy, Peterhouse, the Pantyfedwen Fund (Saint David's College, University of Wales Lampeter), and the Maison des Sciences de l'Homme, Paris.

The extract on p. 169 from *The Gaze of the Gorgon* by Tony Harrison is reprinted by kind permission of Gordon Dickenson.

Maison Suger, Paris, 1992
Tawelfan, Talsarn, 1995

AN INTRODUCTION

Here will be outlined the purpose, scope and viewpoint of this book. It is meant as a guide to a discipline and its objects. Considered will be the themes found in Classical archaeology and the questions most usually asked. A genealogy of where they come from will be provided: an inquiry into the historical and conceptual origins of the themes and questions. A rudimentary ethnography of the discipline will be attempted, describing the institutions and people and their practices. Some elements towards a social archaeology of Classical Greece will be dealt with. There is also an analysis of the discourse of Classical archaeology: an account of the writings to be found and the conditions of their production.

There are those introductory guides to Classical archaeology which narrate the Classical past of Greece in the fifth and fourth centuries BC as in a history book, describe its spectacular finds, or provide a guide to ruins and museums. This is not one of them. Much reference will be made to the historical context of the middle of the first millennium BC in the Greek world of the Mediterranean, as would be expected, but the purpose is not to provide a coherent narrative or typology of materials that archaeologists find. That can easily be found elsewhere. The focal point is the interests and energies which lead to people working upon, thinking about and making so much of the remains of times now long gone.

So this book might be profitably considered alongside historical accounts of the life and times of Classical Greece: it will work in counterpoint, and give some insight into why the discipline which deals with ancient Greece has come to look the way it does. It is also intended as an accompaniment to a book of mine (*Art and the Early Greek City State*, forthcoming) which deals with the art and archaeology of an early city state, Korinth. Both form an encounter with the discipline, with the separate work on Korinth being an attempt to work with archaeological materials in constructing an account of the past which joins others in breaking the disciplinary mould a little.

Given this, Korinth and its archaeology will be used as an illustrative focus throughout this book, exemplifying many of the general points. In this way there will hopefully be an interplay of detailed treatment of issues, which is

1

so necessary for deeper understanding, with broader strokes sketching the forms of the discipline.

For the history of receptions of the Greek past it should be pointed out here that reliance has been mostly on secondary sources, though with thorough cross-checking and reference of important opinions to original works. I am convinced of the soundness of the general stand taken and account given.

A basic aim is to further what may be termed a prehistory of the ancient Greek past. This is to shift back behind the historical accounts of this time and region, which sometimes appear so familiar, almost a façade, to attempt to defamiliarise on the grounds that what is often taken for the real past is a partial construction, in all senses of the phrase. Here is introduced the term 'metanarrative' which refers to narratives, dispositions, ideological, philosophical and methodological systems which subsume the particularities of local historical textures. All too often Classical archaeology becomes part of grander stories of art or reason or civilisation or European origins. It is important to be wary that these familiarities do not prevent the independence, difference and life of the past from answering back with a challenge to the present. A term that has been used for this is effective history.

Classical archaeology is usually taken to involve an interest in the cultural riches of the fifth and early fourth centuries BC. But it is also part of wider archaeology of Greece, which includes notably Aegean prehistory, the so-called Dark Ages and their archaeology, Hellenistic times, Roman Greece, Byzantium, and the several subsequent cultural epochs. It may be difficult to separate these methodologically in an excavation, account needing to be taken of all. Attention has also come to focus on the Dark Ages (the earliest centuries of the first millennium BC) under the proposal that they are important for understanding what comes later, and here have been made some notable advances in archaeological method and approach. The development of Aegean prehistory from the late nineteenth century is closely connected to Classical archaeology. This book also makes a philosophical case for taking full account of historical continuity. Nevertheless it will deal primarily with archaeologies of Greece from the tenth to fourth centuries BC, that is the study of the period covering the emergence and early maturity of the city state. Reference will also be made to earlier Aegean prehistory. This is the scope of the book.

In order to make the viewpoint of the book as clear as possible, it will be helpful to give some account of the personal background. The project began during seven years of teaching Classical languages and ancient history in a high school in the north-east of England during the 1980s. I had first encountered the fascinations of Classics in a traditional education, learning Latin and Greek from the age of 11. After a first degree in archaeology and anthropology, I worked as an archaeological fieldworker and draughtsman for a year before Richard Smith, of the School of Education, University of Durham, reintroduced me to the importance and potential of Classics. I owe a great deal, and more than he probably knows, to his humanism and energy.

Two authors brought my thoughts on the place of Classics and writing in contemporary culture into focus: Tony Harrison, the poet and dramatist, and the historical novelist Gore Vidal. The former I deal with in the last chapter. Here I need only say that his mediation of schooling and education, a background in a class-based, post-war Britain, and a facility for vital translation and verse represents to me a model of creative appropriation of the past. Gore Vidal's novel *Creation* is a story of one who travels from the fifth-century Athens of proto-anthropologist and historian Herodotos into the rich cultural worlds of Persia and the east. Greece and Europe, historical trajectories, and the scale of an individual's creative agency are brought into perspective.

My ideas on prehistory and matters of archaeological philosophy having taken shape in books with Christopher Tilley, whom I had met at college, I next wanted to explore the potential of a body of material for constructing different archaeologies. Classical Greece, or rather its archaic lineage, seemed an appropriate field. First because I saw how Classical studies has immense evocative power even among those pupils I was teaching, who in no way could have been said to have had a commitment to high cultural prejudices or an interest in European common heritage, both of which are frequently associated with interest in Classical Greece. They just liked the stories and gained immensely from them. Second, Classical studies seemed appropriate because the field is in many ways marginal. Archaic Greece comes between prehistory and historical archaeology; it has been the focus of anthropological, literary, philological, historical, art historical and archaeological interest, and is in this way marginal in a disciplinary sense.

I chose to study Protokorinthian pottery (a stylistic class of the late eighth and seventh century BC) because it comes between eastern stylistic influence and experiment on the part of Korinthian potters, and because the pottery has been interpreted as at the beginning of the Greek artistic miracle, at the edge of Geometric style and the Classical tradition. Edges are frequently creative areas where frictions generate clarifying controversy and debate: different sides are forced to state their position clearly. New ideas start in the gaps of old systems. I wanted to make something of this potential, exploring the new perspectives which were being developed in Classical studies and Classical archaeology, relating these to new thinking in prehistoric archaeology (particularly developments in the understanding of material culture design), and also to explore the effect of the Classical past on the present in a way that I had not been able to do with the wonderful students at my school. So I left teaching, managed to obtain funding for doctoral research, and returned to my college Peterhouse in the University of Cambridge.

There I worked with Ian Hodder in the Department of Archaeology and Anthony Snodgrass in the Museum of Classical Archaeology. Ian Hodder has come to stand for humanistic interpretation of archaeological materials with an anthropological perspective. Anthony Snodgrass has helped pioneer new archaeological approaches to Dark Age and Classical Greece, overcoming disciplinary divisions between archaeology, philology and history, and asking questions of the relation of ordinary archaeological finds (not necessarily high art or fine architectures) to historical understanding. Both have supported cross-disciplinary fertilisation of ideas for constructing social archaeologies.

French Classical studies has had a big influence on my work through its anthropological perspective; the way it seeks to make sense of ancient *mentalités*, delving beneath the surface into basic dispositions towards self and other, society and history. Getting beneath the skin is surely one of the fascinations of the archaeological, dealing with the ineffable material basis of past human experience.

Another relevant perspective is that of a body of philosophy which has been developing in a number of disciplines, including archaeology, and is often termed Constructivism. It can be summarised quite effectively with the following illustration. The remains of that late archaic cemetery lying in the ground will not speak up for themselves, will not appear on their own account. The cemetery needs to be excavated and worked upon in many different ways for it to become history. The past needs the interests of the present. Archaeological desire is the condition of the very existence of the past. This means that there can be no pure and straightforward account of the way the past was, no matter how good the evidence may be, because it always depends on people doing something with the remains of the past. The past is constructed. Some worry a great deal about such a viewpoint, thinking that if it is held that archaeologists construct the past in the present, this means that the real past, back in its own time, is compromised at the least. But to argue that archaeologists and historians make the past does not mean they make it up; it does not make the past any the less real, does not mean that archaeologists spoil the past with their interests. A television set is manufactured, but few people get worried about whether the black box sitting in the corner is real or not; the important questions are whether it works and how people get on with it.

The book thus follows the argument that the past is not simply discovered in archaeological remains. Archaeologists deal with source materials and these require interpretation. How interpretation proceeds depends upon amount of evidence, the ideas and preconceptions of the archaeologist, their interests and aims. And, of course, interpretations differ and change. This is the experience of archaeology: not a set of static images of a past gone by, but a process of detection and supposition, following connections, constructing plausibilities forever rooted in uncertainty. Archaeologists do not discover the past but take shattered remains and make something of them. This is what makes archaeology so fascinating, and it is with this that the book attempts to deal.

More so Classical archaeology, because the history of Classical studies and its archaeological subdiscipline, with their relationships to the cultural dispositions of Classicism and Hellenism, their cultural politics and evocations which run through the social imaginary, form a deep and richly textured genealogy. Within are conjoined history and definitions of national and European identity, measures or standards of cultural excellence. The Classical past is a foreign country that many people have wanted to visit and make their own.

There is thus in the book an interest in sources and an emphasis upon source criticism. But sources are not held in a traditional sense to lead to the past, if the scholar is sufficiently critical. The independence and irreducibility of sources is stressed. The remains of the Classical past are decayed ruins; they are not to be seen primarily as 'expressions' of something else (such as a Greek spirit, or the social practices of the fifth century BC). Our sources, material and ruined, are both partial and indeed not identical with 'the past'. The ruins of the past are *resources* with which knowledges may be constructed by archaeologists, historians and indeed anyone with the interest and energy to acquire the necessary skills.

So this is a book about Classical archaeology from someone who has taken an unorthodox route into the subject and is as much interested in the reception of the remains of Classical Greece as in stories of what happened in some hectic centuries of the first millennium BC in a sunny country at the margins of some great eastern empires. It is a viewpoint from a social archaeologist who has moved from prehistory to study Greek materials, and who has learned from approaches to material culture taken elsewhere, accepting that a significant aim is to reconstruct and understand the social context of material things, rather than stopping at their inventory, dating, classification and admiration. That this is something of a marginal view of Classical archaeology is proposed as a strength, because people looking in from the outside often see things of great value and importance which those on the inside have overlooked or forgotten.

It is claimed that no apologies are necessary for such a personal, committed, incomplete and provisional viewpoint. If the above arguments are accepted, there is a need for archaeologists and others to take responsibility for the knowledges they construct; they should not hide behind ideas such as objectivity, the way things really were. This is being more and more accepted in world archaeology in the context of different types of interest and claims on the archaeological past. A native American nation may have a very different claim on the remains of its past as compared with an academic anthropologist. The former's spiritual traditions and interests may contrast markedly with the scientific aspirations of the latter. There is a strong ethical argument for resolving differences of claim by recognising the right to have different interests, based upon the past being a multiplicity rather than a singularity. There was no one particular past, nor was there ever, even in its own present (to appreciate this, simply try to answer the question 'What is happening now?' – there is no one answer).

It may be noted that the book is stressing relationships between archaeology and history. This, of course, is not at all new, but with the rise of anthropological archaeology in the 1960s, the initiative in archaeological thinking passed to prehistorians and others who wished to escape what was seen as naïve descriptive historical narrative. The task was to develop generalising knowledges (for example relating the remains of a particular society to a set of relationships commonly found at a certain phase of cultural evolution, or relating them to variables of relationship between society and environment). Other archaeologists assumed the disciplinary highground by claiming that historical archaeology was easy because of written records, and that the proof of new approaches needed to be found in prehistoric case studies. Now there is increasing interest in modes of historical narrative which has accompanied criticisms that the aim of explaining a particular event in the past by subsuming it beneath some general social process may often be inappropriate and miss a full understanding. Critical historical archaeology in the United States has produced some fine examples of interpretation which escape this (false) polarisation of approaches into anthropological and generalising or scientific, and those that are historical and particularist. The interpretations of early colonial America via its material culture immediately come to mind. I suggest that a historical archaeology (stressing the links between archaeological and historical projects) does not depend upon the existence of written sources. Another aim of this book is to help show how this can be so.

It is therefore an appropriate time for a guide such as this: the interpretive (a word which summarises what has been outlined above) and historical character of archaeology generally is being more widely accepted; foregrounded is the relationship between past and present, as in heritage interests. Also approaches in Classical archaeology and Classical studies are developing readings that challenge or refresh traditional and entrenched accounts. A guide shows the way forward as well as back. This book is intended as an introduction for the future, providing a set of tools and observations for others to make something of the discipline for themselves.

In this increasingly interdisciplinary field it is not appropriate to assume specialist knowledge of the reader: the book is written for anyone who shares a fascination with the material traces of those who created and lived in the city states of Greece and who wishes to understand what archaeologists and others make of them.

Chapter 1 is anecdotal in character, aiming to give impressions and flavours of the discipline. The intention is to show the intersection of an extraordinarily varied assemblage of experiences and cultural themes. The word *poikilos* (many-coloured, changing and ambiguous) captures this density, which is also, I believe, the reason for the cultural power of the Classical – this is the resonance.

Chapter 2 deals with the standard art histories and approaches to style. Connoisseurship, typology and iconology are considered in some detail and an interlude on the methods of the Classical archaeologist as detective looks forward to later discussions of the sources with which archaeologists deal and the methods appropriate to a historical understanding of them. The nineteenth-century museum collections and aims of the big excavations are also covered.

The interests and ideologies which have constituted the Classical archaeology of Greece are the subject of Chapter 3. Brief histories of antiquarians and travellers introduce some root metaphors of the discipline (philological and scientific aims). A main topic is Hellenism, an ideological complex which can be traced through Winckelmann and the cultural movements of Classicism and Romanticism, with related matters of taste and German scholarship. That ancient Greek artefacts may be classed as high art is partly examined here through the work of Michael Vickers and David Gill. Other ideological contexts are tourism, modernity and metanarratives of European origin. Bernal's critique *Black Athena* is brought in. Overall the chapter is one of the cultural politics of Classical archaeology in historical perspective, sketching constituting interests.

Interest leads to discourse. With the proposition that the past cannot be understood without considering the present, Chapter 4 moves to provide the tools for an analysis of the discourse of Classical archaeology: its practices, practitioners and products. The context is the branch of the sociology of knowledge mentioned above: Constructivism.

Chapters 5 and 6 together develop some elements which could be held to lie behind a project which aims to use archaeological remains to reconstruct society. Emphasis is on contextual analysis and the mediation of broad social modelling with an attention to the textures of everyday life. Style and approaches to material culture feature prominently, while there is a running commentary on the character of archaeological sources. The purpose is not to provide a programme of research but to consider from where a social archaeology of Classical Greece might come.

The final chapter develops the case for a Classical archaeology conceived as effective history. The discussions about the character of archaeological sources, constituting interests in a study of the Classical past, and relationships between Greek past and 'European' present are drawn upon to argue for pluralism and provisionality, shifting ground and perspective to avoid the petrifying gaze of ideological systems.

An important note about quotes, references and bibliography

I have not considered it worthwhile to overburden the text with referencing, because it would be out of keeping with the purpose of the book as outlined above. There are many reasons for quoting and citing references, and some points about this and other matters of academic writing are discussed in Chapter 4. I quote simply to illustrate, not to call in authorities. In all cases there are many other passages I could have used as illustration, so the reader should not be concerned about following up literatures from the quotes in the main body of text, which is meant to present a flow of ideas. For routes into the discipline the reader is directed to the bibliography at the end of the book. Some remarks about using the bibliography will be found at its beginning.

1

A SEARCH FOR SOURCES

Through the village of Anaploga the road becomes a track that takes you into one of the shallow ravines that divided up the ancient city of Korinth. Off to the left and westwards, skirting a field and grove of citrus trees (where must have been found the burials of the Geometric period I had been told about), brings you to the site of the American excavations. The publications from 1948 deal with what they call the Potters' Quarter. It was here that the Korinthians produced many of the ceramic wares which, in their seventh and sixth century BC heyday, travelled right across the Mediterranean Greek world.

It was the spring of 1991. Wild flowers were everywhere. Hellmut Baumann's pleasant little book (1981) *Die griechische Pfanzenwelt in Mythos, Kunst und Literatur* [Greek Wild Flowers and Plantlore in Myth, Art and Literature] tells all about the connections between many of the 6,000 native species and ancient Greeks. I was sure I found a species of larkspur, *Consolida Ajacis*, called Aias, after the hero at Troy. The story goes that after the death of Achilles, Aias and Odysseus quarrelled over his armour and weaponry, forged by Hephaistos. Aias won the argument, but Athena forced him to cede them to Odysseus. Driven mad at the affront, he committed suicide, falling on his sword. The Roman poet Ovid, in his *Metamorphoses*, tells of the transformation of his blood into a flower inscribed with the letters AI, the cry of anguish and mourning, the first letters of the hero's name. And sure enough, the letter A, flanked both sides by the letter I, can be seen on the purple petals. A drawing on a tiny ceramic perfume jar, now in a museum in Berlin, is considered by some to be the earliest depiction of the story.

I was in Greece as part of my research into these pots, made in ancient Korinth in the seventh century BC. Technically termed Protokorinthian, they are part of various changes in Greek society and culture, times of the early city states and when many ideas were being borrowed from eastern design; hence the term *Orientalising* art. The perfume jars (aryballoi) are covered in tiny figures and many variants of lotus and palmette flowers.

The remains of the so-called Potters' Quarter and all around were covered in wild thyme; some bee-hives were positioned up the ravine towards the rock

Figure 1.1 The Potters' Quarter, Korinth

of Akrokorinthos, presumably to take advantage of this. There was not much to see, as I had expected. Excavation had taken place to investigate the defensive circuit wall when considerable quantities of pottery attested to a site of manufacture. But the excavations only investigated a narrow strip parallel to the outer wall, so there are no complete plans of the area, only enough to give a rudimentary understanding of the potteries; this is compounded by confusing recording and descriptions – it is difficult to work out what came from where. They may not even have been specialised, purpose-designed potteries. I checked out a cutting in the bed-rock which the present Head of Excavations in Korinth, Charles Kaufmann Williams II, reckons is evidence that the city may have been walled at an early date, in the seventh century BC. As well as being in the forefront of pottery design, Korinth was pioneering new settlement planning and military organisation. The Greek helmet that

10

everyone first brings to mind – completely covering the head, with cheek-pieces and nose-guard for the face, eyes cut out from sheet-metal, crest nodding on top – was a Korinthian invention.

The modern town of Korinth is in the angle of the Isthmus and the northern coastline of the Peloponnese, the southern mainland of Greece. It was completely wrecked by an earthquake in 1928 and looks homogeneously modern with its antiseismatic buildings; tourist guide books tell you to avoid the town. A few miles away towards the great rock Akrokorinthos and on its northern slopes is Archaia Korinthos, the small village of Old Korinth. The central square is right by the centre of the ancient city.

Korinth was proverbially wealthy. Thucydides wrote in the fifth century BC:

> Because the Korinthians had their city on the Isthmus they have always had a market. In ancient times the Greeks travelled through the Korinthia to make contact with each other rather by land in and out of the Peloponnese than by sea, and the Korinthians were powerful through their riches, as is shown by the ancients; for they called the place wealthy.

Its reputation in the ancient world was one of this smart opulence and business finance, combined with commercialised pleasure along the lines of

Figure 1.2 Korinth from Akrokorinthos. Nineteenth-century engraving.
(Courtesy of the Museum of Classical Archaeology, Cambridge)

Las Vegas. Osbert Lancaster calls the ancient Korinthians the advertising men and motor-car salesmen of the Greek world. Korinth was, however, known as the place where painting was invented. At the time of its capture by the Romans (Lucius Mummius razed the city and killed or sold its inhabitants into slavery in 146 BC), Korinth was stuffed with works of art. Pliny as connoisseur and antiquarian later collected Korinthian bronze statues. One of the earliest works of Korinthian art, which retained its celebrity in later times, was the chest of Kypselos, tyrant of Korinth in the seventh century BC, made of cedar wood and adorned with figures. It was dedicated to Zeus at the sanctuary of Olympia where Pausanias, the Roman writer of the most famous tourist guide to Greece, saw it and described it in minute detail.

Korinth had various reputations as a centre of craft and design. Athenaeus writes of rich garments from Korinth and there is mention in Antiphanes of Korinthian *stromata* – rugs or blankets. Remains of a large dye works (vats and concrete dying floors) have been found in the city centre. Korinth was also famous for perfumeries. Plutarch, writing in Greek in the first century AD, recalls that an exiled tyrant of the Sicilian city of Syracuse, Dionysios II, whiled away his time in the famous perfumeries of the city. The pots I was interested in are certainly small oil jars. Did they indeed contain perfumed oil, as has long been supposed? Some scientific studies have found traces of resins appropriate to perfume in similar types of small pot. Humphry Payne, a British archaeologist, sometime Director of the British School at Athens, wrote in his great book on Korinthian pottery, *Necrocorinthia*, that one aryballos, upon being opened, smelled of scent two thousand years old!

The project which brought me to Greece on this occasion concerned Korinthian manufacture. The aryballoi of seventh-century Korinth are an important class of artefacts to Classical archaeologists for various reasons. As I have already mentioned, they are at the forefront of changes in design in the late eighth and seventh centuries BC. Art historians consider this 'Orientalising phase' a crucial one in the development of Greek art. Aryballoi have been collected by the great art museums for nearly two centuries. I had already visited collections in London and Boston and spent much time working through the series of books *Corpus Vasorum Antiquorum*, which record and illustrate the Greek pots to be found in museums around the world.

The style of these pots is very distinctive, regularly changed, and is easily recognised. There is a clear sequence through time from fat and globular shaped to pointed aryballoi. This makes an aryballos a good index of the relative chronology of an excavated archaeological context, such as a grave, temple rubbish dump, or whatever, within which it was found – a corpse accompanied by a globular aryballos was most likely laid to rest before another found with a more pointed base. And aryballoi have consistently been found in the cemeteries of early Greek colonies in Sicily and southern Italy; in antiquity they were taken to religious sanctuaries and out to colonies and settlements in the west, Magna Graecia (Great Greece as southern Italy came to be called). Absolute dates of foundation seem calculable for some colonies from references in later Greek authors, particularly Thucydides. So Protokorinthian pottery provides a chronological scheme for the late eighth and seventh centuries BC, and one which is so useful because aryballoi turn up all over the Greek world, enabling cross referencing of disparate stylistic groupings and local relative sequences.

I was interested in a wider question: why did the Korinthian potters start drawing people and animals and flowers upon these new designs of pots? Greek art is so focused on the human body. I wanted to know how this interest started. Why did the Korinthians need images like these?

I had arrived in Korinth with a friendly Aegean prehistorian, a Greek Cypriot (who looked like Telly Savalas) based in the British School of Archaeology at Athens. He was interested in the prehistoric remains which predated the city state, or *polis* of Korinth. Together we were going to

Figure 1.3 Temple of Apollo, Korinth, with the North Market in the foreground

approach the Director of the Korinth excavations during this busy excavation season. Charles Williams was working on a part of the city centre, to one side of the Roman forum, in Frankish levels. One of the American graduate students told him of our arrival. He helpfully supplied an offprint of an article of his about the early development of the city, told me of the problems and inadequacies of the excavations of the Potters' Quarter, and took me over to the dig house. In this smart villa is a small working library. There are various doctoral dissertations on the shelves forming a record of a coherent research programme, coherent because most theses were produced at the suggestion of a few Directors of the American School of Classical Studies at Athens. They certainly benefited considerably from their patronage. And, as if to remind me, the chairs were labelled with the names of the excavating professors: Blegen and Broneer and others. Photographs of the same decorated the walls.

The foreign schools of archaeology and Classics in Athens have dominated excavation in Greece over the last 150 years. Their activities have been restricted for some time now, but the financial resources of the Americans still have great pull. Excavations continue, notably at Isthmia, down the road from Korinth and originally one of its sanctuaries (to Poseidon), and on the prestigious site of the market place (*Agora*) of Athens. The big excavations in Greece have concentrated on the centres of the famous cities, and on the great sanctuaries such as Delphi and Olympia. A couple of years later I heard Mr Williams (as I was told by a knowing research student to call him) give a fascinating talk reconstructing the architectural features of a Roman building in Korinth.

I spent some time exploring what little was left of the Greek city. The walk over to the Potters' Quarter from the city centre was not a short one; as I indicated, it is beyond the next village to Archaia Korinthos. It is clear that the early 'city' was not at all the conventional image we have of urban settlement. There were few scattered sherds in the cultivated fields by Anaploga, before the Potters' Quarter at the circuit wall – something inconsistent with densely populated areas, however ancient (ceramic materials are notoriously durable). The consensus is that Korinth began as an association of scattered villages, much as the region is today.

Another favourite type of site has been the cemetery. I had already read of the North Cemetery at Korinth, again excavated by an American team. Ian Morris and others have adopted approaches to cemetery analysis taken in prehistoric archaeology with the aim of using archaeological evidence to reconstruct the structure of ancient society. Not here an interest solely in the artefacts found buried with the dead, nor in city centre architecture, nor in the fine dedications found in religious sanctuaries. The idea is that the pattern of finds in a cemetery reflects the organisation of society. Lack of finds and poor evidence of dates meant that Morris couldn't do much with Korinth.

Before coming out to Korinth I had spent some time in Athens, at the British School, using its library and visiting the National Museum with its collections of Protokorinthian pottery. Most foreign archaeologists use the schools in Athens; they are legally required to be attached to a foreign school if they are to do any serious work beyond intelligent tourism. The Assistant Director of the British School had written, for example, after I had registered that year, asking whether I needed any permits or museum passes. Since most of the material I wished to look at was now in Italian museums, I had declined the offer.

The British School at Athens is an erstwhile colonial establishment of learning, set in gardens shared with part of the American School of Classical Studies, its bigger neighbour, in Kolonaki, the embassy district of Athens. Let me try to give some idea of the character of the place. It was founded in 1886 after high-level negotiations and initiatives involving the Prince of Wales, Gladstone, Lords Salisbury and Rosebery, the academic Jebb, and Macmillan from the wealthy publishing family. The Greek government granted some land on the slopes of Mount Lykabettos, a large house was built; and Francis Penrose, member of the old aristocratic Society of Dilettanti, became the first Director.

The school is now centred upon the hostel; the old house has become solely the Director's. Here is to be found the accommodation for the students, dining room, offices and library. Photographs of the Queen and Prince Philip greet you in the foyer where is also to be found the visitors' book (lots of distinguished names of academics and others). The offices house a secretary and the Assistant Director who is responsible for the day-to-day management of the place (surveying tripod by the door). The common room is known as the Finlay Library (still containing many old books on topographical subjects). I remember from earlier visits late afternoon drinks (iced tea and coffee) on the terrace. The ouzo flasks were empty on this visit and the chairs in sorry repair. The fine Penrose Library was the reason why I was at the school, checking up on books and periodicals. It has been said that if it weren't for the library, the school would be little more than a youth hostel (albeit a smart one with plenty of connections, a nice garden and tennis court). There is also the Fitch Laboratory, for archaeological science. This has become an expanding and important field. Particularly popular are characterisation studies: scientific determinations of the character of archaeological materials such as ceramics (knowing the precise composition of a clay can help establish where it came from, if a map can be made of clay deposits).

There is a community at the school all year round. Students arrive from parent universities in Britain to follow their various research projects, using the library and the School as a base. The school has its own students (funded independently), including the Greek government scholars and British students supported by Greek bursaries (notoriously meagre). As I have mentioned, the visitors' book records many more temporary stays by affiliated students such as myself.

Regular lectures are held here and also in other foreign schools with which there is regular contact. During my short stay in 1991 an invitation to an evening lecture and reception came from the Goulandris Museum. The Canadian school was presenting its year's work at this private museum centred on the art collection of a Greek shipping millionaire. I felt distinctively under-dressed among the social set of Kolonaki.

A small portrait of Humphry Payne, another Director of the school in the 1930s, hangs on the wall of one of the rooms in the library (named after him). Just below is shelved a book, a general account of ancient Greece by an author now obscure, whose inside cover is inscribed 'winner of the Leslie Hunter Prize for an essay in Classical Archaeology – Winchester July 1922 – signed M.J. Rendall (Informator)'. It belonged to John Devitt Stringfellow Pendlebury, Curator of the British School's outpost at Knossos on the island of Crete, 1929–34. Various other distinguished ex-members of the school have given their books to the library. A sun-tanned young lady, fresh in from Egypt, told me she was writing Pendlebury's biography. Having read Classics at Oxford, she was grateful to her family whose wealth gave her the opportunity to travel and here record the life and times of this British archaeologist who had immersed himself in Aegean prehistory and had been shot by the Germans in 1941 for helping with the resistance. She was off to Crete for a party commemorating the fiftieth anniversary of his death.

A Greek government scholar was interested in the ancient Greek army. He read me a passage from an early Greek poet and mercenary, Archilochos, with some reference, he explained, to short cropped hair. Having been in the marines himself he felt he sensed what Archilochos was on about in his lyrics. I took this to be representative of a relatively new interest, after the work of Victor Hanson particularly, in the experience of ancient soldiering; so much effort has been invested in the history of tactics and battles and campaigns of conquest, but little in understanding the life of the ordinary soldier.

Others were engaged in studies of the imagery on Mycenaean pots (second millennium BC bronze age) and Mycenaean ceramic animal figurines. I asked what they thought they were about. 'I must leave interpretation to someone else', a student from Basel told me. Not all were academic researchers, how-ever: someone was seated in the spring sunshine on the roof of the school, painting pictures of Greek scenes.

The weekend before I left, many of the people at the school were off to the Mani, a relatively remote part of the southern Peloponnese, to immerse themselves in the rural Greece of old. They were after the experience of authentic Greece, the fascination of the peasant medieval world in the late twentieth century, and well away from the tourist trail. So many of us must feel this urge to escape commercialised and conditioned experience, but they seemed to be setting out on an anthropological trip whose character concerned me. There were strong undercurrents of Rousseau – observing noble savages, aboriginal Greeks, and a sense of voyeurism. These members of the British School were in a foreign country which nevertheless was culturally familiar to them through their studies, through their institutional links and interests. But Greece in the remote south was an opportunity to escape to experience and learn about the unfamiliar, or another premodern time. Learning can be seen as a process of absorption. It may be conceived that knowledge of the past lies in meticulously observing, measuring and describing pottery. (A Japanese archaeologist in Athens described to me his seven-year project of recording all marine scenes, and especially those containing octopuses, upon Mycenaean pots. He had devised a framework which fitted around a pot and gave a fixed and standardised position from which to photograph. He was building up an archive of slides. There ended his project.) In anthropology there is a long tradition of participant observation – fieldwork where the anthropologist aims at immersion in another society to observe what it is all about. These questions of learning and gaining knowledge had interested me in my time as a high-school teacher and afterwards in university teaching. Is education about absorbing a body of knowledge? Criticisms have been levelled at anthropological fieldwork on the basis of the imbalance in the relationship (the anthropologist has the knowledge and expertise, the right to ask the questions, not the observed exotic specimen of cultural otherness), and the point has been made that there is a need to *engage* with the indeterminate uncertainties of cultural experience. (Societies are not just a set of rules to be observed and described; the anthropologist is in a moral relationship with the people they seek to understand.) All this has led me to believe that this model of absorption is not what learning about other societies, present or past, should be about.

Instead I think of it as something like a conversation, an exchange of opinion. Consider that a good conversation depends on the mutual strength of character of both parties to the relationship, involving sensitivity and the ability to take what the other is saying and *change* it by relating it to themselves and their understandings. The conversation is thus a creative act, after which both parties come out differently. And there is no end to it, never a point when one side really knows the other, because the conversation is a relationship which constantly changes those who are a party to it. This is another reason why we can never simply absorb the character of someone else, or what they have done or made. I hoped that the trip down to the Mani would give something to the locals.

From the libraries of my universities in England and France; to museums and their collections; to Korinth where the pots were made; and then out to Italy, where many of the pots ended up in antiquity, only to be later excavated, hoarded and written about by antiquarians, collectors, museum curators, art

Figure 1.4 The panoptic gaze and a view from Akrokorinthos. The ancient city is in the middle distance

historians and archaeologists: I saw this as a journey of interpretation. The idea was to follow the life-cycle of the perfume jars, from their design and manufacture, through their exchange and consumption as goods fit to dedicate to a divinity or the dead, to their deposition and later resurrection as the objects of archaeological interest. Tracks led off in all sorts of directions, concrete routes from libraries to excavations to museums, but also journeys of the interpreting imagination, all in an attempt to understand what the perfume jars were about.

Following a structuralist school of anthropology, some French Classical archaeologists have been considering the images upon Greek pots. Their method is not to try to understand any one image in isolation, or to attempt to ascribe a single meaning to any one design (such as a picture being the illustration of a myth or a goddess). Instead they bring together in their interpretations all sorts of imagery and evidence about ancient thought and society to attempt to reconstruct the way the ancient Greeks looked at the world, how they conceived of relationships between people and gods, humanity and the natural world, men and women, for example, to understand the underlying structures of meaning which lie behind the images and artefacts remaining of the ancient world.

So the aim was to pay close attention to the perfume jars and let them suggest connections which I could follow up in a collection of source materials, following connections through the life-cycle of the pots. The result is this book and another, mentioned in the introduction, more specifically about the perfume jars.

Scenes of soldiers and violence upon the pots led me to consider warfare in ancient Greece and Korinth's relationships to military changes, its war-machine in the seventh century BC. Heroic literatures seemed related in terms of subject matter. The general absence of women and their minor presence in iconography as threatening amazons led to questions of gender relationships; strange threatening monsters such as centaurs and sphinxes led to conceptions of the animal world. Were these pots art? How are archaeologists to deal with the design of artefacts? This led to questions of archaeological method and interpretation and how it has changed. Are the pots really to be understood as part of a sequence of design, an art history of Greece and Rome which has come to be identified, through Classical traditions, with western Europe? Patterns of trade involved questions of the character of ancient economy and its relationship with religion (the pots were dedicated to the dead and to divinities, altered states of being at the edge of human society) and with lifestyle (wealth, resources, the ships which carried goods). New public spaces and environments featuring figurative imagery were another context of the aryballoi, as were the political revolutions much discussed by ancient historians. Some scenes on the pots led to myths and legends. I needed to think about Greeks and flowers, Greeks and connections with the east, and the significance of the many bird forms.

All this was traced through whatever sources dealt with it: these are questions of a social and historical archaeology, modes of reconstructing past societies. I was to treat the aryballos as a total social fact, knitted into the new worlds being constructed by the people living and working in ancient Korinth. The task was to string together the cultural fragments into a story or account that would make sense of it all, make sense to us now.

I could not miss a walk up Akrokorinthos, the great mountain acropolis of Korinth which dominates the area. The Sanctuary of Demeter and Kore lies halfway, with its cult dining rooms and open public area of rock-cut seating (at least that seemed to be the interpretation). It is mostly left to the lizards now, at least at this time of the year; the tourist buses drive by. In his topographical travels around Greece at the beginning of the nineteenth century (ten thick volumes 1821–46), military man William Martin Leake surveyed the height of Akrokorinthos as 1,886 feet, rising almost straight up from the coastal plain. It has an encircling wall of not less than one and a half miles, with the single approach to the top guarded by triple line of gates. On ancient foundations are to be found Byzantine, Frankish, Venetian and Turkish construction. All over are ruins of Turkish houses, Byzantine chapels and brick-vaulted cisterns amidst rampant thistles and flowers. Conventional chronologies and histories seem inadequate to account for this tumble-down decay combined with the extraordinary energy of plant and insect life. There is no easy answer to the question: what date is this structure? The whole place is shot through with different times and histories: temporal continuities.

In a corner, by the Turkish barracks, are the remains of the upper fountain of Peirene, by which Korinth was also known (Korinth is the city of Peirene in the poet Pindar). Down in the lower city is now a relatively well-preserved Roman courtyard with six arches fronting the caves which lead back into the water-bearing hillside. On Akrokorinthos there is a stairway down to a Hellenistic chamber which has been reroofed in modern times. The surface of the still pool is invisible in the dim light, only appearing when the visitor meets it taking steps down into the lower chamber. It was here that Bellerophon, heroic offspring of early legendary Korinthians, found the winged horse Pegasus. A scene of Bellerophon riding Pegasus and fighting the Chimaira, a creature part lion, goat and serpent, appears on another of those perfume jars I was following.

Not far away from the fountain is the site of what was a splendid temple of Aphrodite, one of the patron goddesses of the city. Here were kept more than a thousand sacred female slaves for the service of strangers: temple prostitutes. This Aphrodite is the Syrian Astarte. There seems to be a Phoenician connection here. Lais, a famous Korinthian call-girl, obtained, it was said, such high fees as often to ruin the merchants who visited the city: 'Not even the rich make it in Korinth', went the ancient proverb, or words to that effect. To call a girl 'Korinthian' was to call her a tart. The word Korinth even became a verb: to Korinth – to play the pimp or courtesan.

I stayed for over a week in Tasos' Taverna. The locals were in at eight in the morning with their coffee and brandy chatting in front of the counter with its pictures of heroes of the war of independence. I had tried to find a ferry or flight to Syracuse or Naples and their museums full of Korinthian pottery, but there was only one of the many boats from Patras to Brindisi. Here I joined the well-worn trail of students, each on their own grand tour with their rail passes and guidebooks to European culture.

Someone later suggested that I should follow the tracks of the *Arimaspea*. In this lost epic poem of the late seventh century BC (reconstructed from its traces and influences in later literatures by Bolton in a scholarly work of 1962), Aristeas of Prokonnesos related a journey north beyond the known world. He told of the Issedonians, whose women were treated equally to men, of a world of griffins, gorgons, the graiai, swan-maidens, cannibals and amazons. Here were to be found the Arimaspoi, one-eyed horsemen, and a land of ever-falling feathers. His journey began, it would seem, when he developed a passion to travel after apparent death and resurrection, in a trance-like state. Bolton connects this with shamanism, divine possession and altered states, and through this achievements of knowledge. It seemed that here was someone associating elements closely connected to and so reinforcing those to be found running through the design and consumption of the pottery: death and otherness, altered states, the avian, monstrous and threatening gender roles beyond, at the edge, reached through the fascinations of travel.

I have myself presented here a metaphor of a cultural or interpretive journey, stringing together or mapping source materials, with archaeology conceived as a mediation of past and present rather than a discovery of what happened in the past. Other metaphors for what archaeologists may be doing appear later. The main features of the book are here: archaeologists as members of communities dealing in Greece with materials which resonate through the western cultural imagination, and with the grand stories of the past (notably civilisation, art and otherness) in an uneasy tension with the actuality of the past, its material place in the present.

2

CITIES AND SANCTUARIES, ART AND ARCHAEOLOGY

Roots in the past

In this chapter will be presented the main approaches that Classical archaeologists have made to the objects and features considered most worthy of their attention.

A HISTORY OF POTTERY STUDIES

Fired clay is durable. Pots turn up in extraordinary quantities on Classical sites. Some 'fine wares' have attracted considerable attention because they have been classified as art or near art, and because their styles are often so recognisable, making them ideal tools for bringing to order the chaos of debris from the past.

Consider the vessel in Figure 2.1. This can be used to illustrate some common approaches and methods of Classical archaeology. The shape and small size mark the pot as what is conventionally called an aryballos or perfumed oil jar (though they were probably called *lekythoi* in antiquity). It is one of those pots mentioned in Chapter 1. At present it is in the Museum of Fine Arts in Boston, Massachusetts.

With the size and shape, the hard, smooth and pale clay fabric indicate that the pot is Korinthian and of the seventh century BC. The character and subject matter of the painted and inscribed decoration confirms this identification. Specifically it is of the style or industry Protokorinthian. The boundaries and coherence of this 'industry' were definitively set and established by Johansen in his work *Les Vases Sicyoniens* of 1923. The German Adolf Fürtwangler had brought a great deal of order to the different kinds of Greek pottery at the end of the nineteenth century, but this book was a work of such definitive systematisation that it is still used today for reference. Johansen gathered and coordinated pots of this shape and fabric, noted their occurrence in excavated deposits with other vessel forms, and defined a set of stylistic points which united them. He also proposed a chronological sequence to the shape of aryballoi – from early and 'paunchy' to late and pointed or 'piriform' through middle of ovoid shape. Most of the pots that Johansen dealt with were from early Greek colonies in Italy, but he considered

Figure 2.1a Protokorinthian aryballos in the Museum of Fine Arts, Boston. (*Source*: K.F. Johansen, *Les Vases Sicyoniens.* Paris: Champion, 1923)

Figure 2.1b Detail of Figure 2.1a

this coherent stylistic group to have been manufactured in the north-east Peloponnese of southern Greece, at Sicyon; hence the title of his book.

A British archaeologist, Humphry Payne, accepted Johansen's grouping and synthesis, but considered that the stylistic similarities with what was known to be later Korinthian pottery were too great to allow there to be different manufacturing centres. With many pottery styles there had been confusion over where they were made because most were found first in Italy (most Attic pots come from Etruscan tombs). The origin of Korinthian pots, however, had been fixed long ago by an antiquarian traveller, Edward Dodwell, who had bought a ceramic box (*pyxis*) in Korinth in 1805. So Payne took the animal friezes, decorative devices and distinctive fabric to be early Korinthian ware, or rather Protokorinthian. These aryballoi were made in Korinth.

So the handbooks of Johansen and Payne sketched the lineaments of Protokorinthian style. The work of traditional Classical archaeology has added little in the way of refinement of the sense, usually and largely intuitive, of this style. The earlier chronological schemes of its development (the change from fat to pointy pots) have been much debated, modified, made more complicated, even challenged. Such debate has been a major concern of specialists. The first reason for this is because chronological sequence is thought to be of primary importance in making sense of the cultural remains of the past. It also lends an appearance of historical substance to this archaeology concerned with classification – the passing of history, even if without any content or narrative, is marked by the changing fashions of pottery design. The second reason why specialists have been so concerned with the sequence of stylistic change was briefly mentioned in the first chapter. Aryballoi like this, and even if not so decorated, are easy to spot and so are the different phases. They turn up all over the Greek world and have been associated with the historical dates known for the founding of some Greek colonies in Italy. These pots have a clear relative chronology and can be attached to an absolute chronology. Aryballoi can be used to tell the time, or rather the date. (This can prove tricky though; it is not as straightforward as it seems – this will be taken up in Chapter 6.)

Ceramic art histories have recounted over and again, and with more or less eloquence, the features and innovations of Korinthian pottery. Pots made in Korinth in the earlier eighth century were decorated in a linear and restrained Geometric canon. But there then occurred the birth of a new style, or rather a radical transformation of Geometric. It is called *Orientalising*. On some pots like that in Figure 2.1, the austerity of the Geometric is abandoned for swirling and animated designs, and with some features apparently borrowed from designs found in the east; hence the term Orientalising. These include floral decoration (lotus and palmette), some mythical creatures (such as a new form of sphinx), ways of drawing others (such as lions), certain 'stock' scenes (the lion hunt, for example), and some Geometric traits (rays at the base of a pot).

The account of the Orientalising movement, with its stylistic diffusion (supposed according to detailed comparison of artefacts from Greece and abroad) and the creative adaptation of Greek 'artists', is an exemplary aspect of Classical art history.

This aryballos is clearly in the Orientalising style, with its figures, animals and rays below. It is part of Payne's 'first black figure style', where detail is added to figures by scratching through the clay slip used to paint the figures. It is this Protokorinthian incised black figure decoration which was adopted by the potters of Attika to the north (the territory of Athens) and is used in the production of the very famous Attic black figure vases. With red figure vases, these form the heights of Classical Greek ceramic art; they are in every international art museum and have fetched high prices in the art market since the late eighteenth century.

So archaic Protokorinthian is, in the accounts of art history, a key style in the emergence of Classical Greek art, indeed in the development of representations of bodily form (drawings of people and animals before this Orientalising style are not reckoned to be of the same order). This aryballos in Boston is representative of its style which provides its artistic credentials. It is not just any old pot but fits into the story of the emergence of the Classical; hence many finer figured Protokorinthian pieces such as this appear around the world in art museums.

Narratives of art history like this have been a major feature of Classical archaeology and they involve the ascription of value. Artefacts are evaluated according to their judged place in stylistic development. There is a search for those pieces that mark the changes – great works, or works of creative innovation. They are the works of 'artists' – those who set the pace and sketch the character of stylistic growth.

TYPOLOGY AND CLASSIFICATION

The illustration brings two interests to the fore. One in ordering and systematising objects, the other in the category of style. The conditioning interests are in chronologies and systematisation, classification and rationalisation. Much effort has been expended by Classical archaeologists on chronological and geographical frameworks, particularly for the art work.

Catalogues have long been a major form of publication in Classical archaeology. These are either of museum and private collections or of particular types of artefact, such as gemstones, Athenian lekythoi or Clazomenaean sarcophagi. A book such as Payne's *Necrocorinthia* (1931) defined a style, Korinthian, and set up a chronological framework. A work such as Coldstream's *Greek Geometric Pottery* (1968) is a handbook of this particular type of pottery, describing the different regional styles throughout Greece and proposing a chronological sequence based on where pots have been found, particularly comparing the associations of artefacts in different graves to

25

establish a relative sequence. Books like this are considered invaluable for the job of the person who deals with finds from an excavation: they facilitate identification and classification.

John Boardman has produced over the years a set of handbooks which present a body of knowledge about the stylistic development of Greek art. The introduction to his *Greek Sculpture: the Archaic Period* (1978) describes the book as follows:

> This little book attempts to present the evidence fairly, but also to propose a pattern by which the development may be better understood. If it did not, the undertaking would have proved as boring for the author as for the reader. Much is *uncontroversial*, but in places the manner of presentation is novel. The narrative concentrates on the history of style by period and region, *as the material dictates*, and it attempts to be as *comprehensive* as space allows rather than so selective as to exclude even the majority of *types, places and names* relevant to the subject. As in the companion handbooks to Athenian black figure and Archaic red figure vases, the illustrations are small but numerous, both aides-mémoires to the familiar and glimpses of the uncommon. [My emphases.]

Indeed, it does appear so uncontroversial and ordered. Another piece of sculpture may come along, but it can be expected to fit into the scheme of things; the 'controversial' debates usually only precipitate a slight alteration of the story, but no more. It is 'as the material dictates', to divide into period and region. Boardman tells the story plainly, with little reference to debate or controversy, and avoiding any possible sources of confusion, to help the book be useful. There are many such books, but it might be asked for whom they are useful – presumably those wishing to acquire a body of knowledge (hence the stress on lack of controversy and fairness – the story probably really was like this). Boardman's book is 'little', but 'comprehensive'. Handbooks of particular classes of artefact are often far from little and go to quite extraordinary degrees to be comprehensive, both tracking down every last example of the artefact type in museums around the world and finding every reference in specialist literatures to each catalogued piece. This is the rigour of scholarship, and I am anticipating some of the points to be dealt with in Chapter 4.

ART AND JUDGEMENTS OF STYLE

Let me return now to the aryballos in Figure 2.1 and use it to illustrate some other approaches to artistic style.

Karl Schefold, a German art historian writes of it so in his book *Myth and Legend in Early Greek Art* (translated from the German 1966) (he has just identified the clothed male figure as Zeus, the mightiest of the gods):

26

The action is seen not merely as a fact or the assertion of a great individual, but as part of a connected whole, the inevitability and duration of which is expressed in the structure of the picture based, as it is, on firm axes and bounded surfaces. The lack of balance between different elements is not to be explained as a result of incompetence but, rather, as the result of the grand scale of the inner conception. The eagles around the tripod may indicate the power of Zeus, but the strange running figure of a sword-bearing daemon has still not been explained.

He then goes on to compare the scene with early literatures, the Homeric hymns of the seventh century, and particularly a scene describing the solemn entry of Apollo into Olympus:

On an amphora from Melos dating from *c.* 650 BC the same spirit pervades the portrayal of Apollo's arrival . . . The scene has the character of a monumental painting. The hymn tells how the island of Delos burst into flower for joy at the birth of the god and, here too, plants of every kind surround the fabulous splendour of the divine procession.

J.L. Benson is an expert on Protokorinthian pottery, a connoisseur of the style. He produced a list of its scene painters in 1953: *Die Geschichte der Korinthischen Vasen,* and another in 1989: *Earlier Corinthian Workshops: a Study of Corinthian Geometric and Protocorinthian Stylistic Groups.* He did much work for the catalogue of finds from the excavations in the 'Potters' Quarter' at ancient Korinth.

In the development of Protokorinthian pottery he stresses artists and workshops struggling with stylistic principles:

The torsional and curvilinear plant ornament of the Cumae and Toulouse Groups constitutes more than a particular theme (though it is one): it was the fundamental deeply felt experience through which Corinthian artists liberated themselves from Geometric habitude. By this I mean the change from a mentality engrossed in rectilinear abstract ornaments to the same mentality caught up in substantive curvilinear ornamentation. I see the first stirrings of this already in the running spiral of the Thapsos Class vases, and then in its implementation in Egyptian-derived plant and animal forms leading directly to the Cumae-Toulouse aesthetic in question.

Benson is writing about artistic and creative personalities and their relationship with 'style'. It is clear that these examples represent another kind of approach to artistic style. Here is needed an explanation of some ideas lying behind a mainly German tradition of art history.

Michael Podro, in his book *The Critical Historian of Art* (1982), distinguishes *archaeological* art history (the search for historical facts about works, focusing on sources, patronage, purposes, techniques, contemporaneous responses and ideals), from *critical* art history, which developed through the nineteenth century and which aims to see how the products of art sustain purposes and interests (timeless experiences or qualities) which are irreducible to their conditions of emergence and yet inextricable from them. He has written a detailed introduction to the work of these critical art historians.

Podro quotes Goethe (active at the time of the first development of critical art history at the turn of the eighteenth century):

> When we would treat of an excellent work of art, we are almost obliged, as it were, to speak of art in general, for the whole of art is contained in it, and everyone may, as far as their abilities allow, by means of such a monument, develop whatever relates to art in general.

The question here, that of critical art history, is of how to regard the art of the past, its diversity, and how it is accessible or retrievable, as more than an object of archaeological interest (which simply explores the place of a work of art in its own time).

The point is one of the two-sided character of the work of art: it was made in the past and so is distant from us. But as an art work it escapes (according to this art history) its own time and communicates across the centuries: the art of the past is appreciated in later times and places. Critical art history thus seeks to justify the timeless qualities of art and explores the relationships between these timeless qualities (such as mystery, devotion) and their material, phenomenal, transient manifestations. For Whitley, in an article listed in the Bibliography, this is a Platonic and idealist agenda, with timeless art as a Platonic 'form' finding its realisation in many material manifestations – works of art. This tradition of art history has strong philosophical roots and is much influenced by Kant and Hegel.

The extraction of a work of art from the social and cultural worlds which produced it does not result in a fomalist history, simply tracing stylistic change through time. There is instead a concern with how particular historical and social circumstances are transformed by 'Art', that is how particular artists react to and interpret art and the stylistic histories and contexts within which they work.

The two central concerns of critical art history are to show the way in which art exhibited a freedom of mind, and to show how the art of alien cultures could become part of the present, through the understanding of art history, placing particular works in the context of changing art styles. Other general features include a historical account of change without reference to the function and purpose of works of art in the societies that produced them. This is an interest in formal change or transformation, with works seen only in the context of each other, as progressive modifications of each other and of certain 'ideal' or 'human' qualities, free from contextual meanings. The rationale or explanation of a particular work is to be found in its place in a developmental sequence, with artistic creativity modifying antecedents and anticipating or carrying imitations of what is to come. Sometimes there is reference to craft traditions, with changes in form explained according to the translation of techniques from one craft tradition to another (for example, metalwork to clay). Sometimes craft tradition is interpreted in relation to the realisation of potentialities inherent in the medium.

Whitley makes the point that later twentieth-century art historians have tended to focus upon post-Renaissance and modern art – a breadth of concern to be found in nineteenth-century critical art historians and which involved an interest in ancient art has been lost. It was this scope of interest which led to the development of critical histories of Classical art.

In some critical histories are to be found Hegelian ideas (crudely speaking) of art as expressions of *Zeitgeist* – the spirit of the age. Alois Riegl, in his work *Stilfragen* (1893) considered the development of floral motifs (lotus, acanthus and palmette) from Egypt onwards for many centuries. He considered that these were not motifs which can be explained as imitations of reality, but the changing depictions of these motifs formed a development with its own internal dynamic, an evolutionary dynamic analogous to those found in the natural world. This is vitalism. Heinrich Wölfflin considered style as a set of formal principles (for example, painterly line).

Whitley presents a useful example of how critical art history has influenced Classical archaeology. The issue is the change from the Mycenaean world of the second millennium BC, with its 'palace' redistributive economies, collective burial and bronze-based technologies, to later Geometric Greece and its radically different material culture. Bernard Schweitzer, in his book *Greek Geometric Art* (English translation 1971), contrasted two amphorae, one Mycenaean, the other Protogeometric, and described the change as one from voluminosity to a sense of verticality which prefigures much of Greek art to come. For Whitley the specification of formal principles which characterise two epochs is the sort of analysis found in Wölfflin. Other characteristics of critical art history are the abstract qualities held to determine the particular form of artefacts, the expression and articulation of forms seen in particular works, the dynamic which leads Greek art from Geometric to Classical. The purpose is historical, the change from Mycenaean to Geometric, but there is no reference to social context. Understanding the relationship of individual art works to formal abstract principles, identified by the art historian, makes them intelligible to the present. This is held to be a rational account of the intrinsic aesthetic properties of a work and its style, and one which is universal, hence scientific.

In the short quote from Schefold (see p. 27) it was clear that this approach can include literatures and other media. Hurwitt has produced a cultural history of early Greece to 480 BC: *Art and Culture of Early Greece 1100–480 BC* (1985), which, in its identification of abstract principles manifested by particular cultural works in various media, shows some influence of this philosophy of art history. Korinthian pottery, for example, is held to display the quality of *akribeia* – meticulousness and precision; Orientalising art is about cultural anxiety upon the meeting of two different cultural orders; the 'archaic' is generally considered as an impulse to pattern, representing an animation of the inorganic, explicitness and passivity, and a domination of surface and plane.

POTTERY AND THE CONNOISSEURS

There is a popular TV programme made by the BBC called *Antiques Roadshow*. The production team travel around Britain, announcing the setting of shows in advance. Members of the public take their antiques along to be scrutinised by one of the team of experts. Someone may have a tattered mantle clock which has been in the family for generations, so long that no one knows anything about it. The clock expert looks at it with his eyeglass and reveals that it is a rare work of a Bavarian master clocksmith of the seventeenth century. The audience hold their breath for the key question. For how much has the owner insured it; do they know its value?

John Beazley is a legend in Classical archaeology. Over a lifetime he got to know tens of thousands of Attic vases and attributed the painted designs, in a series of catalogues, to artists, schools of artists, artistic manners, circles and the like. It was a vast programme of ordering and systematising. But it was more than this, because here was a Classical archaeologist getting to the heart of style – the individual hand of the artist and the different relationships of influence between them. Not all of these artists have names known from antiquity, in which case Beazley supplied one. A favourite of his, for example, was the 'Berlin painter': vases had found their way from Greek and Italian findspots to collectors and museums around the world, including Berlin. Beazley kept himself out of the art market, but he could look at an Attic vase and tell you where there were ten others painted by the same 'artist'; he might even have been able to give you their name. Beazley was a connoisseur.

Beazley's work is a story of tremendous success; it seems complete: there is nothing more to be done with Attic vases, simply fill in the few gaps. Narratives have been attempted, for example by Boardman in his vase handbooks, and notably by Martin Robertson in his book *The Art of Vase Painting in Classical Athens*, published in 1992. Pseudo-biographical works have been produced: one, for example, is called *Papers on the Amasis Painter and his World*.

Beazley has been the model for much work on Protokorinthian figured pottery since Payne's book *Necrocorinthia* (1931); indeed Payne was a pupil of his at Oxford. Martin Robertson and Tom Dunbabin produced a list of Protokorinthian pot painters in 1953, as did Benson for all Korinthian pottery, publishing in German in the same year. Darryl A. Amyx capped his life's work on Korinthian pottery in 1988 with a three-volume catalogue of attributions and descriptions of Korinthian style.

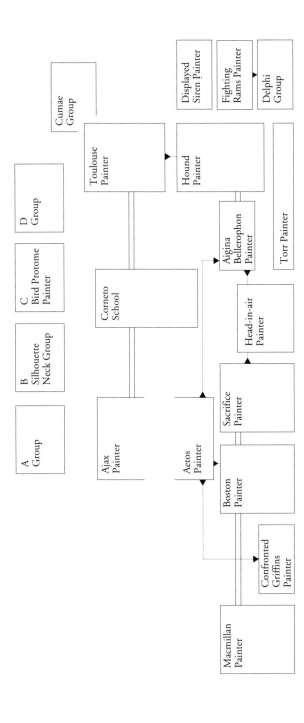

Strong (workshop) association: =
Influence: ▶

Figure 2.2 The connoisseur's choice: painters and workshops of Protokorinthian. *Source:* (based on T. Dunbabin and M. Robertson. 'Some Protokorinthian vase painters', *Annual of the British School at Athens* 48 (1953): 172–81)

These Classical art connoisseurs delve into the particularities of style, noting the rendering of figure detail, shapes, forms and subject matter, surmising that different artists, otherwise anonymous, can be distinguished on this basis. Behind the apparently dull but scholarly lists of pots and sherds are artists' hands, masters and pupils and schools traced in the evolution of style.

The aryballos of Figure 2.1 (a and b) has been attributed to the *Maler des Gesticulierenden Reiters* a name coined by Benson in 1953, or, as he or she is more usually known now, the 'Ajax painter'. The painter is named after another aryballos in Berlin, upon which is a figured scene which includes a man lying upon a sword which apparently runs through his body. This is taken to be Ajax, the epic hero, who committed suicide in such a way. The painted frieze upon the Berlin aryballos is not particularly accomplished and it is hard to make out the scene at all. Perhaps there is some (latent) wish for Protokorinthian pottery to aspire to the 'art' of Attic black figure: there is a very famous, dramatic and finely drawn scene of the death of Ajax on an amphora by Exekias, one of the potters whose name is known. The aryballoi of the Ajax painter (four or more depending upon connoisseur) have common features such as cabling upon handles, neck ornament, and particularly figure form – quite full-bodied with distinctive long arms at an acute angle at the elbow, hairstyles and beards incised cross-wise (Figure 2.3).

Beazley never came clean about his method, but attribution proceeds as follows. The archaeologist, as connoisseur, gains familiarity with the minute and particular detail of as many pots within a stylistic category as possible: noting hairstyles, lions' paws, lotus petals, ears, and the way fingers hold swords – anything in fact. The task of attribution depends upon diagnostic traits, a symptomatic logic: particular stylistic traits are considered to be conscious or unconscious symptoms of a painterly hand. So a painter is identified by any little details that give their individuality away.

It is clear, however, that attention is more often paid to the subject matter of scenes: a different symptomatic logic. Consider the problems surrounding the separation of painter from a group or school (less tightly similar paintings?). The latter cannot be identified so consistently according to the idea of style being a symptom of the individual. For example, Amyx has identified a Chigi group as well as a Chigi painter, which confuses and eliminates the Macmillan painter of Dunbabin and Robertson, identified mainly, it would seem, on the grounds of subject matter. This is the sort of thing that connoisseurs debate.

To the concept of painterly hand the aryballos (back to Figure 2.1 again) is subordinated and referred. This aryballos is 'lucky' and a diagnosis can be made. But for many, indeed the majority of Protokorinthian pots, there are too few diagnostic stylistic traits and no attribution can be made. These pots seem somehow less than the aryballoi of the Ajax painter; they have no hope of diagnosis; they contain no trace of that which would explain them, their originator or author. In having fewer stylistic traits they are less 'artistic'. Attribution, the work of the connoisseur, ascribes value.

Figure 2.3 Figures from pots by the so-called 'Ajax painter'

There are two sorts of value here: one, the value accorded to individuality, the other being the symbolic value of the cultured individual artist. So it might be noted that, without the aesthetic connotations, such a search for individuality through the identification of idiosyncrasy was proposed by Hill and others in the volume *The Individual in Prehistory* published in 1977. The devaluation of the anonymous is a lament for the loss of the individual in the past, or at least their mark. Attribution is a search for the autonomous individual who has escaped the passing of time. Value is accorded to the individual as an ego signifying itself in the artwork. This is a distinctive and modern (bourgeois) conception of the individual; anthropologists and historians have recorded other conceptions of what it is to be an individual. The 'I' which is valued and pursued by the connoisseur is that which struggles for identity (in a power struggle), for permanence (the individual against time). The devaluation of some pots is the fear of anonymity, the ego dispersed, fragmented, lost (in the flow of time, in the *mass* of ordinary people, of un-distinguished, 'coarse' pottery).

33

Concomitantly valued are signification and the signifier: the idiosyncratic detail signifies the artist; the attributed pot marks or signifies the individual and their art. This is all about *meaning*. The connoisseur pronounces on the meaning of detail, marking the signifier (significant squiggles) in this symptomatic logic of attribution. But this signifier, in fact, can be seen to return the connoisseur to himself, the cultured (artistic) individual. The mark of the artist, signifying individuality, etches order into the mass of detail, ineffable disorder. This signifier, and pronouncements upon it, represent the compulsion (we all now feel) to be an ego, a somebody.

So, wrapped up in this process of attribution of artefacts and artists is a series of distinctions:

art	anonymity
high culture	low culture
permanence	loss
signification	non-sense
order	disorder
ego	mass
identity	messy chaos
meaning	absurdity

It will be shown that these are far from neutral. In particular, it can be noted here that the distinctions between high and low culture, fine arts and other 'crafts' are very contentious ones.

As has been indicated, procedures of stylistic attribution are ill-defined; much is to do with intuition arising from long-term handling and reading around the material – it depends on becoming aware of the ineffable qualities of design and manufacture. The non-verbal component accounts for the near absence in listings of explanation for particular attributions; seeing the pots together is argument for their affiliation. The idea of visual rather than verbal argument is an attractive one, given the character of archaeological materials. But many criticisms have been made of attribution.

The esoteric expertise of the connoisseur, which is founded on the rare facility of being able to study a body of disparate and often obscure material over decades without any immediate return, is open to the charge of elitism and of being obscure to the point of mysticism (part of the Beazley legend perhaps). The connoisseur senses the essence of style on the basis of expertise and familiarity with the material; the rest of us have little ground for empirical disagreement. There is also the charge of ethnocentrism and cultural imperialism. The Classics connoisseur, pronouncing ego, roams the museum vaults and auction rooms of the 'cultured' world (sometimes literally), seeking the bearers of 'Style', but without reference to social, political or historical context, only that of his own academic evaluation. The conditions of this practice relate directly to a notion of art being timeless and universal, a transnational culture.

Expertise and practical knowledge gained through familiarity ('pottery sense' as it is sometimes called in archaeology) are indeed valuable, as any excavation team knows. The lack of rigour, however, the role of intuition, the lack of quantification (statistical control of such large bodies of information), and the apparent absence of reflection on the theoretical and philosophical assumptions of stylistic attribution (such as the categories of style and artistic personality in relation to social and historical change) are disconcerting.

Some of the identifications of artists' hands do seem reasonable: the figure drawing and choice of design elements of the pots attributed to this Ajax painter seem to form a coherent unity (see Figure 2.2 and discussion above), but only of *four* pots (Dunbabin and Robertson do list more). However, for Protokorinthian pottery, it is clear that stylistic attribution just does not work.

I considered all the 164 attributions to painters' hands in a sample of 1951 Protokorinthian pots. Between the three main listings (those of Dunbabin and Robertson, Amyx and Benson's second of 1989), there is agreement on hardly more than one in four pots.

Full agreement on attribution	44 pots; 26.8%
Agreement between two lists	44 pots; 26.8%
Three separate attributions	76 pots; 46.4%

Given that the 164 pots in the sample are whole and well published, a considerable degree of agreement might have been expected. The figures are undoubtedly affected by there being new material available since Dunbabin and Robertson's list of 1953 (but not enough to invalidate the result), but the reason for the disagreement is quite clear: the connoisseurs are all doing different things. Benson, like many others now, is willing to consider Geometric decoration as well as figured (the others here are not); Dunbabin and Robertson were less cautious than Amyx, looking a great deal at subject matter; while Benson's basis for deciding attribution seems markedly different to the others. Benson is more conscious of the validity of a particular painter in relation to the evolution of style as a whole (the German tradition sketched above), and relies less on simple comparison of figure detail; the theoretical basis for his attributions does seem more formulated and explicit.

I have used Korinthian pottery as an example here, but is there any reason to think that the results are exceptional and incidental to the practices of attribution? Some disagreement is reasonable, but it might be asked: How expert are the experts? How refined are their sensibilities? And if stylistic attribution is such a subjective exercise, on what basis have these people been authorised the luxury of cultivating and pronouncing their expert opinion?

Other standard criticisms relate to the vague notions of schools and artists. Just what do the stylistic groupings represent? I have already anticipated this question somewhat in proposing that the desire is for personality, an ego self, whether this is explicitly acknowledged or not. I have indicated how some are prepared to think of relationships between masters and apprentices or schools of followers (see Figure 2.2). However, the desire for the artist seems to efface consideration of motivation, in the following sense. That a design is somehow a symptom of an artist's identity assumes that the artist is a unitary and, crucially, expressing entity, unconsciously, or even consciously expressing *their* view, interpretation, reality. This may indeed be the case, but equally it may not. The artist may wish to experiment with styles and subject matters. I can see no objection to the 'Ajax painter' of this aryballos of Figure 2.1 being the anonymous painter of a plain Geometric cup the next day, and then experimenting with different shoulder garlands and animal scenes such as those that characterise the so-called 'Corneto painter' and 'school'. The painter's *motivation* (to express whatever) may change or be absent. The idea of self may be absent, as implied above. Such motivation, unconscious or not, can only be understood by relating concepts of the individual to wider social contexts, forces and structures. It may well be that there is social and economic pressure upon a contemporary craft or fine artist to express a distinctive 'style' and identity; this is not at all universal, but a function of a particular mode of production of artworks, particular market relations and values.

But its meaning does not really matter to the practice of artistic attribution. It is in many ways a *pragmatics* – intuition picks up various ways of distinguishing one Attic scene or Protokorinthian frieze from another – twitches of a painter's brush (the paws of the 'Hound painter') to a supposed predilection for animals with a particular bearing (the 'Head-in-air painter' for example). Stylistic attribution has little bearing on anything other than the discourse of style to which it belongs. Beazley's painters and artists are just another set of classificatory taxa which mean very little, though they do have friendlier names as Morris puts it: Oikopheles sounds better than something like Late Helladic IIIa. Mary Beard has observed that nothing can be said about the so-called painters and potters that cannot be said of the pots themselves. So when Beazley did talk about production, potters and social contexts he relied on written sources. So there is only the appearance of a humanistic story and creative artists in the practices of attribution.

More seriously, the concepts of style and artist, at the root of such practices, can be criticised as idealist, in the following way. The hand or mark of the pot painter is meaningful only in relation to the art style to which it contributes. This idea of the primacy of art style has already been introduced. Many Classical art histories consider, define, and refine style; the social, physical, intellectual context of production of the pots is either omitted or relegated to a chapter on technology. In this it does not matter how they are conceived (as personalities or workshops), because they are abstract constructions. The style exists in relation to the artistic efforts of potters who commune with it through their struggling with form and decoration, concept and content in the figured scene. The overarching whole of style, beyond the mainly incidental act of the potter, allows *teleological* explanation (here explaining the past through the future, potential causes through effects): a painter or pot may be explained, evaluated or given significance by its contribution to the future, to what is to come stylistically. In this way style is largely detached from the social and political reality of people; though there is art history – its evolutionary momentum and cycles.

INTERLUDE: SHERLOCK HOLMES, THE DOCTOR WATSON AND JOHN BEAZLEY

'I can never bring you to realise the importance of sleeves, the suggestiveness of thumb-nails, or the great issues that may hang from a boot-lace . . .

Never trust to general impressions my boy, but concentrate yourself upon details. My first glance is always at a woman's sleeve. In a man it is better first to take the knee of the trouser. As you observe, this woman had plush upon her sleeves, which is a most useful material for showing traces. The double line a little above the wrist, where the typewritress presses against the table, was beautifully defined. The sewing-machine, of the hand type, leaves a similar mark, but only on the left arm, and on the side of it farthest from the thumb, instead of being right across the broadest part, as this was. I then glanced at her face, and, observing the dint of a pince-nez at either side of her nose, I ventured a remark upon short sight and typewriting, which seemed to surprise her . . .

I noticed, in passing, that she had written a note before leaving home but after being fully dressed. You observed that her right glove was torn at the forefinger, but you did not apparently see that both glove and finger were stained with violet ink. She had written in a hurry and dipped her pen too deep. It must have been this morning, or the mark would not remain clear upon the finger. All this is amusing, though rather elementary . . .'

(Sir Arthur Conan Doyle, *The Golden Pince-Nez*)

Beazley's method was that of the Italian art historian Giovanni Morelli (died 1891), who developed the skill of distinguishing individual painters and originals from fakes on the basis of tiny details (overlooked by imitators more interested in larger, more conventionally stylised characteristics of a school or artist). So Morelli could distinguish Renaissance artists even though they did not sign their works. This involved no necessary concern with aesthetics, no need to judge artistic quality: it is a method with no necessary connection with art. Indeed, it has more to do with conceptions of disease and crime and semiotics, the science of signs.

For both Morelli and Beazley, an artist is given away by details of eyes, ears and knees, just as a criminal might be spotted by a fingerprint. The art connoisseur works as a detective who discovers the perpetrator of a crime on the basis of evidence that is imperceptible to most people. This is the connection with Sherlock Holmes, whose method is exemplified in the passage above: trifling details lead to deep insight. It is not that Holmes is a methodical scientist who calculates all possibilities, never guessing until the truth is clear. Sherlock Holmes in fact depends on inspired guesswork, and this is what makes him so fascinating: he observes, makes a guess on the basis of what he thinks is likely, then tests out the guess. The difference between ourselves and Holmes is that we don't guess as well as he does.

Beazley's method was described above as a symptomatic logic, according to which small details are treated as symptoms of the artist. The connoisseur makes a diagnosis like a physician; it is an exercise in semiotics. Details are noted and treated as signs of an underlying condition (diseases are not immediately visible in themselves). Freud's psychoanalysis is an analogous method of interpretation based upon discarded information, marginal data, which are revealing because they are instances when control of the self gives way to what lies beneath.

Conan Doyle was a practising physician until Holmes made him rich enough to give up his practice. His detective was modelled on Dr Joseph Bell of Edinburgh Royal Infirmary; Doyle, as a student, had been his outpatient clerk. Doyle followed Bell in extending the practice of diagnosis to the entire life and personality of the patient. As Bell put it: 'In every essential they resemble one another; only in trifles do they differ – and yet, by knowing these trifles well, you make your recognition or your diagnosis with ease. So it is with disease of mind or body or morals.' We are not far here from physiognomy, reading character and history from the features of a face, the relics of experience, characteristic features of a person.

How is a face to be read? How are traces, symptoms, clues, pictorial marks to be interpreted? How does the physician know what to treat as symptoms; how does the connoisseur know what gives away the artist? No answer can be given in advance. Testing a hypothesis concerning the identity of an artist or disease of a person through the collections of clues always involves a certain amount of guessing, hence the philosopher Charles Pierce calls it 'speculative modelling', a mixture of imagination and reality.

In this field of forensics, detection, crime, diagnosis and connoisseurship, Beazley is semiotician; the doctor becomes detective; Holmes a brilliant physician to the body politic whose disease is crime; and the art museum comes to resemble a rogue's gallery. It is a wonderfully fascinating mixture exploited so well by semiotician Umberto Eco in his novel *The Name of the Rose* (1983): his detective monk William of Baskerville traces clues through a wealth of misleading signs in the great library of a monastery peopled by all sorts of curious physiognomies. Detection is also a root metaphor of the archaeological project: reading the signs of the past.

The historian Carlo Ginzburg has proposed that a conjectural model for the construction of knowledge emerged towards the end of the nineteenth century in the sphere of the social and human sciences. It is of the form which has just been outlined – using obscure or remote clues in a speculative manner.

The process of reasoning is one called abduction – rules are postulated to explain observed facts until causality is proved, that is, the hypothesis or 'guess' tested. Everything at the scene of a crime may be relevant: where is the detective to look? Consequently a cultural or experiential knowledge is required to codify this method: there needs to be a basis on which to postulate the rules or make the guesses. This is the field of experience of Holmes. This is where every good detective has a 'hunch'. Hence that term mentioned in connection with connoisseurship, 'pottery sense'. These are types of knowledge which are very difficult to codify effectively.

Everything at the scene of a crime could be relevant, as could anything in a painting. Into this chaos reason moves with careful observation and experience, allowing conjectures about the object of interest (crime, criminal or artist). A rule is postulated which will explain certain facts about the object, then the rule is checked out independently. Holmes, in the extract above, knows from experience to observe a woman's sleeve carefully. He notes certain features, makes a conjecture that these are the effect of a typewriter, tests this out against the signs of spectacles, requisite for close work, and further tests it out with a question. The connoisseur begins with a pot, supposes (from experience) that certain ears mark out this pot and its type (read painter), then checks out the supposition against other pots. Abduction is this process of reasoning backwards, studying tracks, and is rooted in all the senses and faculties. Every dimension of experience and memory may be helpful in making the imaginative conjecture. Abduction is the work of intuition, defined not as extra-sensory perception, but as a lightning re-capitulation of rational processes. After all, anyone could do what Holmes does – it is elementary; only he does it so quickly.

Note should be made here that abduction does not include the substantive link proposed between idiosyncrasy and artistic personality, for example. All sorts of problems have been noted with this already. Abduction refers simply to the process of reasoning involved.

For Ginzburg, speculative modelling unites history, archaeology, geology, physical astronomy (i.e. not nuclear physics) and palaeontology, as well as medicine, forensic science and divination. The relationship with time is interesting: these are all diachronic disciplines using this conjectural or divinatory paradigm of reading signs. The logical structure of abduction is one of forecasting retrospectively. Divination reads signs in the present for the future. Medical semiotics deals with past, present and future in prognosis and diagnosis. Forensics and archaeology read present signs to reason about the past.

Abduction is a form of *scientific* reasoning which involves generalisation and testing. It is also creative and embodied, thoroughly rooted in subjective experience, not eschewing this for notions of pure logical reasoning. So it is interesting to contrast deduction, a form of reasoning championed by many archaeologists since the 1960s who have wished archaeology to be more scientific. A deductive project of stylistic analysis could take the following form:

- hypothesis: a rule associating details and a painter's individuality;
- test against data;
- confirmation or rejection of the hypothesis on the basis of results.

Deduction deals with generalisations. Meanwhile induction could look something like this:

- gathering of pots;
- scrutiny of pots for patterns;
- supposition of rules on the basis of the patterns.

The basic distinction becomes one between two fields of reason, two scientific fields. First there is mathematics and empirical method concerned with quantification and the repetition of phenomena. Then there is indirect and presumptive science, using repetition merely as an instrument to understand individual cases. Abduction tends to go with the latter. Ginzburg traces the distinction back to Galileo in the sixteenth century, and the establishment of a mathematical basis to science. This was a strategy which opposed anthropocentric and anthropomorphic reasoning and interests. Ginzburg contrasts the new physicist deaf to sounds, insensitive to tastes and odours, dealing in geometry and algebra, with the physician hazarding diagnoses by placing ear to wheezy chest, sniffing faeces and tasting urine. The latter has an individualistic focus, a scientific knowledge of the individual case. Physics makes its primary purpose the establishment of repetitive processes.

Whence the split? The tendency to obliterate the individual traits of an object is directly proportional to the *emotional* distance of the observer. A science of pottery may establish certain rules which govern its manufacture. Adherence to the rules brings success. This is the degree of involvement in making a pot according to a mathematically based or physical science. The craft of making a pot is based on another form of reasoning rooted in experience or know-how. To use another example, the ability to discern a hostile intention by a sudden change of expression is not something that can be easily learned from a book. Such knowledge is practical, rooted in experience which is not distanced but involved. This is, I believe, a crucial point because archaeology fascinates in its degree of involvement and immediacy: the presence of the past in the thumbprint on the pot. And it is more so with Classical archaeology because many have and do see the ancient Greeks as like themselves, ancestors of Europe. It may be held that all baboons look alike and we can experiment upon them retaining an emotional distance. But we are like the Greeks; this is our past. Beazley and the connoisseurs find themselves sensitive aesthetes.

The fascination of the detective story or TV doctor series is that we too are the detective or hospital physician, living the case. It engages; we too follow the clues, appreciate the symptoms of the person. There is a potential here of a humanistic, socially and politically engaged scientific method. The use of generalisation in the service of understanding individual phenomena is opposed to grand systems and total explanations of phenomena. Here are connections with the aphoristic reasoning found in Nietzsche and Adorno, which will be discussed in the final chapter.

The speculative modelling of the human sciences also has origins in modernity. A need to classify the criminal elements (with the criminalisation of the class struggle, as Ginzburg puts it), accompanied social control and surveillance in the nineteenth century. This has been famously covered in Michel Foucault's study of the birth of the prison (*Discipline and Punish*, English translation 1977). The creation of a criminal class and concern with their identification led to Bertillon's anthropometrics in the late nineteenth century and the development of fingerprinting by Galton. The work of detective fiction and indeed policing arrived too.

Hence a problem with Beazley could well be that his method of bringing tens of thousands of pots to order according to a spurious humanism of painters' hands (disguising a general taxonomics) was more to do with the panoptic gaze of state surveillance and control of the abstract 'individual' (what lies behind the potters' names, after all?). Perhaps there is a lack of imagination here or an unwillingness to harness method to a humanistic purpose different to recognition and control. Beazley's catalogues are not to be read; they are boring, and, at the same time, fascinating monuments to a legend.

ICONOGRAPHERS AND ICONOLOGISTS

What are figured designs about? Classical iconographers compile examples of different kinds of figured subject matter, painted, modelled or sculpted. Iconologists attempt to make some sense of the subject matter, identifying figures, and reflecting upon the structuring of figures, for example in pictorial narratives. The latter has become a major topic. Let me illustrate these practices, again using Korinthian pottery and the aryballos in Figure 2.1.

There are studies of the iconography of Korinthian pottery which, like the connoisseurs of attribution, also display a concern with the fine particularities of the rendition of detail and figure. Johansen's defining work of 1923 included much description of the variety and type of things painted upon his proposed style (this has been followed by Payne and Amyx). Strictly speaking, iconography is merely descriptive, and need not be restricted to any one style: there are general studies, published as monographs or catalogues of the depiction of griffons, sphinxes, centaurs, lions and panthers, all of which are to be found within other styles of decoration as well as Protokorinthian. Types

41

are defined and classifications proposed, lines of development induced or deduced. The meaning of the things painted upon the pots is secondary to iconographic work.

And so to meaning. Something seems to be happening in the scene upon this aryballos from Boston in Figure 2.1. A man-animal or centaur is confronting a warrior who brandishes something which is not immediately recognisable. Behind the monster is a stand for a *krater* or *dinos* (a mixing bowl) with four birds of prey. Another animated swordsman and various 'decorative' devices complete the scene. Is this the depiction of some story or myth? This is a question posed of all figured scenes by conventional Classical art history. Meanings are often sought in the literatures of ancient Greece and indeed Rome. Something seems to be happening in the main frieze, so there is the potential of discovering sense; whereas the frieze of animals upon the shoulder of this aryballos seems more mundane, merely a frieze – what narrative can there be? Sense and meaning are thus contrasted with the decorative. For this particular aryballos there has been considerable discussion of possible myth represented. Much has been made of the object in the hand of the figure opposing the monster, whether it is a thunderbolt, the weapon of god Zeus, who is therefore facing some enemy of his – Kronos, or Typhon, or a giant. The trouble is that there are no mentions in ancient literature of Zeus battling with a creature that looks like this, so various attempts have been made to explain away the look of the 'centaur'. Others have abandoned the identification of the figure as Zeus, accepted the iconography of the centaur, and found an enemy for it – Herakles.

Such a specification of myth and narrative depends on attributing meaning to particular details. But in this case the object in the hand of the swordsman is rare and a mystery for its date. There seems little prospect in deciding a secure interpretation. The tortuous discussion surrounding the identities of the figures could be called indulgent; for what does it matter when discussion and identification are related to nothing other than narratives of the development of Greek pottery painting? (Although, significantly, colour and detail are added to the art history.)

Mythological attribution is again a pronouncement of meaning, following a search, a desire for the sign that means something. Klaus Fittschen's superlative and critical study *Untersuchungen zum Beginn der Sagendarstellungen bei den Griechen* (1969) is defined by this desire to find out what the figures stand for. There has commenced a great encyclopaedic study of iconography and iconology – the *Lexicon Iconographicum Mythologiae Classicae* (1981–): a comprehensive dictionary. Searches such as these work through comparing scenes and representations; both iconography and mythological attribution use a comparative method whereby the meaning of a representation established in one context is transferred to another whose significance and meaning is in question. The strange weapon brandished by the figure upon the aryballos (Figure 2.1) may be interpreted as a thunderbolt in the hand of

Zeus because thunderbolts later and elsewhere are depicted comparatively similarly. Such a method crucially depends upon the definition of a 'meaningful context' – the space within which it is legitimate to make comparisons. This is usually 'the Greek': artefacts and representations are compared across a broad spread of geography and time which is thought of as Greek, with due note taken of supposed influences exerted by one design upon another across space and through time. The meaningful unity of this context is assumed. It can be argued that this marginalises significant difference in the pursuit of similarity (and so meaning); or rather difference is understood within a supposed higher unity (the Greek).

There are indeed clear lines of development and continued use of some figures and representations. This is the starting point for the work of iconography: fighting figures and centaurs not only appear on Protokorinthian pots such as this aryballos, but also have extensive currency in Greek art. However, this unity of Greek art is not 'natural'; it needs interpreting. The unity (the idea of the Greek) is one that is certainly conceived and made by people. Note has been taken of the interplay between cultural regionalism in Greece (inhabitants of some parts of Greece consistently seeing themselves as different to other Greeks) and notions of common Greek cultural identity, particularly stemming from the construction of aristocratic pan-Hellenism with the rise of the great sanctuaries in the eighth and seventh centuries. Identity is not natural but the result of desire, a desire to be the same, to join in opposition to another. However, iconographic studies and these attributing mythological meaning make this unity natural and do not ask questions of it. Why, it should be asked, do these studies accept the unity? Is the context 'Greek' accepted as meaningful because Classical archaeologists are involved in constructing their object as a unity, or are party to giving their object of interest an identity?

The designation of a mythological meaning involves transferring a meaning associated with a figure from one context to another. A centaur looks more or less like this; Zeus looks more or less like that. (The 'more or less' is, of course, open to debate.) Criticism of this one-to-one equation of a figure or point of style with an identity and meaning, mythological or other, comes from those who favour Structuralist and Post-structuralist interpretation, which sets a particular cultural item in context, but in a structured logic of difference (in contrast to the similarity required of a comparative method). This form of approach will be illustrated in Chapter 6.

IMPERIAL COLLECTIONS AND THE BIG DIGS

The *Blue Guide to Greece* by Stuart Rossiter lists and describes interesting places to visit. There are museums and archaeological ruins. A lot of the content of the former comes from cemeteries. The latter falls into two distinct classes: ancient town centres, and temples with their sanctuaries.

Classical archaeology has been dominated since the eighteenth century and before by a search for things to put in museums and by the excavation of the public buildings of city states and their sanctuaries.

The race for collections of Classical antiquities to be housed in the new national museums of European and American capitals took off in the nineteenth century. In 1811 a group of northern European aristocrats and architects, among whom was Charles Robert Cockerell, designer of the Ashmolean Museum in Oxford, found the sculpted marbles of the temples of Bassae and Aegina. The Aegina marbles went to adorn Ludwig of Bavaria's Munich, housed in Leo von Klenze's new museum in Grecian style, the Glyptothek. The Bassae marbles were sold to the British Museum in 1814, which, in the following year, purchased Elgin's Greek statues looted from the Parthenon in Athens.

The new designs, by Robert Smirke, for a British Museum in Grecian style were agreed in 1823; though it was not opened until 1852. Its interior clearly needed to vindicate the claims of its external appearance, a great Classical portico. So Charles Fellows was in Asia Minor in the 1840s collecting the marbles from Xanthus, which went to the British Museum. Charles T. Newton, later Director of the Museum, discovered and acquired various bits of the mausoleum at Bodrum, one of the seven wonders of the ancient world. This is how he describes the eleven-tonne coping sculpture of the tomb:

> While he had been lying grovelling on the earth we had never seen his face at all; so that, when we had set him on his base, and our eyes met for the first time his calm, majestic gaze, it seemed as if we had suddenly

Figure 2.4 Baron von Stackelberg. *Der Apollotempel zu Bassae in Arcadien* [The Temple of Apollo at Bassae in Arcadia]. Rome and Frankfurt am Main 1826. Plate 9

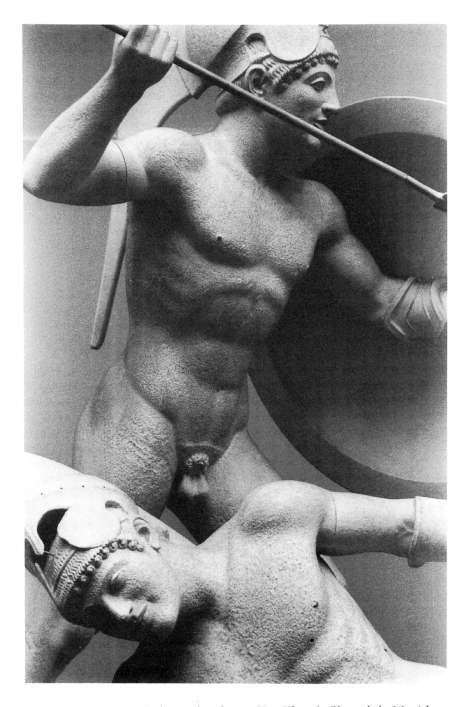

Figure 2.5 Aegina. Pedimental sculpture. Von Klenze's Glyptothek, Munich

roused him from his sleep of ages . . . When I stood very near the lion, many things in the treatment appeared harsh and singular; but on retiring to the distance of about thirty yards, all that seemed exaggerated blended into one harmonious whole, which, lit up by an Asiatic sun, exhibited a chiaroscuro such as I have never seen in sculpture; nor was the effect of this colossal production of human genius at all impaired by the bold forms and desolate grandeur of the surrounding landscape. The lion seemed made for the scenery, and the scenery for the lion.

It ended up in the museum in London.

John Turtle Wood, railway engineer backed by the British Museum, discovered and spent ten years excavating the Temple of Artemis at Ephesos, another famous wonder of the ancient world with its 127 massive columns, 19 metres high. Excavations ended in the early 1870s after the removal of 132,221 cubic metres of deposit, according to Wood's own calculations. There were further excavations under Hogarth in 1904–5, and later by Austrians. After 1966 explorations of the temple site took place under Eichler and Bammer.

Ludwig Ross, a German, supervised clearance and excavation of the Athenian Acropolis from 1834, accompanied by Leo Klenze, a neo-Classical architect. The Parthenon, the temple of Athena on the Acropolis, was restored as far as possible for the capital of the new independent state.

The all-Greek archaeological society *Arkhaiologiki Etaireia* was founded in 1837. It dug the Tower of the Winds, the Thrasyllos Monument, Propylaia and Erechtheion in 1839–40 and the Theatre of Dionysos on the slopes of the Acropolis in 1840–1. After various financial and other crises, the society excavated every year in Athens from 1858–94. However, excavation in Greece in the nineteenth century and long afterwards was dominated by the foreign schools of archaeology, based in Athens, which had access to the financial power of the great colonialist and imperialist states of western Europe.

The French school was founded in 1846 as a spin-off from the mainly German-sponsored Instituto di Corrispondenza Archeologica in Rome (1829). It was conceived as an important political link between Greece and France. German influence in Greece did not decline with the toppling, in 1862, of Otto of Bavaria's rule in Greece and the institution of a Danish monarch. From 1874 they had the German Archaeological Institute in Athens.

Ernst Curtius, who had been one of the key figures in establishing the Institute, undertook the excavation of the home of yet another wonder of the ancient world, Olympia. The site given to German control was two square miles of the hill of Kronos and by the river Alpheos, much of it under 5 or 6 metres of mud. Curtius and Adler began in October 1875 with 450 labourers. After two months of digging the first of the sculptures from the temple of Zeus was unearthed. The agreement with the Greek government meant they were to stay in Greece, though the Germans had sole rights for five years to any casts taken from them. Curtius, significantly, valued more the 400 inscriptions. Olympia was given over to careful but lavish publication, about which there will be more in Chapter 4.

Carl Humann, whose elder brother was Minister on the island of Samos, dealt with the restoration of the great Altar of Zeus built by Eumenes III in Hellenistic Pergamon. It was on display in Berlin in 1880. Though an amateur, Curtius had him made a Fellow of the German Institute.

The American School was digging by 1886. Its first project, under Waldstein from 1892–5, was investigation of the Sanctuary of Hera which had belonged to Argos – the Argive Heraion. This continued what was becoming a tradition in Greece of 'big digs', typified by the Germans at Olympia. These massive and expensive projects were only possible when undertaken by the foreign schools of the great world powers seeking their cultural roots.

The French, eager to restock the Louvre, had acquired the Venus de Milo in the 1820s, and became involved in a competition to dig at Delphi, foremost sanctuary of the ancient world. The Germans were claiming rights to dig on the basis of previous interest, as were the French. The 1,000 houses of the village of Kastri, which overlay the site, had to be moved at great expense. The Americans were tempted by the Greek Archaeological Society, and the price of the site went up from $25,000 to $80,000, but the French made trade concessions (over Korinthian raisins), voted a million francs to Greece, and received the right to excavate (from 1893). '*On fait de nous des chercheurs de truffes*' ('We are become truffle-hounds') complained a marquis in the Senate.

The Americans had founded their school in 1882. Britain followed in 1886, the Austrians in 1898, and the Italians in 1909. Private money played an important role in these, less directly attached to state interests. So prior to 1914 a geography of excavation had been set in place which has scarcely changed since; the French at Delphi and Delos, Thasos and Argos; the Germans at Olympia, Samos and in the Kerameikos of Athens; the Americans at Korinth and the Argive Heraion; the British in the Peloponnese, at Megalopolis and Sparta, also Crete and Knossos; the Italians at Gortyn, Ida and Phaistos on Crete; the Austrians pioneered exploration of Samothrace.

The time was appropriate in 1924 to excavate the Agora, the market area and centre of ancient Athens. More and more people were moving to a growing modern Athens. It was going to be then or never. Various Greek territories had been surrendered to Turkey and immigrants were arriving; there was a need for cultural integration, to be achieved perhaps by focusing attention on common roots and heritage. The Greek monarchy had been abolished by plebiscite and the government needed the prestige of a great cultural work. But the state had no money to buy out the 7,000 to 10,000 residents of the Agora. Then in 1927 an anonymous gift of $250,000 from

Figure 2.6 Korinth in the snow, before the excavations. (Courtesy of the Museum of Classical Archaeology, Cambridge)

John D. Rockefeller allowed the Americans to win a concession to evict and dig. Between 1931 and 1939 another million came from Rockefeller. In total, 365 buildings were demolished, and 16 acres cleared of 250,000 tons of earth.

As might be expected, the excavations generated a wealth of material. This allowed Leslie Shear (Senior) to train a generation of excavators. It still keeps researchers busy. The momentum of the sheer weight of finds means that there is no time, space or indeed need for questioning approaches and priorities. The school from 1928 held a monopoly on excavation (all projects had to be approved) and exclusion from unpublished artefacts meant exclusion from the discipline. These points will be taken up more generally in Chapter 4, which deals with discourse.

Arguably the sanctuaries have not been well excavated or treated. Their stratification and contexts are very complex: the result of temple officials regularly clearing out material, and the long-term use of the sites. Much is often missing: rich items were taken away. What is more, the artefacts have been pre-ordered by the discipline; its art historical interests going back well before excavations started in the nineteenth century. Hence there are superb catalogues of isolated classes of artefacts from these great excavations, but contextual associations are often missing. Under architectural interests, individual buildings, even very fragmentary, have been measured, recorded and planned to an accurate degree, but there is still now little understanding of how a sanctuary worked. This is shown by Cathy Morgan's book on the

Figure 2.7 The Stoa of Attalos, Athens. Rebuilt with American money, mid-twentieth century

origins of the great Greek sanctuaries, *Athletes and Oracles: the Transformation of Olympia and Delphi in the Eighth Century BC* (1990); remarkably little of sound historical understanding arises from the century and more of large-scale excavation of Delphi and Olympia.

Excavation techniques have, of course, changed immensely for the good in recent years. Note can be made of the development of field survey, about which there is more in Chapter 6. This has involved a re-evaluation of the priorities of archaeological research. The pressure from urban development is, however, considerable, and much effort in Greek archaeology now goes simply into mitigating its effects with rescue or salvage excavation.

ANCIENT HISTORY, THE HISTORICAL EVENT AND DESCRIPTIVE NARRATIVE

En voyageant dans la Grèce, il faudrait avoir Pausanias à la main pour trouver les choses remarquables, parce qu'il a fait autrefois ce voyage par la même curiosité; prendre les vues de Tempé en Thessalie, du Parnasse, du temple de Delphes et des ruines d'Athènes; rapporter le plus d'inscriptions qui se pourra.

[In travelling round Greece have a copy of Pausanias with you to help find the most significant things, because he made the journey with the same interest; take a look at Tempe in Thessaly, Parnassus, the temple of Delphi, and the ruins of Athens; bring back as many inscriptions as possible.]

(Minister Colbert to M. Galland 1679)

As one goes up to Korinth (from the Isthmus) are tombs, and by the gate is buried Diogenes of Sinope, whom the Greeks surname the Dog (the 'Cynic' philosopher). Before the city is a grove of cypresses called Kraneion. Here are a precinct of Bellerophontes, a temple of Melaenis and the grave of Lais, upon which is set a lioness holding a ram in her fore-paws . . . The things worthy of mention in the city include the extant remains of antiquity, but the greater number of them belong to the period of its second ascendancy. On the market place, where most of the sanctuaries are, stand Artemis, surnamed Ephesian and wooden statues of Dionysos, which are covered with gold with the exception of their faces; these are ornamented with red paint . . .

(Pausanias, *Guide to Greece*)

Why this interest in sanctuaries and town centres? There is a simple answer. The Classical archaeologists who established this pattern in the discipline were guided above all by Pausanias and his detailed descriptions of the remains of the city centres and sanctuaries of Greece in Roman times. More generally the blueprint has been supplied by ancient literatures. Archaeology

Figure 2.8 Stuart and Revett. *The Antiquities of Athens*, Volume 3. London 1787. Chapter 6, Plate 1. Korinth

has often been seen as an illustrative addendum, or parallel art history, to 'real' history – archaeological materials fleshing out the main features of ancient times found through scrutiny of written accounts. The amount of effort expended into establishing fine-grained archaeological chronologies, often for no sake other than chronological control, can be mentioned here (and is discussed above). Criticism may be raised that this interest is only in the construction of what David Clarke called 'counterfeit history books', that is an interest which does not heed the character of archaeological materials and the sort of interests appropriate to them.

There are all kinds of tricky issues here about relationships between history and archaeology, and many are dealt with throughout this book, but the idea that archaeology is merely an illustrative addendum to history remains.

The point is made clearly in an article by Paul Cartledge summarising archaeology in Greece in a book entitled *Greece Old and New* (ed. T. Winnifrith and P. Murray, 1983). He provides a historical background of travellers to Greece and Hellenists, and then picks out several recent archaeological finds he regards as important. The choice is very revealing. Under some paving stones of the sacred way at Delphi, excavations mounted by the French School found in 1939 some fragments of three chryselephantine statues and a lifesize bull. They are now on display in the museum at Delphi. Chryselephantine statues were the composite constructions of precious metals and ivory which so characterised the ancient sanctuaries. They are an artistic medium about which much has been conjectured. So few have survived because they were dismantled and plundered in antiquity. Hence Cartledge marks out these finds.

Between 1954 and 1958 the Germans at Olympia found debris from the construction of one of the seven wonders of the ancient world, the chryselephantine statue of Zeus made by Pheidias, the sculptor of the famous pedimental marbles of both Olympia and the Parthenon. Pausanias had been used to guide the excavators to the site of the workshop of Pheidias. To the south was found ivory and bone, obsidian, rock crystal, amber, tools, clay matrices for hammering out the gold dress 'and even moulds for making glass ornaments not mentioned by Pausanias'. What clinched it all for Cartledge was a pot inscribed with 'I belong to Pheidias'. Other pots allow the debris to be dated after 435 BC. The chryselephantine Athena in the Parthenon, also by Pheidias, was completed by 438. 'So his Athena set the standard he had to surpass at Olympia to produce a "Wonder" of the ancient world'. Here Cartledge is continuing an interest long established in historical personages, artists, and written roots of the archaeological. It will be argued later that this is a wholly inadequate way of conceiving of archaeological materials.

Michael Grant has considered the relationship between archaeological materials and ancient history in his book *The Visible Past: Greek and Roman History from Archaeology 1960–1990* (1990). He recognises the difference between archaeology and historical studies, but the book is all about archaeology contributing to a *story* of the past which is how, basically, he conceives of history. Hence the title: history *from* archaeology.

Contacts are being sought here with political-military narratives or historical narratives more generally. Archaeological materials are frequently thus considered as passive mirrors of a social reality known from literatures, needing no explanation in terms of social action. This point will be developed through Chapters 5 and 6.

To temper this criticism, mention should be made of the social and economic histories produced particularly under the influence of Moses Finley's Marxism. There are also French anthropologies of Classical antiquity, and new art histories. Classical studies generally is setting new agendas which have done much in the way of reassessing the relationship between archaeological and written sources. But here I am anticipating following chapters.

CONCLUDING REMARKS

In the last 200 years of Classical archaeology there has been a consistency in the questions asked and answers sought from certain accepted classes of evidence. It has been the purpose of this chapter to give some idea of these. Things are changing though; there is a considerable broadening of outlook – an aspect that will feature in the discussions of later chapters. But the raw materials with which these new archaeologies work remain largely the product of excavations and collection strategies whose principles and values were established in the nineteenth century. So, for example, upon deciding to consider the design of artefacts made in Korinth at that time of change in the seventh century BC, I was drawn into 200 years of connoisseurship simply to get to the perfume jars in which I was interested. And with the aryballoi come all sorts of underlying attitudes, cultural outlooks and ideologies. It is the purpose of the next chapter to consider these further.

3

GREEK MYTHS
AND METANARRATIVES
From Winckelmann to Bernal

COLLECTORS AND ANTIQUARIANS

It is often held that the 'rediscovery' of Greece came in the eighteenth and nineteenth centuries. Indeed, it is true that until the late eighteenth century most educated west Europeans probably regarded their cultural origins as Roman and Christian. Language (Latin) was an important factor in this. An earlier rediscovery of Roman roots had occurred with Renaissance Italian artists drawing inspiration from Roman art. Yet, as studies like Richard Stoneman's show (and in a different way that of Alain Schnapp: see Bibliography), there is a continuity in the reception of the remains of the past and those of Greece in particular. One manifestation of this is Classicism.

In the 1500s François I of France was collecting Roman statues and Roman copies of Greek (as especially did Louis XIV) as part of a French claim to be the new Rome. A great collection of bronze copies was formed at Fontainebleau (marble at Versailles). To own a cabinet of medals became popular in the same century. By 1550 there were 380 collections in Italy alone, 200 in the Low Countries, 200 in France and 175 in Germany. Collections too were started of drawings of antiquities and inscriptions. Two famous rival collectors in England of the seventeenth century were the Earl of Arundel (died 1646) and the Duke of Buckingham (assassinated 1628). Charles I was another. At his death Arundel had 37 statues, 128 busts and 250 inscriptions as well as sarcophagi, altars, fragments, coins, books and manuscripts. Neglected on his death, some of the collection eventually reached the Ashmolean Museum, Oxford, in the nineteenth century.

Mention has already been made of Louis XIV (1638–1715). During his reign a series of agents were sent out by Chief Minister Colbert to Greece and the Levant to collect books, manuscripts, medals and inscriptions. This French interest in Classical antiquities continued past the death of Louis. The Abbé Michel Fourmont notoriously claimed the discovery of many important historical inscriptions at Sparta. They were later realised as forgeries at the end of the eighteenth century.

Fourmont records in 1730:

> For a month now, despite illness, I have been engaged with thirty
> workmen in the entire destruction of Sparta; not a day passes but I find
> something, and on some I have found up to twenty inscriptions. You
> understand, Monsieur, with what great joy, and with what fatigue, I
> have recovered such a great quantity of marbles. . . .
>
> If by overturning its walls and temples, if by not leaving one stone
> on another in the smallest of its sacella, its place will be unknown in
> the future, I at least have something by which to recognise it, and that
> is something. I have only this means to render my voyage in the Morea
> illustrious, which otherwise would have been entirely useless, which
> would have suited neither France, nor me.
>
> I am becoming a barbarian in the midst of Greece; this place is not
> the abode of the Muses, ignorance has driven them out, and it is that
> which makes me regret France, whither they have retreated. I should
> have liked to have more time to bring them at least more than bare
> nourishment, but the orders I have just received oblige me to finish.

Edward Dodwell on his later visit to Sparta in 1801 reported that Fourmont
was still remembered as ordering the defacement of inscriptions he had just
recorded.

Bernard de Montfaucon (1655–1741) was part of the great tradition of the
Benedictine monks of Saint-Maur. His *L'Antiquité expliquée et représentée en
figures* compiled 30,000 pieces of antique art. It reveals something of a
funerary obsession, but also an extraordinary and systematic collection of
material to do with the life of antiquity. In it the image plays a fundamental
role, but as a complement to the text. Schnapp contrasts this with the work
of Francesco Bianchini, working in the Vatican, at the end of the seventeenth
century. He treated the image as of a separate order of perception and knowledge and opened a new route to the past, that of comparative iconography.
Through close scrutiny of imagery, Bianchini presented the decisive role
of figuration in antiquity, with historical periods represented by particular
emblematic images. Instead Schnapp detects in Montfaucon a Platonic
element, a distinction between the world of ideas (represented by text and the
subject of history) and that of the senses (images, the subject of archaeology):
each object was connected to a body of text which gave it meaning. Thomas
Carlyle was not impressed by Montfaucon's project, calling it 'mere classical
ore and slag'.

Anne Claude Philippe de Turbières de Grimoard de Pestels de Lévis,
comte de Caylus, spent three years travelling in the eastern Mediterranean
from 1714–17. Active member of the Académie des Inscriptions et Belles
Lettres (an antiquarian and historical association founded in 1701), he built
up a large collection, becoming a leading antiquarian of his time. From
1752–67 appeared the seven volumes of his *Receuil d'Antiquités égyptiennes,*

étrusques, grecques et romaines. This was not just a monument to antiquarian relics; as well as the art of the ancient world, contemporary art interested Caylus. The key point for Schnapp is Caylus's project of replacing the philological model of antiquarian or archaeological studies, which assumed the priority and metaphor of textual interpretation. For Caylus the antiquary was a sort of physician of the past with an experimental paradigm. In criticising the textual model of interpretation applied to monuments, he asserted the priority of observation and insisted on the positive experience of the artefact, that it was not just a supplement to history or something like an isolated text to be deciphered. Objects were clues or symptoms, diagnostic tools for recognising cultural and geographic origins, and for establishing sequences of change. In Caylus can be found a cultural determinism founded on observation and quantification, the basis of typology.

TRAVELLERS

By the 1670s English and French travellers were visiting Greece. The country had largely been ignored apart from Ciriaco Pizzicolli, known as Cyriac of Ancona, who, with antiquarian interests, had made several journeys from Italy in the fifteenth century and brought back many drawings of temples and reliefs.

Jacques Spon and George Wheler became travelling companions in 1675–6. The former's authoritative account of their travels became a benchmark for a century. For Spon, the past was a book to be read. This active metaphor, according to Schnapp, laid emphasis on medals and inscriptions; Spon can be treated as the inventor of numismatics and epigraphy, applying a philological model to the past.

George Wheler in the Preface to his account of their travels, dedicated to Charles II, wrote the following:

> A country once mistress of the civil world, and a most famous nursery both of arms and sciences; but now a lamentable example of the instability of human things, wherein your majesty's discontented and factious subjects, if their own late calamities will not sufficiently instruct them, may see the miseries that other nations are reduced to, and behold, as in a picture, the natural fruits of schism, rebellion, and civil discord.

There are several elements present here of a nascent set of attitudes towards the Classical Greek past: time and the past; order and disorder; state unity versus political diversity; Greece as the ideal of liberty and excellence lost and crushed. More will be made of this throughout this chapter.

Spon and Wheler were among the last to see the Parthenon in Athens relatively undamaged. In 1669 Pope Clement IX gave his blessing to the fleet which sailed against the Ottoman Empire. As part of the campaigns the Doge of Venice, Morosini, moved against Athens. The Acropolis was bombarded,

with the Parthenon, at that time a mosque, being used as a powder magazine
. . . bits were blown hundreds of metres.

JOHANN JOACHIM WINCKELMANN
AND GREEK ART

Johann Joachim Winckelmann, born at Stendal near Berlin in 1717, was a
main figure in an eighteenth-century revolution in attitude towards the
ancient Greek past: an attitude which still has effect today. His *Gedanken*
of 1755 was translated by Fuseli into English (as *Reflections on the Imitation
of Nature in Greek Art*) in 1765. He became Librarian and President of
Antiquities at the Vatican, and in 1764 was published his two-volume work
Geschichte der Kunst des Alterthums. This was a chronological account of antique
art which had never before been attempted; Winckelmann produced a stylistic
chronology where others had only undertaken iconographic commentary. For
example, the most celebrated ancient statues in the Belvedere courtyard in the
Vatican or Florence's Tribuna had been considered simply as being of the 'best
period'. A four-stage scheme, adopted from Scaliger's for poetry (1608), was
proposed for Greek sculpture: pre- and early Classical was straight and hard;
the High Classical of Phidias was grand and square; that of fourth-century
Praxiteles was beautiful and flowing; then art was imititative.

Winckelmann's stylistic analysis was not, as for Caylus, a technical instrument,
though both, according to Schnapp, stood for an evolutionary model of art.
Winckelmann certainly describes an evolution from primitive beginnings
to perfection. The scheme derives ultimately from theories of rhetoric and
had been applied to the arts by Vasari in the Italian Renaissance. For
Winckelmann, stylistic analysis was the key to aesthetic understanding. So
rather than just explain works of art as artefacts, Winckelmann sought
to explain a culture by its works of art. In Greek art he found an idealised
pagan soul, a noble simplicity and calm grandeur (the famous '*eine edle Einfalt
und eine stille Grösse*'). Greece was to be seen as the childhood of Europe, the
foundation from which all European culture sprang. This had a great influence
on intellectuals like Goethe, Herder, Fichte and Schiller, for whom Winckelmann's heritage was the sublime mystery of Greek art. For others like Thomas
Jefferson and Jacques-Louis David, the neo-Classical painter of the French
Revolution, he stood for the freedom of Greek artists.

Winckelmann developed a way of writing about art which foregrounded
questions and issues of taste. In a full philosophy of art transcending mere
archaeology, art was inseparable from morality. Here is his rapturous adula-
tion of the Apollo Belvedere (a Roman copy, in the Vatican collections, of a
Greek original):

> an eternal spring clothes with the charms of youth the graceful manliness
> of ripened years, and plays with soft tenderness about the proud shape

Figure 3.1 William Blake's Laocoön

of his limbs . . . My breast seems to enlarge and swell with reverence . . . for my image seems to receive life and motion, like the beautiful creation of Pygmalion.

On the Belvedere torso (a fragment of a statue, again in the Vatican):

Ask those who know the best in mortal perfection whether they have ever seen a flank that can compare with the left side of this statue . . .

57

You can learn here how a master's creative hand is able to endow matter with mind. The back, which appears as if flexed in noble thought, gives me the mental picture of a head filled with the joyful remembrance of his astonishing deeds, and, as this head full of wisdom and majesty arises before my inner eye, the other missing limbs also begin to take shape in my imagination.

These are exercises in an old Classical literary genre, the *ekphrasis*.

Winckelmann's method involved a close scrutiny of statues by torchlight. His alertness to details anticipates the later connoisseurship of the likes of Morelli (discussed in the previous chapter). He made observations on the size of knees and nipples; notable is his concern, amounting to anxiety, about the depth of the navel of the Venus de Medici, and the importance he attached to a barely perceptible flaring in the nostrils of the Apollo Belvedere. This was all part of a methodical stylistic analysis of anatomical parts; but parts of Roman copies, not Greek originals. Winckelmann never went to Greece. And whereas he considered mainly sculpture, Winckelmann worked largely from ancient literature about art.

The importance attached by Winckelmann's connoisseurship to such close scrutiny can be related to a decline in the fashion of restoring ancient statues. Lord Elgin, for example, had originally hoped that the marbles which he had acquired from the Parthenon would be restored. (Thorvaldsen, the noted neo-Classical sculptor, restored the pedimental sculpture of the temple of Aphaia on Aegina which had been bought by Ludwig I for Munich.) Winckelmann valued the original fragments over later work, stressing, in a reverential attitude as towards sacred relics, that the excellence of ancient Greek sculpture could not be imitated.

In a recent short history of Classical archaeology, Ian Morris joins others in seeing Winckelmann as representative of a German elite resisting French assertions of its Roman roots and credentials. Here the role of German Protestantism is important, with ideas of getting back to the simple Greek original unencumbered by Latin and papal commentaries. By the late eighteenth century in Germany and elsewhere, ancient Greece was a meta-historical construct, something more than simply a part of history, and one of the methods considered appropriate to understanding ancient Greece was connoisseurship.

Winckelmann articulates a *metanarrative* which came to dominate study of and attitudes towards the Classical past. A metanarrative is a grand system, often taking form as a structure of emplotment, but may also be a body of theory or explanations, often approaching myth, which lies in the back-ground of particular accounts and provide general orientation, framework and legitimation, conferring meaning. One of the operative metanarratives in Classical archaeology is Winckelmann's Hellenism.

CONSTITUTING THE ART OBJECT

After Winckelmann there developed in the nineteenth century a Romantic attitude to Greek art. The new international art museums worked all out to gather collections. The Getty Museum in Malibu is the latest to join the big league who have taken over from the older aristocratic and royal collections.

Sculpture and pots are considered not just as archaeological relics, but works of art with no need of interpretation (for the educated viewer). The visual and aesthetic language of art has been presented as transparent. Whereas ancient literatures need careful commentary and critique, this has not been considered necessary for art. This attitude is clear in the mode of presentation found in all of the world's big international art museums.

The Classical artefact is presented free-standing as art, with minimal supporting information, in the museum detached from the exigencies of day-to-day life – in splendid isolation from the prosaic. Art is presupposed as an immanent 'humanity', with artefacts formally identical according to spiritual truth, universal values expressed in the exceptional artefact. History is thus unified, and museums are free to roam the whole productive past, juxtaposing whatever is considered art. The viewer need only approach with finely tuned sensibilities.

This lack of interpretation of art (other than in more or less idealist art histories) is compounded by the effects of the art market and lack of contextual information. Classification of artefacts considered as art so often becomes circular and a wholly unenlightening exercise. A pot arrives on the art market. Without provenance it is classified by the (saleroom) expert as, say, typical early Hellenistic. It then enters the literatures as an early Hellenistic piece, and as part of an art historical corpus it provides justification for the schemes that allowed its attribution.

Attributions of the expert connoisseur are central to this attitude to 'Art', providing distinctions between authentic and fake, and passing judgements of quality, as explained in the last chapter. Critical art history (also discussed in Chapter 2) places importance on the sequence of works and so depends on contextual information to supply secure dates. But the ideology of pure works of art, which feeds the art market and which treats social and historical context as secondary, is an extremely dangerous threat to serious and critical understanding of artefacts.

VICKERS AND GILL AND THE CRITIQUE OF CERAMIC ART

Winckelmann concentrated on sculpture. A typical image of Greek art is also the fictile vase. Michael Vickers, of the Ashmolean Museum, Oxford, and David Gill, lately of the Fitzwilliam Museum, Cambridge, have made a long and carefully documented stand against the idea that Greek pots are high art.

Sir William Hamilton was posted as Envoy to the Court of Naples in 1764. He was there for thirty-six years, during which time he indulged his passion for antiquities. In 1774 he sold his first collection of Greek 'vases' (still thought to be Etruscan or Campanian) to the British Museum for the extraordinary price of 8,000 guineas. He had had engravings of the collection published prior to the sale in sumptuous folio with a text by Pierre d'Hancarville. Vickers and Gill argue that this was a clever marketing job involving a confidence trick played by d'Hancarville. The claim was made that the vases were extremely expensive in antiquity. Winckelmann was involved. He did not produce such an argument, but was convinced of the superlative art of the vases and did argue, flimsily, that the Greeks competed for vases at games. The Greeks were artists: the British Museum was convinced; Winckelmann and Goethe were convinced. The art market developed its tastes for Greek vases.

Why should pots be taken as expensive works of art? The context of such a shift in taste was right. Porcelain factories, such as Meissen, Sèvres, and at Vincennes, had been developing in eighteenth-century Europe. Many were established by royalty; all were patronised by royalty and the aristocracy. Porcelain design catered for aristocratic tastes and those of the emerging middle classes eager to emulate their social betters. Indeed, the techniques of porcelain manufacture had only recently been discovered at Dresden, though they had long been known in China; the art of Greek potting was similarly lost and unknown to eighteenth-century Europe.

So Greek vases could be compared with the royal porcelain of Europe. They also met certain new requirements of taste. Josiah Wedgwood was pioneering factory production of ceramics and new principles of marketing, manufacturing taste as well as cheaper wares for the new middle classes. Relations between the radical industrialist Wedgwood and antiquities are very clear. He commercially exploited antique design. His model factory in Staffordshire was named Etruria (vases such as Hamilton's were found in Etruscan graves). On the opening day of the factory, 13 June 1769, Wedgwood threw six 'Etruscan urns'. Encaustic techniques were used to imitate Attic red figure, and scenes were taken from one of Hamilton's vases.

Greek vases also suited changing tastes. In a reaction against decorative Baroque and Rococo, tastes were moving towards greater simplicity. Caylus in 1752 stressed the simplicity of Greek art, as did Winckelmann and d'Hancarville, one of whose comments on the Hamilton vases was 'the Elegance of the outline . . . the Character of their distinguishing simplicity'. Goethe's *Italian Journey* of 1817, a successful and influential work, had the motto '*et in arcadia ego*' – an allusion to the simplicity of the way of life in central Peloponnese and something Goethe found in the kingdom of the two Sicilies. This Romanticism coming together with neo-Classicism will be discussed below.

Vickers and Gill do not stop with the accusation of an art market. They

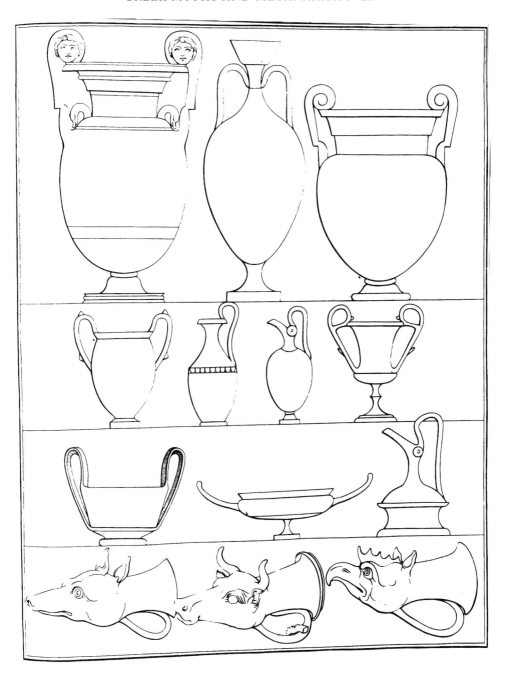

Figure 3.2 Part of Sir William Hamilton's second collection, published with
Tischbein in Naples, 1791

have also aimed to show the scale and character of elite consumption and lifestyle in antiquity: that it had nothing to do with painted pots. It was all about precious metal plate and bullion.

Some of the 300 top Athenian families of the fifth century BC were millionaires in today's terms (Vickers and Gill draw such comparisons using clever calculations around gold values). But they were not as rich, by any means, as Persians; standards of wealth and luxury were set out east. The richest man in the Persian Empire of 480 BC was a certain Pythius, who possessed more than 50 tonnes of silver and 33 of gold: more than £220 million. These people did not use ceramic tableware.

Sanctuaries, the storehouses and treasuries of the ancient world, were stuffed full of metal plate according to contemporary accounts. Croesus of Lydia, for example, in the middle of the sixth century BC gave to Delphi (according to Herodotos): a huge gold shield; two craters of enormous size, one gold and another of silver that could hold 600 amphoras of wine; four silver casks; two lustral vases, one of gold, the other silver; a gold statue, three cubits high, of a woman; and many lathe-turned bowls of silver. Herodotos then describes a display of conspicuous consumption, a great sacrifice almost along the lines of what anthropologists call a potlatch. The ancient Greeks and Romans thought highly of metal plate, not ceramics. Connoisseurs in the late Roman Republic, when antiquarianism was, for once, popular, thought most highly of silver plate.

What happened to all of this wealth of the ancient world? It was stolen and/or melted down for recycling throughout antiquity. What does survive comes from the margins of the Greek world, in Thrace and Macedon, and particularly in the so-called Scythian tombs. Plate does not appear in Greek tombs because capital wealth was passed on to heirs. Etruscan tombs, in which have been found, according to Hemelrijk, perhaps 90 per cent of surviving Attic vases, provided a show of tokens and symbols of wealth in the vases, but not the expense of what really was valued.

Ceramics were, according to Vickers and Gill, skeuomorphic, that is copies or imitations of metal vessels. They claim that the reason why this possibility has not been seriously entertained is because of a doctrine that great art (read ceramics) deals with 'Truth' and is true to its medium and does not imitate another. But the position of Vickers and Gill is that ceramics were not art. Various aspects of the shape of many pots imitate techniques of metal manufacture. This has long been recognised and they point again to thin-walled vessels, handle shapes, ribbing, attachments and false rivets. They admit that Geometric pottery seems to obey a ceramic aesthetic, with its loose forms, otherwise ceramic form follows that of sheet metal. The main contribution to this line of thought about skeuomorphism concerns colour. Why is this pottery black or red figure? Why did potters go to extraordinary lengths to achieve the colour effects they so valued? Vickers and Gill argue that the colours imitate metals.

So black is silver, because the metal was allowed to tarnish. Taken alone this thesis can appear a little strained. The goddesses Thetis and Aphrodite are described as silver-footed. And consider this reference, made by Vickers and Gill, to bad water at Athens:

> Bad water, adduced by Athenaeus as a reason why silver might become oxidised, was a problem. Vitruvius describes how Athenian water brought by conduits had 'a foam floating on top, like purple glass in colour' so that people only used it for washing and took drinking water from wells. This sounds like a recipe for oxidation. Fumigation too, would have had a similar effect on silver, for if Homeric precedent was followed (as it seems to have been) both houses and storerooms might be cleansed by burning sulphur. Both sweaty hands and flatulence would have also contributed to making silver dark.

According to this skeuomorphism, red figure is gold figure. There are indeed many references to ruddy gold: in the poet Theognis, for example, refined gold is ruddy to look upon. Next, purple is copper, and white is ivory.

Pots in antiquity were also cheap, and ridiculously so. The highest recorded price for any Attic painted pot is 3 drachmas, or £5.40. In comparison, a cup of silver with gold figures, according to its weight, would cost more than £450. A commercial graffito on the underside of a red-figure pelike in Oxford and attributed by Beazley to the 'Achilles painter' can be read as 'four items for 3.5 obols' – 26 pence each. There was no money to be made in pots. Indeed, it is beginning to be held that trade in pottery in antiquity was probably a by-product of trade in other materials or of other activities (see below on the ancient economy in Chapter 6.

For Vickers and Gill the real artists were metalworkers. The signatures on pots are copying signatures on their metal models – Douris, Exekias, Euphronios and the others were working in metal. Hence some of the writing is garbage, not understood by potters, and some pots bearing the same signature are clearly by different hands: the example of Douris is cited. Sotades signed his name in many different ways and it seems that Phintias (Phintis, Phitias, or Philtias) and Memnon (Mnememnon, Memmnon, Memnoon, or Memon) could not spell their names!

A division of labour is indicated by the signatures. For example, a stand in New York bears the inscription: '*Kleitias egraphsen Ergotimos epoiesen*' [Kleitias drew this; Ergotimos made it]. Vickers and Gill suggests that *grammata* or *graphides* were designs in parchment or wood shown to a client before a metal vessel was made. This would not be appropriate for pottery, whose cost would not warrant it. Ergotimos would then be the silversmith in this case, while Kleitias designed the *gramma*. These were the artists who determined changes in fashion, and potters followed suit: the switch from black to red figure was a shift in fashions of metal plate.

There is a faulted and circular logic in treating pots as art. The line of thought goes as follows. The draughtsmen who produced Attic ceramics rank alongside Renaissance artists, therefore their work is amenable to the same sort of connoisseurship that is applied to Renaissance painting to discern artists. Therefore the work of potters must have been socially important and valuable; therefore their makers would have earned a good living. But lowly craftworkers were not valued in antiquity (according to Herodotos the Korinthians *despised* them least!). Here Vickers and Gill have Beazley, who adopted the method of Renaissance expert Morelli, as a Romantic, influenced by the Arts and Crafts Movement (1880s onwards) in creating new attitudes towards craftsmanship and the 'art' of studio ceramics. Beazley here is depicted in the same light as Charles Norton, seeing the study of ancient art as an antidote to materialism and industrial consciousness.

So attribution studies, in treating pots as art and in searching for artists, have only confused matters and diverted attention away from understanding ceramics for what they were. But the connection between connoisseurship and the art market has already been mentioned. From the early nineteenth century a considerable investment of symbolic as well as monetary capital was placed in the growing art market in vases. John Beazley conveniently provided artists' names, and I have discussed this search for the creative individual. Here may be introduced the point that attribution deals with the distinction of original artist from derivative imitator or forger, matters at the heart of art market values. Here lies a major problem with the model of pottery workshops and schools. Beazley's artists influence and imitate one another (this is assumed by other attribution studies too, such as those produced for Korinthian pottery and discussed in Chapter 2). The notion of artistic style depends upon a genealogy of iconography with one potter being influenced by another. But the ceramic vessels of Attica went to be consumed in Etruscan tombs. One pot design could hardly be influencing a potter in Athens if it were underground in Etruria.

Vickers and Gill claim that the high status of ceramic artefacts is nothing to do with the ancient world; the pots were not considered works of art:

> Once it is widely recognised that the study of Greek pottery is largely conducted within an intellectual vacuum which has little point of contact with the values of the ancient world, there should be a decline in the extent to which Etruscan (and other) cemeteries are looted in order to supply museums and collectors – and behind them the market-makers and ancient-art consultants – with works of 'Art'.

In this argument artistic value is not an abstract constant, but related to social context. While this does throw doubt on the validity of artistic evaluation, and directly threatens the basis of a contemporary art market, the symptomatic logic of attribution and concepts of art style are left untouched.

Hence Vickers and Gill can concur with most of Beazley's attributions; '[b]ut what has tended to be obscured is the degree to which there is an overlap of motifs between the work of one pot painter and another.' They explain this as a result of the copying of the designs of silversmiths. They still adhere to something of a hagiograhy of Beazley: 'Without Beazley's eye (and in the absence of his strict ethical code with regard to the art market), attribution studies become less worthy of respect.' Nor do Vickers and Gill challenge the notion of art: potters may not have been artists, but metalsmiths were. There is here a distinction between art and craft which will be taken up again and criticised in Chapter 6.

TASTE AND THE GREEK

Taste is a central concept in the construction of Greek artefacts as art. So far I have considered some aspects of the development of Romantic Hellenism. Here may be introduced the case of Lord Elgin.

At the end of the eighteenth century Elgin was building himself a house, Broomhall, on the north side of the Firth of Forth. In 1798 his architect Thomas Harrison persuaded him that books were not enough for contemporary design – casts and originals could change art. A diplomatic job in Constantinople was opportunity to do something about this; hence the Parthenon marbles ended up in Britain. But by 1803 Elgin had spent £40,000 of his own money on the sculptures, and when they went on exhibition in 1807 many connoisseurs and antiquarians did their best to belittle the works, though some artists seem to have been enthralled. The Pheidian marbles were contrasted with hitherto exemplars of Classical taste such as the Apollo Belvedere: they were decidedly less ideal and more naturalistic. The marbles demanded a complete re-evaluation of taste which did not come too soon for Elgin. Elgin worked on public opinion, but it was the acquisition of the Aegina pedimental sculpture by Bavaria that had the significant effect on matters of taste (and the price that Elgin eventually received for the marbles). Ludwig I had staged a cultural coup in acquiring original Greek sculpture (not merely copies) for his capital Munich. He was known to be willing to buy the Parthenon marbles. The Trustees of the British Museum did not want to be upstaged twice and Elgin got £35,000 in 1815, less than half of what he had eventually spent. The sculpture became the symbol of Greek excellence, far surpassing, according to opinion, the Aegina marbles, and as naturalistic originals, outshining the ideal encapsulated by Roman copies such as the Apollo Belvedere.

When first visiting Athens in the late 1970s I was intrigued by some of the ancient sites of Athens listed as so significant by 'authorities' such as the *Blue Guide*. The Tower of the Winds (technically the Waterclock of Andronikos) and the Lantern of Demosthenes (the Lysicrates Monument) seemed inconsequential details of the Plaka compared with the Acropolis. I wondered why they were listed as so important and not to be missed. The reason is two English architects of the eighteenth century.

Figure 3.3 Stuart and Revett. *The Antiquities of Athens*, Volume 2. London 1787. Chapter 1, Plate 1. The Parthenon

The Society of Dilettanti was founded probably in 1734 as a dining club for aristocrats who had visited Italy. In 1751 they funded James Stuart ('Athenian' Stuart as he became) and Nicholas Revett to go to Setines, as Athens was then known. Their aim was to produce a scholarly record of the buildings of ancient Greece, as Antoine Desgodetz had done for Rome in *Edifices antiques de Rome* (1682). The result was *The Antiquities of Athens* (four massive and handsome volumes and a supplement; Volume 1 was published in 1762). These set new standards of accuracy in antiquarian recording and provided architectural models for the next 50 years. The Greek Revival was underway.

They had made much of the Tower of the Winds and the Lantern of Demosthenes, and these were used as source models for all sorts of neo-Classical buildings. Copies were even made: the Radcliffe Observatory in Oxford (James Wyatt, 1773–94) is a Tower of the Winds which is also to be found in the middle of a lake in Lord Shugborough's estate in Staffordshire (1765).

The Classical Greek is here being used, as antiquity had been for so long, as a tool in the construction of taste and cultural identities. These matters of taste are about what it is to be a cultured individual. They are about the constitution of types of self or subjectivity. In Chapter 2 I dealt with the character of the connoisseur, finding themselves mirrored in the past as

Figure 3.4 Stuart and Revett. *The Antiquities of Athens*, Volume 2. London 1787. Chapter 2, Plate 17. Drawing of Erechtheion, detail

transnational artistic personalities. We move on in this chapter to see how the Greek has been used in the construction of much more.

GERMAN ACADEMICS AND THE IDEALISATION OF GREECE

For Winckelmann and many after him ancient Greece was a cultural pinnacle. This idealisation of Greece was carried through the nineteenth century by the unmatched rigour of German Classical scholarship.

There were radical changes in German higher education in the eighteenth century, instituted, for example, by Heyne at Göttingen, and overseen by Alexander von Humboldt, Prussian Education Minister from 1808–10. Education was a crucial part of Prussian political ideology. Key features of von Humboldt's Hellenist *Bildung* were skills of source criticism, producing a science of the ancient world *Altertumswissenschaft*. The Greeks were enshrined as beyond historical criticism. Classically educated graduates came to monopolise jobs in the state sector, in education and law. While the idealism of the early nineteenth century, centred upon the metaphysical concept of *Zeitgeist* (spirit of the age), gave way to a hard-headed realism and learned historicism, the German University set the intellectual agenda.

In the United States after 1850 it was considered by many that Germany was the place to go for a serious education. There was an impetus to emulate the Germans coming largely from within the American academies. In France in 1896–7 fifteen universities were opened on the German model. Despite these direct influences, major differences existed in the middle-class educational systems of the western nation states, but German scholarship was recognised as supremely rigorous and Hellenism held sway. This held that (an idealised) Greece was the origin of Europe, and access to it was through original Greek. And whatever the political ideologies of the early Romantic champions of Hellenism, Classical education was conservative.

CLASSICISM, ROMANTICISM AND NEO-CLASSICISM

The counter-enlightenment of the eighteenth century came to idealise a simplicity and spontaneity seen to be the characteristic of ancient Greece. Roman art, so long the model, was now considered uninspired and derivative compared with Winckelmann's account of the liberty and spiritual simplicity of the Greek. The Greeks were free; the Romans decadent and corrupt.

This cultural shift is to be seen as part of a complex interplay of ideologies of Classicism and Romanticism; another term, Hellenism, has already been introduced. This is not the place to give a definitive account, which is anyway impossible, for the terms are not fixed, but have been constantly subject to rhetorical changes of meaning. It is important, however, to raise some broad issues.

In his book *The Classical Tradition in Art* (1978), Michael Greenhalgh defines Classicism in art as an approach to various media founded on the imitation of antiquity, and on the assumption of a set of values attributed to antiquity. Francis Haskell and Nicholas Penny have documented the importance of copies and collections of plaster casts in this tradition. For many centuries it was accepted by everyone with a claim to taste that the heights of artistic achievement had been reached in a limited number of antique sculptures. Many were displayed in the Belvedere courtyard in Rome and in Florence's Tribuna. Later Naples and Paris came to hold significant pieces. Art schools everywhere acquired plaster cast copies for study. Winckelmann and the early antiquarian collectors can be considered in this context. In another interesting twist these sculptures now mostly attract our attention transformed into kitsch tourist souvenirs.

Most arts from Renaissance up to nineteenth-century Romanticism were governed by this retrospective ideal of antiquity. Furthermore art was considered governed by rules determined by reason. Beauty was truth, and art therefore had a moral aim. Renaissance humanism had placed man at the centre of things, as the measure of all; this was above all though a concern with the ideal, with the typical (eschewing the individual) and with morality in the widest sense.

Much of this Classicism is expressed in Raphael's frescoes in the Stanza della Segnatura 1508/9–1512, a private apartment in the Vatican. Its style is that of the noble simplicity and calm grandeur so praised by Winckelmann. Its iconography is of the life of Man pictured as a search for Truth, with four ways to achieve it: Theology, Beauty and Art (the Muses and Mount Parnassus), Reason (the School of Athens) and Law (Figure 3.6).

Romanticism

> High towers, fair temples, goodly theatres,
> Strong walls, rich porches, princely palaces,
> Large streets, brave houses, sacred sepulchres,
> Sure gates, sweet gardens, stately galleries
> Wrought with fair pillars and fine imageries;
> All those (O pity!) now are turned to dust
> And overgrown with black oblivion's rust
>
> (Edmund Spenser, *The Ruins of Time*)

The Romantic component of this cultural nexus enveloping ancient Greece involves conceptions of the picturesque and historicity (the sense of history and time). David Le Roy was visiting Greece at the same time as Stuart and Revett. His book, *Ruines des plus beaux monuments de Grèce* (1758) is also concerned with taste, but in a very different sense – with respect to the representation of ruination. The ruins of the Greek landscape are pictured as a

Figure 3.5 Plaster casts in the old Museum of Classical Archaeology, Cambridge, 1977. Now the library of Peterhouse

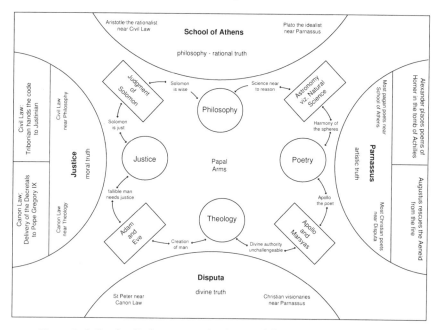

Figure 3.6 Raphael's frescoes in the Stanza della Segnatura 1508/9–12. The encompassment of Classicism

Figure 3.7 Robert Sayer. *Ruins of Athens.* London 1759. Plate 10. Temple of the
Winds, Athens and the Temple of Korinth

field of meditation and reverie, symbols of the passing of time, the disappearance of civilisation, the permanence of nature.

In 1776 Comte Marie-Gabriel-Florent-Auguste de Choiseul-Gouffier
travelled to the eastern Mediterranean. *Voyage pittoresque de la Grèce* (two
volumes, 1782) appeared under his name, though he had employed various
draughtsmen, artists and antiquarians. He was an aristocratic collector as of
old: consider this letter to his agent, the Consul Fauvel, in Athens: 'Take everything you can. Don't neglect any opportunity to pillage everything that can
be pillaged in Athens and its territory . . . Spare neither the living nor the
dead.' But the work of Choiseul-Gouffier does not belong with the scholarship of Caylus or Montfaucon. Few plates in the *Voyage* are of antiquities. His
interest, shared with many later, was in topography.

The encyclopaedic treatments of antiquarian relics of the likes of
Montfaucon and Caylus are replaced by the monographic study, by travel
literatures, as interest shifted from artistic models and taste to landscape, its
aesthetics in relation to history. Here fit the fantastic Roman ruins depicted
by Piranesi and the paintings of Hubert Robert, 'Hubert des Ruines' as he was
known. The picturesque was developed as an aesthetic theory. While William
Wordsworth and William Gilpin speculated upon its character in the Wye
Valley of the borders of England and Wales in the 1780s and 1790s, ideas of

nature and the aesthetic changed English landscape gardening. Painters and artists began visiting Greece from the end of the eighteenth century: Thomas Hope in 1795, Charles Eastlake in the 1820s, Edward Dodwell from 1801.

Fanny-Maria Tsigakou, in her beautifully illustrated *The Rediscovery of Greece* (1981), comments that Romantic paintings of Greece at this time owed more to the hazy light of paintings by Claude Lorrain; Richard Stoneman comments on the superficiality of their vision, together with a contrasting importance for Greek studies:

> The painters, naturally enough, had their eye on the pictorial possi- bilities of the scene. No melancholy here over fallen beauty, no Turnerian sublime but the charm of ruin and of pretty girls, of camels, and of exotically clad Greeks and Turks to adorn the ruins and the hills. . . . But the young Englishmen who visited Greece rejected the rococo not, like Goethe or Diderot, for its superficiality and irrelevance to deeper human concerns, but for its inadequacy towards the real landscape and their sense of history. It was the discovery of the Greek landscape that changed the understanding of Greek history. And it was the historical sense that gave the Greek landscape its especial importance in picturesque theory.

Here is a new sense of history, beyond simple reflection upon time and mortality. These were ruins that not only attested to the ravages of time but also were traces of a great past to be recalled. This is an attitude found also in Pausanias: there is little interest in contemporary life; Greece is a landscape whose meaning is its ruin. As Edward Dodwell expressed it in his *Travels*:

> Almost every rock, every promontory, every view, is haunted by the shadows of the mighty dead. Every portion of the soil appears to team with historical recollections; or it borrows some potent but invisible charm from the inspirations of poetry, the effects of genius, or the energies of liberty or patriotism.

This topographical interest found its embodiment of efficiency in the British Army officer William Martin Leake, who established the location of so many sites mentioned in Classical authors between 1805 and 1810.

For stories of the Romantic adventure of archaeology, reference must be made to the association of aristocratic treasure hunters, mentioned above and including Cockerell, John Foster, Karl Haller von Hallerstein, Jacob Linck and Otto Magnus von Stackelberg, who discovered the sculptures of Aegina and Bassae. This international association broke up over disposal or rather sale of the sculptures in a series of events worthy of an Indiana Jones movie, including Turkish intrigues, power politics, armed violence and a special agent of Ludwig of Bavaria – Johann Martin von Wagner. Mention here must also be made of the Romantic association with nationalist move- ments, which found its notorious embodiment in Lord Byron, who had been on the fringes of the association in Athens. Winckelmann's death was

Figure 3.8 Baron von Stackelberg. *Der Apollotempel zu Bassae in Arcadien.*
Rome and Frankfurt am Main 1826. Plate 2. View of the Temple

an intriguing and romantic end: on his way back to Italy from Vienna,
drawn as ever by the Classical Mediterranean, waiting to take the boat from
Trieste to Venice, he was murdered in a tavern.

Neo-Classicism

The reaction against the Roman accompanied the Greek Revival in architecture and neo-Classicism more generally. The latter was at its height from 1770
to 1820. Neo-Classical taste prized austerity of ornament, frieze-like compo-
sitions, sculptural surfaces, and whiteness (it was not yet realised that Classical
sculpture was painted). The influence of Winckelmann's reassessment of the
Greek in art is clear, and points also to some complex interactions with
Romanticism.

It was an international style, and didactic, aiming at a purification of
society. A central concept was that of *la belle nature*. This was a Platonic
notion, defined by a Royal Academy lecture of this time as:

the general and permanent principles of visible objects, not disfigured
by accident or distempered by disease, not modified by fashion or local
habits. Nature is a collective idea, and, though its essence exists in each
individual of the species, can never in its perfection inhabit a single
object.

73

For the sculptor Canova, the Parthenon marbles displayed '*la verità della natura congiunta alla scelta delle forme belle*' [the truth of nature united with the selection of beautiful forms].

John Flaxman produced severely simple sculpture. Angelica Kaufmann painted pretty pictures in the Grecian manner, while Jacques-Louis David and Ingres produced great epic paintings for the New French Republic, political allegory of the age of revolution. David produced a series of morals for the revolution, with Roman republican virtues dressed in Grecian style. His *Napoleon on the Imperial Throne* (1806) was much influenced by recent archaeological reconstructions of the chryselephantine statue of Zeus at Olympia. Canova's white statues are almost archetypal; Mario Praz called him the erotic frigidaire. Ingres was not the last artist to learn antiquity from direct contact, but one of the last in a long line to make this exploration a basis for his art.

Neo-Classical architecture was popular all over Europe and the new world, particularly between 1790 and 1830. Buildings copied Greek temples and porticoes; monuments of Athens were turned into glorified banks, museums, town halls, court houses, universities and government buildings. A fine example is St Pancras New Church, London (W.H. Inwood 1817–22), whose design replicated the Erectheion; the Caryatid porch looks uneasy in London grey.

In Munich Leo von Klenze, Ludwig's architect, designed the Königsplatz and Glyptothek, the museum for the Aegina marbles. Neo-Classical buildings with copies of ancient statues were constructed even, or perhaps especially, in Athens. Along the Leoforos Venizelos are the National Library, Academy and University designed by two Danes (the Hansens) and paid for by an Austrian. 'They gave dignity to a small town that had only one well-preserved Classical building of its own', as Donald Horne puts it. In the United States there is, notably, the Tennessee State Capitol (1845–59; William Strickland), the Lincoln Memorial (1911–22 and based on the Parthenon), and the Jefferson Memorial (1934–43; again white marmoreal Greek).

Neo-Classicism found champions in twentieth-century fascism. At the Berlin Olympics of 1936 film-maker Leni Riefensthal reincarnated the famous statue of the Discobolus as Aryan manhood. Hitler loved the statue and bought it for 5 million lire in 1938 (it was returned to Rome in 1948). Albert Speer, official architect, designed the great parade grounds of Nazi Germany, the Thingplätze, in clean neo-Classical style. Plato and fascism were united in their idealisation of heavy-metal Sparta. The similarity of fascist paramilitary youth organisations, Italy's Gioventù fascista and the Hitlerjugend, to Sparta is no coincidence.

TOURISM

The Temple of Poseidon at Sounion on its headland is one of the great sites of Greece visited by tens of thousands of tourists every year. The marble

Figure 3.9 The stadium in Fritz Lang's *Metropolis*

Figure 3.10 Sounion, Greece. Nineteenth-century engraving.
(Courtesy of the Museum of Classical Archaeology, Cambridge)

stones are covered with graffiti two centuries old. Byron must have used a hammer and chisel to carve his name; it is no idle scratching. Just around the stone from his name is another. The name now escapes me, but I do recall that the visitor recorded his home town; it was North Shields on the river Tyne in northern England, not far from where I grew up. I am intrigued by this combination of someone from a provincial town making their mark on history, now forgotten, and a roving international aristocrat whose name stands for a cultural movement.

Donald Horne has considered the tourist trails of Europe in his book *The Great Museum* (1984). He calls the sites such as Athens, Olympia, Delphi and now the treasures of the tomb of Philip of Macedon dreamlands, dream factories, after André Malraux, strung together in a ceremonial agenda. Tourism is centred upon movements, travels through real and imagined geographies and histories; the difference is incidental.

He interprets the tourists of Europe visiting the national museums, sites and cityscapes, from the Louvre to the Nevsky Prospect and Leningrad, from the Parthenon to Auschwitz as on a secular pilgrimage. The secular relics began with the collection of antique works of art by the Renaissance popes and princes of Europe. Things often never meant to commemorate anything were turned into monuments, loaded up with meaning, becoming modern relics, objects of sacred fascination and veneration. The result is a collocation of fragments forming undifferentiated pasts across Europe.

Focal points of the ceremonial agenda are familiar: Christianity, aristocratic luxury and patronage, folk and peasants, the workers, the people and revolutionary change, images of national belonging, identity and pride, imperialist triumph and brutality. Neo-Classicism and the Classical heritage, the international style of the nineteenth century, feature prominently.

Much of this experience is captured in ascending the Acropolis. The crowds on a Sunday, when admission is free, ascend as to a temple of culture. At the top is veneration of site and cult objects, with spectacle and the aura invested in the stone. The Acropolis thus stands as focal point in the centre of the twentieth-century *nefos*, the Athenian smog, standing central within the Agora and Pnyx (economy and politics), the theatre of Dionysos (culture), the reconstructed stadium (sport and pursuit of physical perfection), the Stoa (the beginnings of philosophy). With the photo-calls, video shots and voices of polyglot guides in seven languages, we are tourists in history.

Horne associates such experiences with changes in public culture, which is now coming to be not a common storehouse of high cultural items, but the experience of the tour. With its reliance on punctuality, timetables, diligence in performing set tasks, and the abrogation of responsibility to an order of management, the ceremonial agenda approaches the experience of the office.

The tourist experience can be related to Postmodernity and its critics. A key feature is the *anticipation* of pleasures: this ties tourism into film, TV,

Figure 3.11 National Museum, Athens

literature, food industries, various other media and experiences, a whole hyper-reality of imaginative pleasure-seeking. The tourist becomes semio-tician, seeking signifiers of notions pre-established in other discourses. A key dimension is authenticity and the genuine – the search for the *real* people, seeing the *real* things, the *real* countryside. But tourist culture is frequently centred upon the pseudo-event (a re-enaction of a false authenticity), stagings for the tourist gaze. This term of John Urry's relates tourism to the culture of the gaze or the look, with observation as surveillance, the one-way look of the tourist. Seeing and being seen are thus constituted as a relation of power between the tourist who has purchased the experience, and the site which is observed. The instability of any notion of authenticity in this set of experiences, the slippage between image and reality, and the manufacture of experience may all be taken as characterics of Postmodernity, as may the collocation of cultural fragments.

Pierre Bourdieu has researched what he terms the aristocracy of culture in a book entitled *Distinction* (English translation 1984). Symbolic capital (closely tied to class and educational capital) is invested in history and culture, laying claim to ownership of those qualities and experiences associated with social standing. But just as many middle-class people are not happy with the operation of high culture, which is supposedly their symbolic milieu, where they should have invested their symbolic capital, so too the secular pilgrimage may engender insight. For Horne the intellectual worth of tourism lies in a

77

Figure 3.12 Nineteenth-century Athens. (Courtesy of the Museum of Classical Archaeology, Cambridge)

vision of the rhetoric that underlies it all, seeing that the experiences are constructed, but not by the hand of god, artistic genius or a historical giant like Napoleon. Escaping the tourist bubble, that tourist reality of guides and hotels, airports and museums which surrounds the traveller, is to come to reflect upon history, originals and reconstructions. 'We can't live without theories of reality that, by giving some shape to existence, enable us to think and act. Sightseeing can be one of the ways in which we can speculate on these "reality-making" processes', as Horne puts it. So sightseeing is simply a special case of a more general predicament within which the task is to try to understand how knowledges, experiences and the past are constructed. In so doing, one becomes a good tourist. Much has changed since the early days of travelling to Greece which I have been describing, and it may be tempting to wish for a romantic trip in the Greece of old, before the contaminations of modernity. But such hopes are always idealisms blind to realities of everyday life, and forgetful that this luxury of the imaginary was an aristocratic privilege bought at the expense of the degradation of whole European populations. If we look positively upon tourism now, there are popularisations of parts of the huge storehouse of goods, ideas and experiences which make up the past. These are rich resources for independent reflection, making them one's own.

MODERN GREEKS INTO THE PAST

In 1835 a column drum of the Parthenon was restored to welcome the new King Otto of Bavaria to his capital Athens. This was a clear symbol of ideological unity between Classicist ideas and the expression of state power. Administrative measures were swiftly taken in the independent state, recently freed from the Turk by the combined effort of European powers, to ensure protection of the Classical Greek past. Archaeological monuments became the very emblems of the new Greek state after 1821. New street plans drawn up for Athens in 1831 and 1834 incorporated the idea of the city as a living museum of European origins. Neo-Classical architect Leo Klenze was brought in when the original plans proved too expensive. He had worked for Ludwig of Bavaria, whose son Otto became the new King of Greece in 1833. The new royal palace, designed by Klenze and originally to have been on the Acropolis, was set at the east point of the new city plan, the Acropolis at the south. A grid was based on streets Stadiou, Athinas, Ermou and Eolou. Settlement was shifted north to expose the area where the Agora was known to have been, but this was soon filled with people moved to make way for the boulevards and by people from Nafplion, the old capital.

From this early date, according to Kostas Kotsakis, reconstruction of the past was tied to a specific political programme. Popularised archaeological notions eventually became deeply embedded in modern Greek state ideology and, at times, were part of actual concrete and powerful programmes of political and social integration.

Figure 3.13 Nineteenth-century Athens. (Courtesy of the Museum of Classical Archaeology, Cambridge)

Nineteenth-century Romantic nationalism, which Bruce Trigger considers to be one of the defining ideologies of modern archaeology (with imperialism and colonialism), took on a unique form in Greece. A nationalism focused upon monuments, history and other cultural phenomena was combined with an international concern for the Classical Greek past stemming not from ethnic interest but from ideas of cultural descent. Ideas of cultural continuity pre-existed this Romanticism in Greece, which operationalised this tradition by bringing in concrete factual evidence of the past running into the present. This diachronic continuity and direct kinship with the past became a prominent ideology in Greece. Anything outside this ideological focus was considered superfluous or an ungainly perplexity; hence official interest in the fate of medieval monuments did not come until 1914 with the foundation of the Byzantine Museum in Athens.

The search for continuity could be extended both forward and backward into prehistory. So Tsountas, founder of Greek prehistoric archaeology, provided an early (1909) discussion of the close relationship between the neolithic 'megaron' of Greece and the Classical Doric temple. With John Gennadius, a one-time Greek minister to Britain, he argued that Schliemann's discoveries showed that the Hellenic spirit was not restricted to the fifth and fourth centuries BC but could reappear in many times and in many forms including that of the late nineteenth century. Works such as Nilsson's *Mycenaean Origins of Greek Mythology* (1932), which read into Bronze Age artefacts myths and legends surviving in later Homeric and Classical literatures, are relevant here.

Kotsakis quotes the preface from the multi-volume *Istoria tou Ellenikou Ethnous* (1970): 'This continuous march of man on the Greek land through millennia, from the first settlements of the stone age up to the present day is followed by the *History of the Greek Nation*. It presents the documented continuity of the Greek World, its cultural unity and the internal integrity of Greek culture.' This continuity, sometimes conceived as cultural, sometimes ethnic, is expressed by George Forrest:

> The best introduction to Modern Greek conversation is not the latest phrase book. It is Plato. Μάλιστα, ἀλήθεια, and so on. And if Plato is the best introduction to the way the Greeks talk, Greek pots are the best introduction to the way they look. Sit on the quayside in Chios or Samos, sit in a café in Thebes or even in Livadia and look at the faces. They come straight from sixth century vases. I make no anthropological, no sociological point, only the assertion: they are the same.
>
> (G. Forrest, 'Two archaic ages of Greece' in T. Winnifrith and
> P. Murray, *Greece Old and New*, Macmillan, 1983)

The supposed continuity of a charismatic culture provided the justification for a 'normal science' focused on the acquisition of facts to the exclusion of deeper questioning. History *per se* constituted an explanation. What needed explanation, the continuity of Greece, was thought to lie outside of archaeology, hence the point that Kotsakis makes is that this is an ahistorical 'historic' reconstruction of Greece which dominated its archaeology for so long, and still does so, except notably in prehistoric archaeology as practised in Greece.

HELLENISM AND CULTURAL POLITICS

Forrest reckons there are two types of student of modern Greece. There are philhellenes who think Greece really is like Periclean Athens, fountain of arts and cradle of democracy. But these people don't really like Greeks, real Greeks. They are worshipped as once they were, not as they are. So Alexander the Great showed his love of Pindar, the Theban poet, by destroying every other house in Thebes except Pindar's. On the other hand there are realists, who shudder at Greeks today, who seem to have nothing in common with the great past. This tension runs through many ideologies of Greek and European identity, as will now be explored.

Ian Morris, in his introduction to his edited book *Classical Greece* (1994), has plotted the shift in Classical archaeology from enlightenment ideas to Hellenism. He defines Hellenism as part of the late eighteenth-century shift from Michel Foucault's Classical to Modern episteme (this will be examined and explained in the next chapter). It is an idealisation of ancient Greece as the birthplace of a European spirit. It is thus a 'continentalist' rather than nationalist view of the past, insisting that the Greek was unique or even superhuman. There is room in Hellenism for dispute over who had the strongest claim on Classical Greece, but it is generally agreed that it was the northwest Europeans.

Morris sees Hellenism developing in the context of nationalist disputes between France and the German states, and imperialist aggression by France and Britain against the Ottoman Empire. The 'continentalist' focus meant that the nationalist use of archaeology by Greeks was problematic, as periods and concepts had been appropriated and defined in advance by external European interests.

Hellenism, according to Morris, had a minimal archaeological component until the 1870s. Winckelmann and most intellectuals responsible for Hellenism after him worked with texts. But he argues that archaeological materials offered insights into everyday life, rather than simply the ideals of cultural excellence; moreover their potential for tracing change through time posed a threat to Hellenism, so Classical archaeology was reconstituted within Hellenism as an unthreatening skill focused upon data acquisition and management. Here his argument applies to that same characteristic of lack of critical reflexivity noted for Greek archaeology by Kotsakis, discussed above.

ANTHROPOLOGY AND EUROPEAN ORIGINS

Morris declares that 'the archaeology of Greece is intimately involved with a two-century-old project of understanding "Europeanness"'. We have come across the different elements of a metanarrative of European origins. Ancient Greece is considered fount of excellence, the home of transcendent artistic values. Modern Greece was liberated from the Turk. European nation states competed for relics and filled their national museums with Greek statues and vases to show their commitment to Hellenism, their civilised status and also their imperialist might.

Greece (ancient and modern) comes between the exotic and the familiar, between the historically constituted symbolic poles of the European and the oriental. Michael Herzfeld has dealt with this ambiguity of Greece in his *Anthropology through the Looking Glass* (1987). He claims it emerged from Eurocentric preoccupations with otherness, the same preoccupations which gave birth to modern anthropology. Herzfeld is an anthropologist and sees Greek nationalism resembling anthropology to the extent that both are historically embedded in Romanticism and a concern to distinguish between identity and otherness. So Romantic Hellenism, an association of European powers and intellectuals, attempted to give a small and politically weak entity

Figure 3.14 Library of Hadrian, Athens. (Courtesy of the Museum of Classical Archaeology, Cambridge)

a foothold in the nineteenth-century scrambles for national identity, and 'the West supported the Greeks on the implicit understanding that they would reciprocally accept the role of living ancestors of European civilisation – the standard, for most romantic writers, of civilisation in the most general and absolute sense'. The Greeks thus came to live out a tension between inclusion and exclusion, similarity and difference, being aboriginal Europeans and at same time oriental vassals. This is the anthropological problem of otherness or exoticism: European colonial powers using other societies to define themselves.

Understanding unity and diversity is seen by Herzfeld as a parallel problem for European identity and anthropology. Europe is conceived as a unity with common cultural origins, yet has simultaneously been divided by nationalisms for centuries. Various ideological solutions have been developed.

European diversity is present in nationalistic movements with their local folklores and folk cultures. And folk traditions have been part of nationalist doctrines of cultural continuity. Herzfeld relates that 'the Greek intelligentsia, in particular, found it useful to treat the local peasantry internally as a backward population while simultaneously presenting folk culture to the outside world as evidence of the glorious common heritage of all Greeks'. The assumption of local archaism within a larger unity such as the modern nation state is part of a long Eurocentric tradition. Other examples apart from the Greeks are the Celts. Both are treated as cultural survivals. This notion is part of evolutionary anthropology, as, for example, in Edward Tylor's *Researches into the Early History of Mankind and the Development of Civilisation* (1865) and *Primitive Culture* (1871).

Winckelmann, who so articulated the Hellenic ideal, never went to Greece, even though he apparently wanted to. He studied copies in Rome, while modern Greece was put to one side for later. Greece was thus in the nineteenth century, in the term of Claude Lévi-Strauss, a 'cold' society, an anthropological case, not part of 'hot' Europe, yet central to its definition, just as anthropology defines its European parent culture in terms of the cultural otherness of 'primitive society'. But the anthropological implies human unity. This is rationalised by evolutionary anthropology of the nineteenth century and after which postulates grandiose and generalising schemes lying behind human culture and history, with progress leaving behind survivals such as modern 'stone age' cultures. Survivalism is thus nationalism writ large: a claim to the moral and cultural superiority of Europe over the entire world.

European identity included reference to Hellenism, with an idealised ancient Greece as the childhood of Europe. But modern Greece was, in Byron's words, a 'sad relic of departed worth'. The romantic love of ruins converts this into an image of a fallen Hellas, the aboriginal embodiment of a European ideal fallen to ruin and the evil corruption of anti-Europe, the Turk. This romantic ruin (of European culture) is suitably timeless, because the opposition is between eternity and history, not two phases of history.

EXPLICATION

DU FRONTISPICE.

La Grèce, fous la figure d'une femme chargée de fers, eft entourée de monumens funèbres, élevés en l'honneur des grands Hommes de la Grèce qui fe font dévoués pour fa liberté; tels que Lycurgue, Miltiade, Thémiftocle, Ariftide, Epaminondas, Pélopidas, Timoléon, Démofthène, Phocion, Philopœmen. Elle eft appuyée fur le tombeau de Léonidas, & derrière elle eft le cippe fur lequel fut gravée cette infcription . que Simonide fit pour les trois cens Spartiates tués au combat des Thermopyles.

Paffant, va dire à Lacédémone que nous fommes morts ici pour obéir à fes loix.

La Grèce femble évoquer les mânes de ces grands Hommes, & fur le rocher voifin font écrits ces mots, *Exoriare aliquis*. . . . .

Figure 3.15b Comte de Choiseul-Gouffier. *Voyage Pittoresque de la Grèce.* Paris 1782. Explanation of Frontispiece

VOYAGE PITTORESQUE

DE LA

GRECE

TOME PREMIER.

A PARIS,

M. DCC. LXXXII.

Figure 3.15a Comte de Choiseul-Gouffier. *Voyage Pittoresque de la Grèce.* Paris 1782. Frontispiece

This metanarrative of the Fall (of the Classical west) affirms, in its Christian metaphor, European civilisation as the secular Eden. It also explains the unity and diversity of European society, represented by transnational European culture and Romantic nationalistic diversity of the nation states. As with the Tower of Babel, diversity comes out of an *Urtext* of European culture. Internal disunity is tied to a transcendent unity with political divisions conceived as a sign of health, the free expression of European individualism.

This individualist character of European identity is contrasted, in another variant of the metanarrative, with oriental homogeneity: the despotic east. Such Orientalism consists again of the reification of a zone of cultural difference through the ideologically motivated representation of otherness. The problem for Greeks, and one which embodies the tension between inclusion and exclusion, is that their 'folklore' or folk history was tainted with the Turk.

Another ambiguity of the Greek came later: primitive survivals rediscovered by Jane Harrison and E.R. Dodds. These Classicists challenged the notion of a purely rational and civilised Greek spirit with elaborations of primitive, irrational and archaic elements in ancient Greek culture: Apollo had his Dionysos. The Greeks again appear the same and different, with ineradicable relics of the past, difference projected into the past.

Winckelmann and others after him, including Marx, saw Greece as the childhood of Europe. Freudian notions of the origins of the person in the child add another dimension to this conception of the Greek: 'Had Greek civilisation never existed . . . we would never have become fully conscious, which is to say that we would never have become, for better or worse, fully human', as wrote W.H. Auden.

The metanarrative of unity and diversity is a basic theoretical stance found in anthropology, archaeology and many other disciplines. It involves the reduction of a culture to a type, or the explanation of cultural diversity in terms of a general scheme. This is the project of nineteenth-century evolutionary anthropology. It is also the roots of state racism: local variation is reduced to being a supposed epiphenomenon of transcendent sameness, so any irreducible cultural diversity within the nation state (cultural pluralism) cannot be tolerated. Only local differences which can be assimilated into encompassing similarity can be allowed. So nationalist history and abstract theory, generalising disciplines and transnational cultures entail the repression of time and contingency in the supposed recapture of an original and pure (read necessary and timeless or divine) state of being or identity. History is denied in its classification and ordering.

For Herzfeld, traditional anthropology consists of an educated transnational culture claiming participatory rights in a local culture to which it is at the same time exterior and superior. This participant observation of ethnography is an intervention in people's everyday lives according to an assumption of common humanity, while at the same time professing a sophistication, rationality and viewpoint which set apart the participant. So attempts to explore otherness have always implied a moral discrimination and inequality – them and us.

An analogous argument has been made by Johannes Fabian in his book *Time and the Other* (1983). The otherness which defines identity is conceived to be back then and over there. So if Greece is central to us as Europeans, it is also removed from us through mythic time; if it is exotic, its distance from us is one of cultural space. In either case the Greek is not us, even though we claim it for our own.

This ideological complex articulated by Herzfeld reaches its extreme in Nazism. While modern Greeks were contemptible and fit only for death and service, Nazi propagandists proclaimed in neo-Classical parade grounds that the present-day Germans and ancient Greeks were the twin pillars of the Aryan race.

ORIENTALISM AND BERNAL'S CRITIQUE OF THE CONSTITUTION OF THE GREEK

Edward Said in *Orientalism* (1978) has made a case against the ideology and metanarrative of Orientalism. As just indicated, this defines the east as a foil to the superiority of the west, proposing that the east consists of incompletely developed cultures, despotic or degenerate, defining what Europe is not. He traces Orientalism through academic disciplines, history and cultural relations with societies east of Europe. It should be clear even from this abbreviation that Said's critique is closely related to Herzfeld's arguments about the anthropological origins of European identity in principles of otherness.

Some of what Said criticises can be seen, for example, in accounts of the Orientalising movement (within which are placed centrally the aryballoi of ancient Korinth). Relationships with the arts of the Levant are clear in artefact design of the seventh century BC (and indeed at many other times). But there is supposed to be little exact copying. A standard explanation of the Orientalising movement is that static cultural forms of the east are taken up and transformed by the fertile genius of the Greek spirit. After all, the despotic empires of the east did not develop the wonders of the Classical Greek city states in the space of three centuries. There must have been something different about the Greeks. More generally, Schuchhardt and Fürtwangler opposed the synthesis of European prehistory presented by Oscar Montelius in the 1880s, which argued for the diffusion of civilisation from the near east. Their claim was that the inspiration for Mycenaean Greece was Aryan and eastern 'semitic' influences were irrelevant. Even accepting Montelius, it was claimed that the east was degenerating by the second millennium BC anyway.

Moving to the nineteenth century, the Greek wars of independence (1821–30) involving European powers liberating Greece, were presented as European youthful vigour versus the sick old man: the Ottoman Empire with its eastern roots. Here an alliance of philhellenes, nationalist interests and academic Hellenists and Orientalists imposed upon the people of the eastern Mediterranaean its own version of their past, present and future. This involved a complex interplay of nineteenth-century Greeks as degenerates, but with their ancestors as aboriginal Europeans – that tension identified by Forrest and Herzfeld above.

At this point it is pertinent to introduce the ideas of Martin Bernal. Bernal's *Black Athena* reached its second (large) volume in 1991. A synopsis of a third volume was given in the introduction to the first, published in 1987; a fourth volume has been promised. This is a major project undertaken by a Professor of Government at Cornell University who specialises in Chinese history and has considerable linguistic expertise.

Perry Anderson, in *The Guardian*, referring to Volume 1 as 'a critical enquiry into a large part of the European imagination . . . a retrospect of ingenious and often sardonic erudition', called it a 'spectacular undertaking'. In *The Voice* the book was declared to be 'the single most important book on black and African history this decade'; 'not only Africa and Asia, but the entire world of scholarship owes Bernal a debt of gratitude' (*South Magazine*). Welcomed by the left, largely ignored by the right in Britain, Volume 1 won the Socialist Book Award in 1987. Since then *Black Athena* has become the focus of considerable discussion and support from black interest groups, particularly on American university campuses; this has included some use by black racists. Bernal has been attacked by right-wing journals in the US. He also reports being compared with revisionist historians who deny the Holocaust took place. Many academics see *Black Athena* as the work of a crank; Oswyn Murray, author of a standard text on early Greece, makes a point of distancing himself from what he calls Bernal's 'fantasies'.

What is this all about? Consider Bernal's argument. Ancient Greece owed much to the east, to Egypt and Phoenicia in the Levant particularly, conduits for ideas and materials from the great eastern empires. This has long been accepted. Bernal proposes conquest, political domination and colonisation of Greece by oriental powers in the second millennium BC; ancient Greece developed under direct and considerable influence from the east. For Bernal Egypt was black; Phoenicians were semitic. If ancient Greece is conceived as the fount of European civilisation, then that civilisation is black and semitic in origin. What is more, Bernal claims that the ancient Greeks knew of their origins. Nineteenth-century scholarship denied the Afro-Asiatic and semitic roots of Greek culture because of racism and anti-semitism. Histories that oppose Bernal's 'revised ancient model' of the diffusion of civilisation from the east are complicit in this racism and anti-semitism. This thesis is presented with energy and verve, documented in tremendous detail. There is a rich mix of metanarratives. No wonder *Black Athena* has attracted attention.

The first two volumes are impressive compendia, covering themes from several disciplines. The first sets out Bernal's project and focuses upon historiography, on the construction, from 1785, of an ancient Greece seen as cultural zenith, pure and seminal, independent of eastern imperial neighbours, and European in character. Much of what I have presented already in this chapter can be found in *Black Athena*, Volume 1. But rather than evaluate this model of a European Greece (with origins in northern Aryan invaders of the second millennium and an Indo-European language group), testing it against empirical evidence and contrasting it with a model of an Afro-Asiatic Greece, in Volume 2 Bernal simply provides 'thick description' of his version of history. Similarities in material culture, in myth and legend between Greek and the east, etymologies of Greek divinities, artefacts and place names, and references in ancient records and authors are marshalled to document what Bernal claims to be overwhelming eastern influence upon Greece, indeed at times direct political domination and colonisation of Greece.

I have already mentioned that contact and influence from the near east have always been recognised, but Bernal polemically divides opinion into

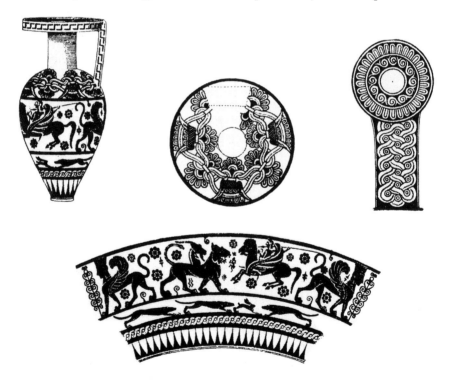

Figure 3.16 Bellerophon and Pegasus fight the Chimaira upon a Korinthian aryballos. Orientalising art. (*Source*: K.F. Johansen. *Les Vases Sicyoniens*. Paris: Champion, 1923)

'ultra-Europeanists', who argue for the purely independent genesis of Greece, those who support invasion from the north, and those like himself. The lines between these so-called opposing factions are drawn firmly because Bernal sees himself as precipitating a major disciplinary change, or to use a phrase explained more fully in the next chapter, a 'paradigm shift', from old models of ancient history to that of Afro-Asiatic origins.

Just what sort of history is Bernal writing? His topic is innovation and acculturation: the way Greece changed and developed in the second and first millennia, and the relationship between societies and polities in Greece and elsewhere – transmissions of cultural traits. But only two aspects of this topic of social change are admitted – indigenous stimuli to change, or those diffused and introduced from outside. Hence the polarisation of models. Bernal is seeking origins. To explain ancient Greek culture, Bernal assumes, is to find the sources or antecedents of its components. For Bernal, most lie in the east, so he calls himself a 'modified diffusionist'.

The second volume of *Black Athena* is dedicated to Gordon Childe, a prominent prehistoric archaeologist of the mid-century, major proponent of an older archaeological project of culture history, which heavily relied upon diffusion as an origin of social change. And indeed, Bernal sounds very dated to most prehistoric archaeologists of the 1990s. He recognises that he is harking back to ideas that were more fashionable in the first decades of this century, dismissing newer thinking as transient. Bernal quite justifiably criticises a metanarrative of European origins. But in not critically considering the character of his sources, and I would include here both archaeological and linguistic materials, Bernal has propagated another metanarrative of cultural origins. To explain this I need to anticipate a little of the next chapter.

The character of Bernal's history is not a shock, but seems very familiar to an archaeologist who has followed the debates in anthropological archaeology of the last thirty years and who has taken seriously what David Clarke called the arrival of critical self-consciousness in the discipline (in a classic article published in the journal *Antiquity* in 1973). To put it simply, Bernal's history and historiography do not hold water after the considerable amount of work which has been directed at rethinking the character of social and historical change, and at understanding the uses and meanings of material culture, the raw materials of archaeological knowledge. Bernal takes no account of this.

His history consists of advanced states conquering and civilising others, of trading empires, imperialism, colonies, a 'Pax Aegyptiaca', international cultures, spheres of political influence. The second and first millennia BC sound very like nineteenth-century Europe. Bernal argues that this is the way it was. It can equally be argued that the basic elements of his story are a function of another nineteenth-century metanarrative, one that emphasises origins and the diffusion of culture.

This metanarrative of diffusionist ideas involves a research strategy of searching for origins and tracing similarities. Without an origin any cultural element is meaningless: the culture to which that trait belongs provides its explanation. Diffusionism also assumes the existence of definable 'cultures': Egyptian, semitic, and the Greek. So it is assumed that Egypt, for example, had a set of authentic Egyptian cultural traits (that is finding their origin in or belonging to 'Egyptianness') to transmit to others. Hence the problem is that, on the one hand, Bernal argues for cultural mixes, against notions of the purity of the European and the Greek. But his new Afro-Asiatic European cultural mix is of elements that have to be culturally tagged and isolated for his argument to make sense. Diffusionism of the sort he practises requires separable 'peoples' who possess culture which influences and is influenced by culture belonging to others. It assumes the categories of race and culture which Bernal seems to wish to deny.

Anthropologists have been challenging this 'proprietary' notion of culture for many years now. 'Culture' is a very awkward category which may confuse as much as it aids understanding of other societies, especially if authentic culture is conceived as having an origin in a particular people or race. As some political groups have realised, Bernal's model of history is as compatible with racism as are those he opposes. It is quite possible within a diffusionist system of thought to demand recognition of cultural purity and precedence on the basis of origins of valued cultural traits traced back, archaeologically and linguistically, to racial origins. Gustav Kossina notoriously did this in the service of Nazism in the 1920s and 1930s. With respect to language it might be asked whether the 80 per cent of the population of Wales who do not speak the Welsh language are not really Welsh, even though many have lived all their lives in Wales, and even though their ancestors lived in Wales, and they consider themselves as Welsh as Welsh speakers. These vital issues of cultural politics are not easily resolved by a formula of simple equation: race=language=material culture. In anthropological archaeology there is now considerable evidence that material culture is not simply transmitted from superior to subordinate culture, or otherwise invented in a creative act. Material culture, with the technologies and economic and symbolic systems that form it, is a set of resources used in all sorts of social strategies. Is a tea cup to be explained by the fact that its design originated ultimately in the far east? What about tea drinking as social lubricant, all the symbolisms of different kinds of tea (tea bags to Earl Grey), tea production and colonial enterprise, tea cups and styles of interior decoration, histories of industrial ceramic design? Nor is social change in any way as simple as Bernal's conquest, invasion and 'influence', whatever nineteenth-century imperialists would have us believe.

Bernal's source materials appear transparent to him; they tell of similarity and this means contact to him. But sources need interpreting. Our present understanding of archaeological sources needs to be related to their political and social context. Bernal does not do this.

Imagine a peasant in a Cretan field in the second millennium BC. Just because they come across things from a very different society does not mean they pack up and start building the extraordinary edifices archaeologists have called Minoan palaces. What did the articles mean to them? To understand innovation and acculturation, archaeologists now argue that account needs to be taken of social contexts of production and distribution. Bernal's history sounds so familiar in its resort to modern experience of social change because he does not consider such contexts and meanings of the appearance and use of the material items of the archaeological record.

What did the articles mean to the peasant? Were they considered as being from another 'society' at all? Perhaps the boundaries which we apply to the geography of the eastern Mediterranean are not sensible for understanding the second millennium BC when there was a widespread cultural mix joining Aegean, Levant and Egypt in a social system which included all three as essential components. I will pick up this point about the edges of societies in a discussion of world systems in Chapter 6. Here might be noted the positive moment to transnational culture. Greek culture conceived as crossing national and racial borders is no longer 'Greek'. Nationalisms and cultural chauvinisms have no place if culture has no specific origin and can be taken up authentically by whoever chooses.

Bernal's project is an admirable and interdisciplinary one of challenging notions of cultural identity in a metanarrative of European origins. He brings past and present together in attacking the racism and anti-semitism of entrenched authorities, but on the basis of another metanarrative of cultural influence and social change which is ironically quite compatible with what he criticises. His social archaeology has been superseded in the last thirty years, and this is the topic of Chapters 5 and 6. The relationship between Classical archaeology and society is taken up in a further consideration of how the discipline works in Chapter 4.

CONCLUDING POINTS

Although this chapter is entitled myths and metanarratives, it is not the intention to imply that earlier travellers, collectors and others have succumbed to ideologies which we somehow now escape. It is to argue that past and present are coextensive, that our interests take us to the past, and its material remains are not transparent but need working upon. Interests are often wrapped up in metanarratives and ideological dispositions. A stronger argument is that disciplines and discourses construct the objects in which they are interested. This will be investigated in the next chapter.

4

SCHOLARSHIP AND DISCOURSE

INTRODUCTION

A professor once declared that I might consider myself to have mastered the discipline of Classical archaeology when I could make sense of Pauly-Wissowa. *Paulys Realencyclopädie der classischen Altertumswissenschaft* (1893–) is a colossal encyclopaedia of *Altertumswissenschaft*, the positive science of antiquity. Closely argued and enormously documented entries fill the pages of its many volumes. There are no plates. It keeps going. It is meant to be complete and definitive. It is a monument to German nineteenth-century scholarship. The point the professor was making is to do with an experience many have upon encountering Classics and Classical archaeology, though less often now in such an extreme form perhaps than in the past. An interest in Classical antiquity may animate you, but the discipline somehow gets in the way and has to be dealt with first. Skills need to be acquired to decipher the very texts which are meant to take you to where your interest lies. The point is not that this is wrong; it is that disciplines are as much about their practices and conventions as they are about their object.

In the last chapter many cases were presented to show that it is important to consider the different types of interest which take people to the Classical Greek past because, understandably, interests condition what is thought and done. So Herzfeld and Bernal have emphasised concepts of identity and Europe. Ideas of art and the quality of ancient art were shown to be vital in understanding Classicism and Hellenism. Then there are root metaphors: the past as a book to be read; the connoisseur as physician performing diagnosis. These profoundly affect the things done with the past and so the knowledges that ensue.

It can, in fact, be no other way: without a set of preconceptions (for that is what an interest is) there would be no study of the Classical past. The term used in hermeneutics for this, the philosophy of interpretation, is prejudgement or prejudice. The Classical past is prejudged as we turn to consider it. We are conditioned by what we already know or have heard and that fires a desire to find out more. This does not mean that what is found is what is desired, a past as wished for; the past may surprise. But that possible surprise depends upon a critical and sceptical attitude, being open to possibility and scrutinising the conditions in which knowledges are constructed. This is being self-reflexive, to use the term of critical theory or the sociology of knowledge.

This chapter considers the workings of disciplines and that of Classical archaeology in particular. A thesis to be examined is that disciplines actually construct their object of knowledge.

TYPES OF TEXT

The aspect of a discipline that is often first encountered is its writings. Some account has already been given of the types of text which went with the study of Korinthian pottery: the handbooks and catalogues, attribution lists and excavation reports, art histories and texts of ancient history. A visit to a research library such as the library of the Faculty of Classics in the University of Cambridge gives an immediate appreciation of the textual character of the discipline. The books are classified and shelved according to artefact type (ceramics, sculpture, metalwork) and period: here are the synthesising catalogues of material, subject matter and iconography. There is the section for the great *Corpus Vasorum Antiquorum* – catalogues of pots in museums around the world. Another set of shelves deals with sites: multivolume multi-part series of reports of sites and their materials, with the famous names of the big excavations: *Fouilles de Delphes, Clara Rhodos, Olympische Forschungen,* the *Korinth* volumes, the *Kerameikos* volumes. Periodicals and publications of the academic associations and learned societies are shelved separately, as, interestingly, are books on 'archaeology' which deal with matters of social reconstruction, interpretation and method.

Classical archaeology's pride of scholarship must surely rest on the authority symbolised by such texts. The cataloguing syntheses (Amyx's *Corinthian Vase Painting in the Archaic Period,* Berkeley: three volumes 1988) make every effort to be as complete as possible: all the pots in this class known in the world, with reference to every article written about them. That Cornelius Neeft produced an *Addenda et Corrigenda to D.A. Amyx: Corinthian Vase Painting in the Archaic Period* in 1991, with further pots, references and some corrections to the list attests to this quest for authority. An excavation report such as *Corinth Volume 7.2: Archaic Corinthian Pottery and the Anaploga Well* by Amyx and Lawrence (1975), published by the American School of Classical studies at Athens, lists pots with descriptions and comparanda – items found elsewhere which look similar; implications for chronology and classification are considered. In the background to these sorts of publications is an ideal of the complete text, the last word (even if only for a moment), the definitive classification to serve as reference point even when superseded by new finds which blur the precision.

Figure 4.1 Lekythoi in the National Museum, Athens

Shorter articles, usually in periodicals, may debate many issues, though most still consider matters related to the projects of classification and synthesis represented by the catalogues and corpora. But whatever the subject matter, there is a format which dominates, and that is the footnoted text. Just as the catalogue multiplies its entries, basing its authority on completeness, so articles multiply references in footnotes. Such references commonly refer the reader to related discussion, previous work and supporting literatures. They are signposts to the *discipline*. These articles look like scientific articles such as those found in scientific periodicals, and they are meant to. This is the technical literature of the discipline, where its key debates take place.

Even the popular art books and exhibition catalogues, defined by selection of choice pieces and sumptuous presentation, defer to an ideal in the background – the sacred authority of the articles displayed, their aura. The mode of illustration (usually studio photography) seems objective and transparent, a direct medium to the article. But this is a rhetoric of the image, for there is nothing 'natural' about studio photography, with the glare of tungsten lighting (albeit with colour temperature adjusted) illuminating with efficiency every nuance, every mark on the surface. The viewer may well want this clinical gaze, but there are other modes of representation, with which many museums now experiment. The *qualities* of light are so distinctive in Greece, as has been noted by several in this book. Why this should be reduced to a one-dimensional relationship between article and viewer says a great deal about a discourse unwilling to experiment.

Classical archaeology is, of course, saturated in historical texts (ancient histories old and new, and literatures from antiquity), but there is a striking absence of archaeologically derived historical narratives. They are simply not the sort of thing that serious academic Classical archaeologists write. (At least that applies to the majority: there are the mavericks, like Anthony Snodgrass, who has used archaeological materials in constructing narratives which come between archaeology and history.)

To understand this range of texts and its characteristics it is necessary to go back again into the nineteenth century when the paradigm was set. In 1850 Eduard Gerhard, a German Classicist, published a series of archaeological theses in the periodical *Archeologisches Zeitung*. He proposed that archaeology was the twin sister of philology. His desire was to free archaeology from the antiquarian dilettantes, from philosophies of art and from aesthetic appreciation, because these were prescientific. Archaeology needed to be made professional against the amateurs and travellers. Presented is the metaphor of archaeology as a science of nature (separate from the aesthetic humanities). Archaeological materials are like literary sources for developing positive historical knowledge of the ancient world. So archaeology is not as Caylus would have had it, a science of antiquarianism, but rather a science of antiquity: *Altertumswissenschaft*. This position adopted by Gerhard was rooted in the cultural success of philology in the German universities, a success which had led to ten professorial chairs of archaeology in Germany by 1848, while there was none in France or Britain. For Gerhard, archaeology's future lay as a positive science producing concrete results and rooted in critical knowledge of literatures.

Schliemann, the amateur outsider, showed the potential of archaeological excavation in his discovery of Aegean prehistory. But it was his enemy Ernst Curtius who brought together excavation and *Altertumswissenschaft*. The aim of the great excavations of Olympia (from 1874) was not primarily to find sculpture but to uncover the entire precinct and understand the relationships between the buildings. Alexander Conze (an Austrian) had had similar aims on Samothrace in 1873 and 1875. Considerable amounts of material were unearthed and demanded new procedures, narratives, texts and new technical languages. These were to draw more on archaeology than the precepts of Hellenism.

Frank Turner, in his book *The Greek Heritage in Victorian Britain* (1981), remarks that leading English Classicists of the 1870s feared that rigorous, comprehensive and detailed archaeological analysis could generate new ways of looking at the past. Morris sums up the response which was not restricted to Britain:

> The solution to the problems which philological-style archaeology might raise was to banish people from its discourse, only to reintroduce them at the end of the story as free Romantic beings who by spontaneous decisions could alter the direction of a passive material culture. The standard text for Greek archaeology was set up as the artefact-centred monograph, describing in great detail the architecture, sculpture, small finds or pottery from a specific site.

Adolf Furtwängler produced a landmark in 1885 with his two-volume catalogue of vases in Berlin. Comprising a list of 4,221 vases according to fabric, period and shape, it was far from a narrative. The analytical text was identified with the scientific text. Olympia provided another model in the five volumes of *Ergebnisse* (1896–7) which reported on the excavations. Narrative writing took second place to non-narrative texts, while narratives dealt with dating and race, ethnicity, and *Zeitgeist* (the Greek spirit). Academic creativity was defined as the list.

In that academic work is part of the biography of academics, this needs to be related to the type and range of interests which take people to the Classical past. Perhaps lists are about the writer wishing to escape into certainties. Whatever, the character structure and subjectivity of the archaeologists is bound up with the work they do. This is the human side of discourse: it is in disciplines that many people become who they are. Hence some theorists, notably Foucault, have linked discourse generally with the creation of particular types of human subject. The implications for educational policy are well known and widely discussed: think only of subject divisions in schooling and how knowledge is distinguished from what is defined as outside the curriculum. Further points will be raised in the final chapter.

Edmund Pottier's *Catalogue des vases antiques de terre cuite* of 1896, was followed by the *Album*, whose 51 large quarto-sized plates illustrated 300 vases in galleries A–E of the Louvre. Further texts and plate volumes followed until the 1920s. The innovation was photographic reproductions, but such work in the Louvre led Pottier in 1919 to develop a plan for the *Corpus Vasorum Antiquorum*, a series of catalogues which would gather every antique vase in the world. This was just the latest of many programmes to publish complete corpora of items, great long-term synthesising and systematising projects dealing with Latin and Greek inscriptions, Attic grave reliefs, ancient coins, the *Denkmäler griechischer und römischer Skulptur* and so on. Not only did they cover artefact types, but also iconographic themes: myths and gods and heroes depicted in the arts of the ancient world. These projects are monuments to the confidence and ambition of nineteenth-century academic discourse.

Under such programmes the field of debate is extremely limited, basically dealing with categories, chronology, classification, comparanda, and the promotion of new classes of item to discussion, or their demotion to irrelevance. Any further types of question threaten to mark as maverick or outsider whoever is asking them. Thus are found ways of defining insiders and those who are not really part of the discipline.

After the conspicuous success of Beazley in simply gathering a vast amount of material in listings, searching for the affiliation of idiosyncrasy of style was, and for some still is, the practice required of the ceramic expert. So consider the specialist ceramic reports to excavations of Korinthian sites such as Perachora (by Dunbabin and others in 1962) and the Potters' Quarter, Korinth (volumes in 1948 and 1984), which focus entirely on the relation of particular pots and fragments to the style Korinthian. To manage the particularity of style in this way is a credential of the discipline; it shows that you are one of the *cognoscenti*. It may even be perceived as required by the discourse – the specialist ceramic report, required of each excavation, necessarily reports (often only) on stylistic affiliation. The newly discovered Korinthian pot is related to style, and if possible, attributed to painter. This is the metanarrative of the connoisseur, scholarship, and the discipline.

Making these points is not, it must be emphasised, to condemn an interest in careful control of detail. As Morris writes, 'the problem with this archaeology is not the level of detail but the idea that in archaeology mastery of a body of material is all that is required'. An interest in the control afforded by information is intimately related to Modernist projects of surveillance and institutional control, summarised in the panoptic gaze, looking into everything and producing knowledges which allow containment and control.

COMMUNITIES AND INSTITUTIONS

Ian Morris and Stephen Dyson have emphasised the importance of institutions and communities of scholars for understanding the discourse of Classical archaeology. (The relevant works are listed in the Bibliography.)

The Archaeological Institute of America (AIA) was founded in 1879 and its journal, the *American Journal of Archaeology*, similarly dedicated to matters of Classical archaeology, began in 1885. So old world Classical remains had their institution before Americanist archaeology. Dyson considers that the constituting ideology (defined as larger justifications) of the AIA was that Classical art and culture represent one of the highest points in human achievement and the task of the archaeologist is to recover and reconstruct as much as possible for the betterment of mankind; this is Hellenism. He goes further with the observation that Classical archaeologists have not, like anthropological archaeologists (with their Society for American Archaeology and American Anthropological Association), been examining the ideological and theoretical basis of their discipline, but have subconsciously accepted the late-nineteenth-century founding ideology of their discipline, while dropping the most imaginative components and not replacing them with any new paradigms.

The first meeting of the AIA was held at New Haven, Connecticut, in 1899. Harvard's Charles Eliot Norton (Lecturer in History of the Fine Arts as Connected with Literature from 1874), who had helped found the Institute and who was an active figure in its early development, delivered a speech. There was a strong underlying sense of disciplinary insecurity to his proposal that American archaeologists were making worthwhile contributions to an *international* discipline. (The foundation of the American School of Classical Studies in Athens in 1881 had been backed by Norton. The explicit purpose of this intercollegiate institution was to contest European dominance, and to make a place in Classical archaeology for American interests.) Norton also articulated what he saw to be the inherent worth of studying Greek and Roman civilisation: 'together they represent the full circle of human affairs and interest. To them all the previous life of man contributes, from them as from their head all the varied full currents of modern life derive.' Greece and Rome are familiarly seen as the origins of the west. Dyson comments that in asserting the superiority of the Greek and the Roman, Classical archaeologists like Norton were claiming for themselves a special place as the interpreters of the origins of the west. With Biblical archaeologists they were dealing with a past civilisation in some ways sacred to the west, and involving sacred objects closely associated with sacred texts. Thus the justification for Classical archaeology was as much from *what* was being studied as from *how*.

By the 1880s American archaeology was split 'because of a near total acceptance of Hellenism among those working on Greek material'. For Dyson, the split with Americanist and anthropological archaeology had occurred because its colonialist attitudes (in the study of non-western societies) and lack of detail made it unappealing to Hellenists.

Dyson has compared articles in the respective journals of the American Institute of Archaeology and the Society for American Archaeology. He notes no interest in theory, method or new approaches in the pages of the *American Journal of Archaeology*, few changes in types of articles over the last few years as compared with *American Antiquity*. With respect to papers presented at the annual meetings, he found that from the 1930s to the 1960s papers about material culture (sculpture and vase painting) dominated the AIA, nothing being said about method, theory, geoarchaeology, floral or faunal analysis, all of which were figuring significantly in the debates of many other archaeological traditions, including that of the Society for American Archaeology. By the 1980s material culture was still dominating, and the programme of the AIA in 1985 was not that different from 1935.

Why is there this lack of change, asks Dyson. The Editor of the *American Journal of Archaeology* had never left the east coast of the US and has never moved north of Cambridge or south of Philadelphia when he was writing: this points to a uniformity of outlook, in contrast with the experience of Americanist anthropological archaeology. Dyson connects this conservatism with control of key power positions in the profession, conservative graduate programmes, the control exerted over graduate and field training. The role of the overseas schools is considered important here, bringing together graduates from various separate parent institutions for access to the sites and materials upon which their careers will be built, ensuring consistent homogeneity in training. So success in the discipline results not only from a mastery of data and the understanding and criticism of theory, but as much from the ability to absorb and articulate the prevalent ideology of the institution to which the academic belongs. This particularly applies to graduates setting out on an academic career. 'In such a system with its strong stress on tradition, innovation is about as likely as in the Chinese bureaucracy in the age of Confucius'; here Dyson is blaming the formalisation of a subdiscipline rather than Classical archaeologists *per se* for the stagnation of the discipline.

Morris too emphasises the importance of hegemonic professionals resistant to change who discipline practitioners and drive out unwanted statements. This is connected to the professionalisation of academic life since the late nineteenth century. The role of journals and academic presses and funding agencies is vital in filtering what gets done and published. He stresses the foreign schools and their role in managing excavations in Greece. Belonging to such a community is often the only sure way to get on in the discipline. A general point is that policing of the discipline and community occurs more through patronage and institutional loyalties than through rational and mutual criticism, just as it is not so much *what* is written that matters, as the *way* it is written.

MAVERICKS

Some do not fit the discourse but get on without being excluded. Charles Newton, Keeper of Antiquities at the British Museum in the middle of the nineteenth century, may be one of these. In tune with anthropologists, he took an evolutionary view of how art changed through time. This emphasis on change was a potential archaeological critique of Hellenism. He also used the British Museum's collection of ceramics to teach students a new way to explore Athenian society.

Jane Harrison at the beginning of this century used evolutionary anthropology, archaeology and French sociology to argue that Olympian gods rested upon an older stratum of demons and spirits. Drawing on Sir James Fraser's anthropological epic *The Golden Bough* (twelve volumes appearing

99

Figure 4.2 The British School at Athens

between 1890 and 1915), she explored Greek roots in the primitive, some-thing which was covered also in Chapter 3 of the present volume.

Newton, like Schliemann, believed that a collection should be exhibited entire rather than in a selection. And Heinrich Schliemann is the archetypal maverick in Classical archaeology. His life has been a best-seller (with more than forty biographies this century). A successful businessman, he was effectively freed him from the authority structures of academic discourse by his fortune. An outsider to the race of empires for Classical credentials, Schliemann could indulge his dreams. In a series of excavations in the last three decades of the nineteenth century he established the site of Homeric Troy, discovered the wealth of Mycenae and began the investigation of Aegean prehistory.

According to William M. Calder III (in his book on Schliemann edited with David Traill, 1986), Schliemann's is a popular story for the following reasons. He was the poor boy who became rich and famous; one who realised his idealistic dreams through hard work and a refusal to be put down by the authorities. He proved all the smart professors wrong by a stubborn and simple faith worth more than their supposed great learning, a faith set in the epic romance of Homer, and wherein Schliemann too had his Odyssey round the Aegean, and a Penelope, his Greek wife Sophie.

In his day Schliemann was opposed by many academic authorities. Ernst Curtius, the German excavator of Olympia, called him a botcher and a conman ('*Pfuscher und Schwindler*'). According to Fürtwangler, 'Schliemann is and remains a half-crazy and confused human being, who has no idea whatsoever of the meaning of his excavations . . . In spite of his passion for Homer, he is at heart a speculator and a businessman.'

What is behind this story? Schliemann's career has been closely examined, and it turns out that not all is as people have been led to think. Eighty-five per cent of the source material about Schliemann's life and discoveries was written by Schliemann himself. On close inspection it is full of fabrication and invention. Schliemann desperately wanted to be accepted as a scholar, but wrote what people wanted to read. His diaries are untrustworthy, yet they are the access to his life and discoveries.

The so-called Priam's treasure was discovered at Troy in May 1873. It came at just the right time at the end of excavation, vindicating Schliemann's theory (that he had found the Troy of Homeric legend) and making a tremendous impact which carried him on to excavation at Mycenae. It became one of the most famous and romantic discoveries of nineteenth-century Classical archaeology and ranks alongside Tutankhamun's treasure of 1922 in the popular imagination. It has been long known that Schliemann got the dates and stratigraphy wrong and that the treasure is far too early for the time of Priam. But there is much more. David Traill made a careful comparison of four reports written by Schliemann and there are telling contradictions. Moreover, a witness to the discovery of the treasure at the end of the last season of excavation also failed to corroborate the diaries. Priam's treasure appears to be a composite of numerous small finds made over the three years of excavation, possibly augmented by purchased items. Further investigations have revealed how much of a fabrication the diaries really are.

In the 1980s there occurred a series of character assassinations of Schliemann. William G. Niederland, a New York psychoanalyst, has interpreted Schliemann's psychopathology, his compulsive need to achieve, and his morbid attraction to the dead, in terms of early familial relationships, including a disgraced clerical father and his being named after a dead brother. Traill has marked off Schliemann against Checkley's symptoms of the psychopath: superficial charm and intelligence; untruthfulness; unreliability; lack of remorse and shame; pathologic egocentricity; general poverty in major

Figure 4.3 Edward Dodwell. *Views and Descriptions of Cyclopian, or Pelasgic, Remains in Greece and Italy.* London 1834. Plate 11. Portal of one of the treasures of Mycenae

affective reactions; unresponsiveness in general interpersonal interrelations. Schliemann fits. He was a lying monster who even manipulated his son's features as an infant so that his profile would be more Classically Greek to match his name, Agamemnon.

Calder reports:

> I am not a psychoanalyst. I am an historian. I can show you that Schliemann lied and deceived, that he altered, suppressed, and forged documents to make falsehoods seem truth, that he bought objects and said that he excavated them, that he fabricated a past that had never been, that he bribed and betrayed to gain his ends. I have never published a moral judgement on Schliemann. I have on his biographers. I consider them lazy and incompetent. But Schliemann was ill, like an alcholic, a child molester, or a dope-fiend.

Yet Schliemann was aware of stratigraphy, aimed to test a hypothesis at Mycenae (that Pausanias was right in describing graves inside the entrance of the citadel), and used excavation to decide a debate in ancient history over the site of Troy, digging first (1868) at the site he did *not* consider to be Troy (Bunarbashi). For Hartmut Döhl this is a very early example of realising the scientific potential of excavation and interdisciplinary links between history and archaeology.

The hagiography and invective is probably not over as Schliemann's life and achievements slip between fact and fiction, discourse and resistance. Here is a reminder that archaeology is not just about the discovery of past things but contains also the romance and realities of disciplinary politics and adventure. The man cannot be separated from the discipline nor from the discoveries, and his writings, as with all others, are conspicuously sources in need of critical interpretation. Schliemann's unremitting persecution of his aims is also a great example of the *will* to truth, the inseparability of knowledge, power and interest.

We are all like Schliemann, after all: imperfect, fudging, human. We should, I believe, beware of the arrogant pomposity of supposed paragons of academic virtue who, with intellects purged of all subjective failings, claim communion with a higher order of reality.

DISCOURSE

Various aspects of the discipline of Classical archaeology, its texts and communities have been covered. It is appropriate to step back and make some more general points. I have been considering aspects of the *discourse* of Classical archaeology.

A key concept for understanding the construction of knowledge is discourse. The term is widely used and often in very different ways. I will emphasise what seems to be most useful. The background to the contemporary use of the term is sociologies of knowledge which have investigated the social location of the construction of knowledge. A related, but distinct, term is paradigm, often associated with Thomas Kuhn. This refers to the working assumptions, procedures and findings routinely accepted by a community of scholars and which together define a stable pattern of scientific activity, and that community itself. The unifying stand taken in such sociologies of knowledge, and based on what is now a considerable body of research, is that there is more to knowledge than epistemology in a narrow sense.

In its technical sense, discourse is not simply text or communicative acts. Discourse is a term that summarises a particular ensemble of social practices through which the world is made meaningful and intelligible, embracing narratives, concepts, ideologies and signifying practices and more. There are three things central to discourses. They are embedded in society. They are situated: partial, negotiated and contested. And discourse conditions what is taken for granted.

The concept directs attention not so much to the content, but to the way something is written or told, and the social and historical conditions surrounding writing and telling. Discourses may consist of people, buildings, institutions, rules, values, desires, concepts, machines and instruments . . . These are combined in heterogeneous networkings – technologies of cultural production which enable and are the conditions within which statements may be made, texts constituted, interpretations made, knowledges developed, even people constituted as subjectivities.

The different elements are arranged according to systems and criteria of inclusion and exclusion, whereby some people are admitted, others excluded; some statements qualified as legitimate candidates for assessment, others judged as not worthy of comment. There are patterns of authority (committees and hierarchies for example) and systems of sanctioning, accreditation and legitimation (degrees, procedures of reference and refereeing, personal experiences, career paths). Discourses include media of dissemination: talk and speeches, books, papers, computer and information systems, galleries, or television and radio programmes. Archives (physical or memory-based) are built up providing reference and precedents. And metanarratives lie in the background, providing general orientation, framework and legitimation.

There is no singular discourse. Pluralism is another key feature of this sociology of knowledge. Discourses may vary and clash in close proximity. In a factory the discourse of the workforce may differ considerably from that of the management. Academic archaeology includes several discourses: near eastern and Classical archaeology being distinct from Anglo-American Processual archaeology, for example. The discourse of commercial excavation is different again.

INTERLUDE: CLASSICAL RHETORIC – A THEORY OF DISCOURSE

Rhetoric is a theory of discourse; it is concerned with the design and production of speech, text, and all things that communicate. Rhetoric foregrounds the relation between author and audience: the act, circumstances, technology and techniques of communication. For Aristotle, rhetoric is the art, skill or faculty of establishing the possible means of persuasion with reference to any subject matter.

Key issues are persuasion and power. Persuasion is arguably ubiquitous; it is an aspect of perhaps every communicative act. Many statements intend to lead the listener or reader somewhere, and even simply accepting a statement as given in order to move on to another is to be persuaded, however temporarily. A blunt statement of fact intends to be accepted, perhaps through its bluntness. Power is involved because an act of communication is intended to get the listener or reader to believe, think, feel or do something, even just to go on listening or reading, or indeed to give up reading.

Another aspect of communicative acts is related to persuasion. This is that much of communication is wholly or partly pre-symbolic; it is *gestural*. When I say 'How are you?', '*Ça va?*', the precise meaning of what I ask is less important than the gesture of attempting to (re)establish a relationship. Many of the gestural dimensions of communication are related to persuasion because the aim of both is to establish and maintain relationships of particular sorts.

Rhetoric reaches out to people; its aim is consubstantiality, building communities.

Rhetoric, being thus about persuasion, includes the construction of arguments and logic and indeed anything else that may persuade: reference may be made to emotion and moral character, for example. It is important to recognise the ethical character of rhetoric. In that the intention is to persuade, there is moral reponsibility regarding the direction of persuasion and consequences. This is simply to recognise that all relationships (the subject and aim of rhetoric) are of ethics. As Winterowd puts it: 'rhetoric focuses on language as suasion, as an act and as a moral consequence. The rhetorician knows that we can literally talk ourselves to death.'

The main departments of rhetoric are traditionally *Inventio, Dispositio, Elocutio, Memoria* and *Actio*.

Inventio: the discovery of ideas and arguments. This is the process whereby subject matter for discourse is discovered. Here are included modes of creative generation and originality. In terms of Classical archaeology, reference may be made to the history of ideas, historiography, to social contexts, and also to interdisciplinary connections.

An important subject here is the theory of *topoi* or *staseis*. These are the places where can be found material for arguments. They are standard issues by which a problem may be attacked, and are often questions. Topoi can take any form. They are simply strategies, ways of staking out common ground (topoi also come under the name commonplaces) in the sense of getting your audience to see what you are up to, to have them follow your line of reasoning and sympathise with your purpose. For example, there is the topos of 'more and less': such arguments concern degrees: if a thing cannot be found where it is more likely to exist, you will not find it where it is less likely to exist. Medieval rhetoric produced books filled with thousands of such 'commonplaces'.

In science the topoi most often concern observation, prediction, measurement and mathematisation: these are sources for persuading people that your version of reality is the correct one. It will be objected by many that these are not matters of rhetoric, but of theory coming up against the realities of nature. Einstein's theory of general relativity predicted that light would bend in a strong gravitational field. This was confirmed by photographs taken during a solar eclipse. Where is the rhetoric? But raw facts never point unequivocally in a particular theoretical direction. Stellar positions need to be interpreted in the light of theory. Stellar positions are the facts of science only under certain conditions, described in certain ways. They are at other times the material of stories and myths. That there are facts that support a theory, that contact is made in science at some point between prediction and reality is a *rhetorical* conviction. People need to be persuaded of the correspondence. In traditional Classical archaeology the topoi are prominently about complete and systematic inventory, and genealogy – tracing back arguments and artefacts through citation. Principal questions are: What class? What others? and Who said?

Dispositio: the arrangement of ideas into sequences and narratives. Logical and aesthetic links may be considered. For Cicero, the parts of a speech were the opening, narrative outline, statement of case, proof of case, refutation of opposition, epilogue. This legal formula is again clearly one that has had considerable influence upon the sciences. Narrative is an important element which, of course, relates to archaeological and historical materials. But narrative is more than simple descriptive chronicle. There are many factors including plot, agency and viewpoint.

Works constructed under Modernist aesthetics have exhaustively interrogated how media may be manipulated and arranged so as to convey senses of reality: from paintings by Picasso through the writings of Joyce to new-wave French cinema. A key method is that of juxtaposition, collage and montage: something which is used a great deal in archaeological texts (the order of listing, for example). The implications of reflection upon the significance and forms of collage have not been considered at all in archaeology to my knowledge. The *technology* of cultural production is another essential concern. We are no longer limited to the speech. So film can use close-up, multiple viewpoints, slow motion, montage and cut, and other forms of interruption and juxtaposition. A technology can enable or facilitate views of nature and society which are impossible to realise without that technology. The role of the image in Classical archaeology has already been mentioned.

Narrative and juxtaposition: these are central to archaeology, yet there has been little experiment or reflection. Conventions are adhered to which are stale and worn out in comparison to cultural production elsewhere (and most of all in heritage).

Elocutio: forms of expression and figures of speech, stylistic treatment. This may be divided into *aptum* – appropriateness to subject matter and context (for example, whether a line drawing is appropriate); *puritas* – correctness of expression (according, or not, to rules of discourse and the discipline); *perspicuitas* – the comprehensibility of expression (clarity and density); *ornatus* – the adornment of expression. Tropes or figures of speech provide a great insight into varieties of text structure within 'elocutio'. Here are included strategies such as antithesis and irony (figures of contrast), metaphor (identity in difference), metonymy.

The contrast between Aristotle's emphasis upon spare purity of expression and Cicero's florid style embracing all possible tropes has severely hindered considerations of style in those disciplines that see themselves as dealing with fact and reality. As early as 1667 Sprat was proclaiming the importance of lack of adornment in science: its communications must 'return back to the primitive purity and shortness, when men delivered so many things in an equal number of words'. So science, with some archaeology included, does not condone tropes like irony or hyperbole which mock and draw attention away from the rhetorical object – nature, or the past as it was. Metaphor and analogy undercut that semantics of identity between word and thing stressed by Sprat and upheld by science, empiricism and positivism. And viewpoint is to be suppressed. As Gross puts it in his book *The Rhetoric of Science* (1990), 'Regardless of surface features, at its deepest semantic and syntactic levels scientific prose requires an agent passive before the only real agent, nature itself. . . . [its] style creates our sense that science is describing a reality independent of its linguistic formulations'.

Purity of expression and third-person report is identified with freedom from emotional appeal, which is considered to undercut the claims of reason. 'But the disciplined denial of emotion in science is only a tribute to our passionate investment in its methods and goals'. The apparent freedom from emotion is not neutrality but deliberate abstinence, the choice of certain stylistic devices over others. There is also the myth of writing for a universal, non-specific audience. In plain scientific prose there is a non-rational appeal to the authority of reason. It is interesting to contrast the affective appeals of Winckelmann with the spare rhetorical demonstrations of Beazley.

Logos and *pathos* (**reason and emotion**): these are two grounds on which persuasion may be attempted. *Ethos* (character) is another. This may include the persuasive effect of authority and it is prevalent in the sciences and most academic disciplines. Academic papers are embedded in networks of authority: journals, grants and funding, institutions, career positions, citation and referencing. These can have a decisive effect. They may be very apparent in styles of writing. The texts of Classical archaeology make prominent rhetorical appeal in citation to authorities.

Memoria: the techniques of storage and the retrieval of speech or text. The scholarly monograph has come to be a standard storage device for the discourse of Classical archaeology. An anecdote will serve to make a point. The excavation of an archaic Greek colonial cemetery recently received long-anticipated publication in Italy. The three parts of Volume I are a testament to the rhetoric of the catalogue format: complete listings with genealogy and comparanda. The price was 2 million lire (£740 or about $1,100). It could have been published electronically for a few dollars or pounds. This is about persuasion, yes, but also the definition of communities who have access to the discourse.

Actio or *Pronunciatio*: delivery, gestures and setting. Included here are the design and delivery of lectures and TV programmes, books and publishing projects, museum displays.

Rhetoric is fundamentally about the recruitment and mobilisation of allies for your cause. It is about making friends. The main point is that persuasion may be legitimately attempted upon *any* grounds, though some are likely to be more effective than others. There is no necessity to style; there is choice, which is only closed down by structures of discipline and authority. Rhetoric is about courtship. Plato, in the Socratic dialogue *Phaedrus*, presents sexual love as an allegory of discourse. Both are acts of relationship with consequences and responsibilities.

IAN MORRIS AND 'POSTMODERNIST CLASSICAL ARCHAEOLOGY'

Ian Morris, as discussed above, has presented an account of the discourse of Classical archaeology which draws on the work of two historians of disciplines, Michel Foucault and Thomas Kuhn. Morris basically makes an equation between Foucault's concept of an *episteme* and Thomas Kuhn's *paradigm* (the latter also introduced above). These refer to a regime or system of knowledge and its acquisition, and the conditions under which knowledges are constructed: the rules and assumptions of disciplines, the accepted practices, and the communities that support them. They are thus clearly part of that general theorisation of discourse described above. It is not necessary to go into detail here about the concepts because the importance of Morris's argument is less to do with the quality of his theoretical definitions and more to do with what use he makes of them in his account of Classical archaeology.

Morris's aim is to relate the history of Greek archaeology to external and internal factors of discourse (social factors and those to do with the organisation of the discipline). He claims there is a crisis in Classical archaeology as the old ways of carrying out the discipline are coming under increasing challenge because they are not providing what more and more people want – they are not attending to new interests. This crisis in Classical archaeology has occurred, he argues, because of the gradual disappearance of the *social* arrangements, those of Modernity, which had made Hellenism an important academic discourse (see also previous chapter, this volume). Hellenism and all it stood for made sense to people. In the contemporary Postmodern world of the new Europe and postcolonial international relations, it no longer does. So the Classical disciplines as a whole and Greek archaeology in particular have been left without adequate intellectual justification.

Foucault has outlined historical shifts since the eighteenth century between three epistemes: the Classical, the Modern and the Postmodern. For Morris, the archaeology of Greece has been part of the Modern episteme and is suffering a crisis because of transitions to a Postmodern episteme. This is something which he describes as a 'huge epistemic shift'. The general cultural changes involved in this shift to a Postmodern episteme include a

Figure 4.4 Caesar's Palace, Las Vegas

fragmentation of disciplines coming with a collapse of secure centres. There has been a

> decentring of the subject, an approach that rejects the panoptic gaze: the piecemeal use of the past without regard for context; and the refusal to accept any totalising 'metanarrative' which would provide coherent meaning in history. One result has been a rejection of traditional ways of identifying truth and objectivity . . . These attitudes are antithetically opposed to the aims of classical scholarship since the late eighteenth century. The central concept of tracing the evolution of the West as the descendants of Greek culture has little relevance to the concerns which are coming to dominate academia.

So Classical archaeology, for Morris, is being marginalised because it is sticking to the authority lent it by its now outdated metanarrative. Hence Classical archaeology needs refiguring.

This is a very interesting comment on contemporary Classical archaeology coming from one of the proponents of new archaeological approaches to the Greek past. A problem that might be raised is that it all appears somewhat too neat and coherent, though Morris does relate and reference much historical detail. More might be made of the tensions and ambiguities discussed in the last chapter. For Foucault, discourse always engenders resistances: they are never total, systematic and without contradiction.

A more serious matter is that of Postmodernism. Morris treats it as a coherent entity, an episteme, the grounds upon which statements are constructed, knowledges established. It is suggested instead that it is best to distinguish *Postmodernity* as an extension of modernity, the cultural condition of late capitalism, from *Postmodernism*, a recent movement in the arts, philosophy, the social sciences, style and popular culture, from a *Postmodern attitude*. These are far from coherent entities but are instead fields of contention: the terms are conceptual tools in the rhetorical postures being adopted in many distinct discourses. They are what people say they want to be or what they don't like. So David Harvey has characterised Postmodernity as a cultural component of a new phase of capitalism, post-Fordist and concerned with strategies of flexible capital accumulation.

The Postmodern condition is characterised as fragmented, dislocated, interested in style, eclectically pillaging the past and other cultures without regard for traditional forms of authenticity, building on the demise of the certainties of old class cultures and institutional forms of the nation state. It is variously celebrated and decried (see Chapter 7). Within Postmodernism, architecture has left the international style of Modernism with an attention to the decorative, to variation of façades with pastiche, diversity of colour, design elements and iconography.

Within the humanities, Postmodern method (notably 'deconstruction') is a mode of *interpretation* which aims to elaborate the multiple relations between

110

culture, class and gender positioning and their effects upon cultural production and consumption, destabilising easy and univocal readings of cultural products. A major criticism here is that the resulting interpretive multiplicity is politically disabling because it challenges single authoritative readings which may provide legitimation for particular cultural or political strategies (a point to be taken again up in the final chapter). This is allied with the more general criticism that a Postmodernist celebration of pluralism may be relativist. A Postmodern attitude is characterised by a radical scepticism towards the claims of grand theory, towards totalising theoretical schemes produced from single and privileged vantage points (for example the claims of positivist *Altertumswissenschaft*). Instead an openness to difference is celebrated, with multivocality, experimentation and the empowerment of marginal political and cultural constituencies.

In not taking account of the discursive location of the terms he uses, Morris seems to confuse matters unnecessarily, ironically by polarising the discourse of Classical archaeology into Modernist and Postmodern. But there is considerable debate, and it is not adequate simply to acknowledge this and leave it at that. My preference is to emphasise the postmodern critical attitude. And with respect to the Classical past, Umberto Eco may be quoted: 'the postmodern reply to the modern consists of recognising that the past, since it cannot fully be destroyed, because its destruction leads to silence, must be revisited: but with irony, not innocently'.

TECHNOLOGIES OF CULTURAL PRODUCTION: RHETORIC, WINNING FRIENDS AND TRUST

What is happening in an academic discipline? Is it to do with critical debate and applications of disinterested reason? The answer of sociologies of knowledge is that this is not the case. In fact, it is much more mundane. I will approach the issue via the products of discourse, namely texts. Various kinds of text to be found in Classical archaeology were described above. Why do they take the form they do?

Consider an article by Michael Vickers: 'Artful crafts: the influence of metalwork on Athenian pottery', published in the *Journal of Hellenic Studies* in 1985. This was the first major presentation of his thesis about black and red figure Attic pottery (see also Chapter 3, above). It is part of a controversy about the artistic status of Greek ceramics, mainly inspired by the article, but nevertheless anticipated by it.

The article is technical and detailed as all sorts of resources are brought in to back up what Vickers is trying to uphold. References and footnotes are multiplied (they must make up more than half of the paper's length). Evidence is marshalled and displayed. What is the purpose? Is it to reveal the truth that Attic potters copied metal vessels, and that their status as art is a construct of Romantic Hellenists? Awareness of the workings of discourse leads to the supposition that the purpose is to isolate the reader who dissents: how can they disagree when presented with all the evidence, the logic, the number of others who agree, attested by references to other writings? Twenty-eight academics are named in the acknowledgements alone, including seven professors. Two of them submitted the paper to their classes for criticism. Even if these people disagree with what Vickers has written, he must have benefited from their comments, it may be thought. As Bruno Latour puts it: 'the power of rhetoric is to make the dissenter feel lonely'. The lonely dissenter has no friends or allies.

Matters of logic, reason and objectivity are, it is suggested, secondary to these matters of relationship. The article attempts to persuade the reader of its thesis. The art of persuasion is about providing only one way for the listener or reader to proceed *freely*. When this happens it is in many circumstances described as logical or reasonable. Logic refers to practical schemes which prevent the reader getting out or escaping the conclusions. Connections of evidence and literatures and points of argument are networked around the reader to prevent him or her straying from the desired path forward.

Another aim may be to appear as a spokesperson for all the 'allies' the author has connected together. A common rhetorical strategy is one of demonstration: 'You may disagree, but let me *show* you'. Demonstration is about the author taking the position of representative of the facts and issues presented. Vickers makes many mentions of features of ceramic vessels which seem uncontrovertibly in imitation of metal. In his book with David Gill, *Artful Crafts* (1994), there are many pictures of pots with metal vessels right next to them and which are of exactly the same form: a more effective visual rhetoric than the journal article with its three plates. Depending on the outcome of the persuasive effort, objectivity and subjectivity may be decided: spokesmen or women become either objective representatives or subjective individuals. 'Being objective means that no matter how great the effort of the dissenters to sever the links between spokesperson and what they claim to represent, the links resist', writes Latour. Subjectivity is when you claim to speak for others and for the facts, but people only think you speak for yourself.

The power of rhetoric relates to the constituencies claimed to be represented by the author. In connecting arguments, people (via references) and things (objects as evidence), the author spreads himself through time and space; this is one of the premises of power. It is about enrolling in a cause and *translating*. The observation of the shape of a pot becomes; it is translated into a proof of a theory. And persuasion is to a great extent about translating other people's interests into your own. There are many hundreds of references to all sorts of other texts and artefacts in Vickers' article and few of these, if any, make the same argument as he does. Translation is a way of making connection. You get things to work for you. Rhetoric is about establishing *heterogeneous alliances* of people and things, arguments and emotions, characters and evidences.

112

This means that a particular response is designed into the technical report which is part of a controversy: this is that it is not meant to be read! Disputes over objectivity lead to the demise of reading. Faced with a dense and technical report most people do not read it; they may or may not believe it but they give up with all the interrelations and networking it presents. Fewer others may go along with the piece and be persuaded. Their interests are translated and they reference or use the work in the future. The report is made more objective and may aspire to being accepted fact. The movement is nevertheless away from reading the report for what it is, a piece of writing. Very few people check up on the report and go through it all, verifying every reference. This is upheld by sociological research, but another point will be made below. In the first response, the text does not count. In the second, the text is abridged and reduced almost to reference. Footnotes and citation can serve to make the author appear trustworthy: there is then no need to check up on things. In the third response, attention is shifted from the text to libraries (checking references), museums (objects stored), and perhaps even excavation (re-establishing the database). The dissenter is faced with establishing a set of connections to counter that of the report; it can be an enormous and expensive effort.

But at points in the article there are no references to certain issues. The social process of emulation, a central point of theory, is left hardly discussed and is unreferenced. The matter is outside the article's paradigm, and readers can be expected not to notice, or not to mind. Readers often need not check references because they are accepted points. Argument and critical debate come to centre upon relatively minor issues. Not all the footnotes are about empirical and scholarly support, as many take a point from the main text and elaborate – often with comment that displays the author's knowledge of the minutiae of the discourse and its community. Vickers thus establishes his credentials and belonging. The reader may again feel isolated.

This is not to question the validity of the critical attention to sources and debate mounted in footnotes. It is to recognise that casual amateurs are not the only ones to be put off by technical literatures. The rhetoric of the technical article is to make the reader who disagrees feel isolated and intimidated by lining up friends and supporters against them. Hence these articles are to be called technical or scholarly literatures *because* they work in this way.

The rhetoric of the catalogues of Classical archaeology involves completeness, finality and genealogy. If logic is a rhetorical strategy which presents a path to the reader which they freely follow, such texts give clear directions. Responses are conditioned by the rhetoric. As indicated above, an item may be added; an attribution to a class questioned. The trustworthiness of the catalogue or report is guaranteed by the comparanda. They mean that it is more likely to be the case because there are others like it. The catalogue fits; it seems appropriate. Substantial questioning of the rationale of such a text is almost precluded, because there is likely to be so little ground for debate. The dissenting reader is excluding him or herself from discourse.

If it is accepted that rhetoric is such a feature of these scholarly and empirically rich writings about the Classical past, does this not challenge objectivity? Surely rhetoric, no matter how skilful, can argue away what happened in the past? I have already made some comment pertinent to this question, but let me introduce an example from Classical archaeology to illustrate the point about the social construction of the past.

Sir William Hamilton's Greek pots and those of similar design were thought to be Italian. Wedgwood's factory was named Etruria for this reason in 1769. But by 1819 enough people thought they were Attic for Keats to write in his *Ode to a Grecian Urn*: 'O Attic shape! Fair attitude!'

What had happened in the intervening years? Consider the debates of the eighteenth and nineteenth centuries about the origin of black and red figure pottery, now accepted as Attica. A.S. Mazochius had spoken up for the Greek origin of Etruscan vases in 1754. Winckelmann had criticised Caylus for treating all painted terracotta vases as Etruscan in 1758. But the debate was still going on when Hamilton arrived in Naples in 1764. The illustrative plates of the Hamilton collection reached Winckelmann in April 1767 and his first collection was sold in 1772. Giovanni Battista Passeri, in his *Picturae Etruscorum in Vasculis Rome* (1767–75), still insisted on Etruscan origin. As well as Hellenism, the issue was wrapped up in Tuscan patriotism and Etruscophilia, and regional rivalries in Italy. In 1749 the Florentine A.F. Gori, author of *Museum Etruscum*, had to agree with the Sicilians Blasi and Pancrazi who claimed that most of the vases in Sicily were Greek. The matter was not resolved in 1800, when a black figure amphora signed by Taleides a Greek was found in Agrigento. But arguments were further shifting towards the theory of Greek origin when Aubin-Louis Millin published his two volumes *Peintures de vases antiques vulgairement appelés étrusques* in 1808–10.

The centre of the art market remained Naples in the early years of the nineteenth century, but many vases were coming to light in Sicily which continued to resist the Etruscomania of the north. Things were not certain at the time of Keats, and his acclaim may owe as much to Hellenism as scholarly consensus. A significant event was the excavation in the late 1820s of several thousand vases at Vulci. Eduard Gerhard of the new Instituto di Corrispondenza Archeologica in Rome recognised the similarity between the Vulci vases and those from Athens, Aegina, Sicily and Nola; moreover he distinguished them from products of Apulia, Lucania and Campania in southern Italy. Before these pots there had been few known inscriptions, and the pre-Vulci vases were not of sufficient quantity to allow such systematisation. After Gerhard the case was fairly settled. An interesting rhetorical point is made by Gerhard's motto: *Monumentorum qui unum vidit, nullum vidit; qui millia vidit, unum vidit* [To see one monument is to see none; to see a thousand is to see one].

Figure 4.5 Stuart and Revett. *The Antiquities of Athens*, Supplement.
London 1830. Frontispiece: Agrigentum

What has happened in these years? Has the truth that pots found in Etruria were made in Attika finally won through? Did Gerhard establish the truth where others had failed to see it? He was right and Hamilton was wrong? Let us turn to the quality called objectivity. What makes a statement objective? The conventional answers are that objectivity is to do with logical coherence, or because the statement corresponds with something out there, external to the statement (here the reality of the past), or because of some inherent quality called objectivity. But who decides on how coherent a statement must be? How exact must correspondence be? It varies. People have to be persuaded that a statement is objective. This explains controversies and debates. Rhetoric, as it has been outlined here, is a way of establishing objectivity.

The archaeological past will not excavate and describe itself but needs to be worked for. If objectivity is an abstract quality or principle held by reality, how does it argue for itself, how does it display its strength? It cannot. People are needed, their projects. Attic pots needed Gerhard. So a statement about the archaeological past is not strong because it is true or objective. However, because it holds together when interrogated, it is described as objective. What then does a statement hold on to, whence does it derive strength, if not from objectivity? There is no necessary answer. It can be many things. An objective statement is one that is connected to anything more solid than itself, so that if it is challenged all that it is connected to threatens also to fall. This is how rhetoric works.

Why do I make this point that objectivity is a social achievement? Why stress that it is not simply a case of people in the past getting it wrong? First, it is perhaps an arrogance to think that what is held now to be the truth has been so for all time, and people were too stupid to know it, or figure it out in the past. Evidences are marshalled by people in particular social and historical circumstances. Classical archaeologists are coming to realise that a lot of pots that are taken to be Greek imports in Italy are, in fact, local copies. This does not necessarily alter the point about Attic wares, but it emphasises the provisionality of knowledge, however certain it may seem. If it is not accepted that the past is a social achievement of the present, the past becomes something that exists for all time, and the Greek becomes a timeless essence separate from us and which we, mere mortals, struggle to get to know. The Greek and material past again slips into that paradox of cultural proximity and distance.

THE WRITING OF HISTORY

Narrative was introduced in connection with rhetoric. Although eschewed in many of the textual formats of Classical archaeology, versions of historical narrative remain for many the ultimate aim of archaeological work – combining the particulars of the archaeological past into meaningful wholes with features such as events and plot. Narrative is not just a literary form found in many nineteenth-century novels. A renewed interest in discourse focuses attention on writing and text. There has been some such scrutiny in archaeology already, with discourse analyses, programmatic statements of the form that archaeological writings may take, and some experiment too. Chris Tilley, for example, has presented an account of Scandinavian rock art with multiple interpretive viewpoints (see his book *Material Culture and Text: the Art of Ambiguity* (1991)). Ian Hodder's *Domestication of Europe* (1990) is a monumental effort to write a reflexive narrative, that is, one that is open about the processes of its construction and writing. The account of the origins of farming makes use of structures of meaning (the *agrios* and the *domus*), interpreted in the material, which condition the narrative of history. The subject of the forms and character of narrative in archaeology (actual and potential) is a wide one. Narrative is a basic human means of making sense of the world, and narratives form a basic component of self-identity: stories are told to ourselves and others about who we are and where we have been. Narrative forms accordingly feature prominently in nationalist and heritage appropriations of the archaeological past: Chapter 3 was about ideological metanarratives.

Emplotment is the process by which elements of historical or other data are brought together (the actions of interpreter or 'storyteller' are required) into a sensible and coherent narrative whole, characterised according to narrativist philosophy by various rhetorical modes or devices. Narrativity is a concept associated with this explicit philosophical concern with the writing of historical texts. It is held by some that meaningful history can only be presented in a narrative form characterised, according to Hayden White, by plot, continuity, agency and closure. Opposed to this is, for example, a deductive covering-law approach which, influenced by positivist philosophy of science, concentrates on historical explanation through explicit causal relationships. (An event is explained by relating it to a general process or causal relationship: to hold, perhaps, that Mycenaean society collapsed because, like societies of its type, its economic base was fragile, would qualify as such an explanation.) As an ideal form of explanation, this was and still is championed by many Processual archaeologists (see Chapter 2 for deductive strategies; there will be more of Processual archaeology in the next chapter).

Art histories of style, of course, take narrative form. Note may be taken of its characteristics: the evolutionary *arrangement*, the *agency* of abstract style and the genius of the exceptional artist, the *focal point* or viewpoint of the sensitive humanist connoisseur. Here is a rhetoric arguing for a particular kind of world. The concept of narrative and philosophies of narrativity emphasise the active character of making sense – constructing meaningful plots out of what was uncertainty, and plots which have or will have meaning and significance for an audience or public.

117

CONCLUDING REMARKS

The question to be asked of a discourse is: Why these statements and not others? Who is allowed to write what and why? Why are some statements and not others candidates for the ascription of (disciplinary) truth? Power is clearly implicated in these questions, as it is in the rhetoric at the heart of discourse: the aim to persuade adherence to a cause, getting people and things to go along with you. Throughout this chapter it has been a concern to explore the relationships between interests, communities of scholars and the things they produce. I have concentrated on texts rather than excavations because the latter are translated into text, but the concept of discourse has been taken to cover all aspects of the heterogeneous connections which enable the production of knowledge.

As expressed in the Introduction to the book, this focus on construction of knowledge does not question the reality of the Classical past. It does, I suggest, make it more interesting, because the past comes to be about the stories of its 'discovery' and the people who have made it. In this way the past is actually more concrete, attached as it is to those people, with their own histories and societies, who have found it of interest.

Nor does this emphasis on discourse and rhetoric question 'scholarship'. What really is required is *more* scholarship, because Classical archaeology has not gone far enough in its source criticism, in its close reading of issues and in its self-critique – the examination of the concrete practices in which scholars engage. Critique may be contrasted with scholasticism. The latter involves redundant citation and argument, meaning the elaboration of texts around issues so thoroughly accepted already by the paradigm – the use of technical formats as strategies of inclusion and exclusion. Critique is an attitude of healthy scepticism and suspicion of easy and consoling answers on the grounds that systems of thought are usually inadequate and never complete, that knowledge is an ongoing process. David Clarke in an article of 1973, 'Archaeology: the loss of innocence', plotted the historical course of disciplines and proposed that archaeology was entering a phase of critical self-consciousness, questioning its rationale and practices, not content with easy answers or accepted traditions of working. Classical archaeology is also entering such a phase.

The Classical past does not reveal itself in its essential character but has to be worked for. This leads to the question: what sort of Classical past do we want? One that is consoling, nostalgic, bolstering up notions of cultural excellence? Or different Classical pasts which question and edify? Classical archaeologists need to take responsibility for their choices and not hide behind notions of the past the way it was and is for all time.

5

RUDIMENTS OF A SOCIAL ARCHAEOLOGY

THE SOURCES

Some questions of archaeology's relationships to philology, to antiquarian interests, to history and to metanarratives and ideologies have been raised. Implicit in many of the points discussed are assumptions about the character of archaeological materials and what can and should be done with them. It was argued that Bernal's reconstructions of social and historical change show little and superficial understanding of archaeological sources. It is appropriate to turn to consider the material remains of the past, archaeological sources, before considering social archaeology, the reconstruction of society through archaeological remains.

According to Anthony Snodgrass, archaeological sources have four assets: independence, directness, an experimental character, and unlimited potential for future expansion. But none of these implies objectivity: he stresses the interpretive character of archaeology and ancient history. A failure to realise this is the source of many problems, he claims. In particular, there is what he calls the 'positivist fallacy'. This holds that archaeological prominence and historical importance are much the same thing, that what can be observed archaeologically is therefore significant. Examples of this fallacy can be found throughout this book.

The asset of independence is that the hypotheses and arguments of archaeologists are independent of historical theory, having been developed in fields that have no written documentation. Indeed, this is true. Many developments in archaeological theory, which deals with the processes of inference which move from archaeological data to statements about the past, make little reference to questions and problems experienced by historians. However, the separation of archaeology from history is an awkward matter to which I shall return.

Archaeological sources, it might be added, are independent also in their irreducibility. It is important to understand the sources for what they are: decayed particles with their own independent character and resonances, with a solidity and density irreducible to the subjective attributes of those with whom sources connect. Artefacts are more than their makers. This is to reject archaeology as a discipline aiming to use sources to discover the reality of which the sources are conceived as traces, a position which often involves an emphasis on method, an alchemy that holds that if you do the right things in the right order the past will appear.

As in detection, at the scene of a crime there is much that is irrelevant. It may not even look as if a crime had been committed there. And, of course, the place is not only a scene of crime. Yet it may, if the detective is sensitive enough, yield particles which may be connected to something that happened; though the carving knife is not reducible to the murder. A scene of crime can be used to tell so many other things – witness the genre of detective stories.

So I contend, and in accordance with the last chapter, that archaeology is an *active* marshalling of resources which are not merely the fortunate by-product of the past, but rather independent materials inextricably linked with societies and peoples through the ages. The archaeologist may pick up the items of the past, taking care to disturb them as little as possible, and work on them. There is an ironic curatorial role here, but one that recognises the active agency of the present, for archaeological materials are as much of the present as of the past, depending upon present interest.

The second characteristic of archaeological sources is their directness. Snodgrass contrasts the sources for ancient history. Herodotos (fifth century BC Athens) is taken as a source for Egypt of the seventh and sixth centuries BC; Plutarch, writing in the Roman world of the first century AD, is taken as

Figure 5.1 Akrokorinthos

120

a source for the life of fifth-century BC Athenian Themistocles. There is a confusion of primary and secondary sources. Indeed, most works used by ancient historians are secondary sources which only happen to be a little closer (chronologically and not necessarily conceptually) to what they write about.

In contrast, archaeological materials are associated with what somebody once did and not what some writer (often a lot later and with distinct agendas) *said* they did. However, all sorts of interpretive procedures intervene between archaeological object and our understanding of it: excavation, cleaning, identification, description, dating, establishment of origin, conservation, interpretation and publication. In the end an excavation becomes a historical record itself, in need of critical interpretation.

The experimental character of archaeological sources is linked to the supply of fresh archaeological evidence. Archaeologists, within the limits of funding and legal permissions and according to the values of the academic community and discipline, can explore ideas or hypotheses about the past by looking for fresh evidence. And this applies not just to excavation, for, in Snodgrass's analogy, thinking that archaeology is excavation is like identifying medicine with surgery. Survey data do not involve excavation, and museums are full of material that has hardly been looked at. Environmental evidence may be quite independent of excavation and scientific studies may produce all sorts of evidence about artefacts and materials.

Archaeologists are often dealing with the remains of past societies (often and not always because there are environmental data for example). Social worlds are thoroughly *polysemous*. That a social act or product is polysemous means that it can always be interpreted in various ways. Meanings are usually negotiated, that is related to the interpersonal practices, aspirations and strategies of people. A good example often used is that of the safety pin, the meaning of which was radically renegotiated by punk subculture in the 1970s. Forms of social life are constituted as meaningful by the human subjects who live those forms. People are constantly trying to make sense of their lives: constantly interpreting.

The sociologist Anthony Giddens has related this characteristic of the social world (that it is to do with interpretation and meaning) to the hermeneutic or interpretive task of the sociologist. He describes the difficult *double hermeneutic* of sociology. First, it aims to understand a world of meanings and interpretations (society). Second, sociologists themselves form a social community with its own practices, procedures, assumptions, skills and institutions, all of which in turn need to be understood. In dealing with the social world of the past, archaeologists are in a similar position, and there is the added factor of ruin and fragmentation. Careful attention to the sources and the practices used to deal with them is very important if sound knowledges are wanted.

New approaches in ancient history are taking account of the character of written sources from antiquity. It is very clear that they are far from

121

transparent windows on the ancient world. Written sources are skewed and require interpretation. Two examples should suffice. That short passage from Pausanias given in Chapter 2 (p. 50) referred to wooden statues of Dionysos, gilded and with red faces, in the marketplace of Korinth. The Greek word for these is *xoana*. The concept of *xoanon*, a primitive wooden image, has long been an important part of theories about the origins of Greek sculpture. There are many references to *xoana* in ancient literatures. It is thought that rude wooden statues of the gods marked the beginning of a Greek interest in statuary. A.A. Donohue, in a book about *xoana* (1988), has examined the issue and found that the word *xoanon* can refer to all sorts of things, from connoting a high degree of craftsmanship in an article of any material, to splendid images of gods, to rude wooden images. The word changes its meanings through time, and context is vital in understanding its meaning. In the place of a single concept, Donohue finds heterogeneity. The idea of the primitive wooden statue which is held to be so significant in the origins of Greek sculpture is shown to be based upon a focus by scholars on certain texts to the exclusion of others. The term *xoanon* may thus now have little archaeological value, but close contextual scrutiny of written sources where the word is found can shed light on Greek attitudes towards images. Donohue's negative findings about the theory of early Greek sculpture turn out to be very positive for the historiography of art.

Rosalind Thomas, in her book *Oral Tradition and Written Record* (1991), has considered the literatures and records of Classical Athens. She argues that to understand the sources used for reconstructing fifth-century Athens (and her argument has wider applicability), account must be taken of the interaction of written histories with the oral histories and tradition on which they were based. (Her topic is thus *memoria*.) She delves into family traditions, official recording, the social significance of writing and its permanent record, manipulations of evidence, and genealogies. There are various mediating factors between event and its record: history is a field of interpretation. So histories are located in Athens' present; sources are situated discourses, material effects and affects of the society in which they originated.

Snodgrass takes the example of Naucratis as an illustration of the differences between historical and archaeological sources. Herodotos, writing about the Greeks in Egypt during the reign of Pharaoh Amasis 569–525 BC, says that Amasis gave the Greeks the city of Naucratis to settle in, that Greek trade was concentrated at Naucratis to the exclusion of other sites, and that Amasis withdrew a settlement of Greek mercenaries from 'Stratopeda' (camps) on the eastern border where they had been established a century earlier by Psammetichus, and brought them to Memphis as his bodyguard.

This is all contradicted by archaeological evidence. Naucratis was excavated from 1884 onwards and it is clear that the Greeks were there before the reign of Amasis. Elsewhere in Egypt has been found Greek material from before and after Amasis. The sites 'Stratopeda' have not been positively identified. But at

Tel Defenneh, and another dozen sites in this region of the north-eastern Nile Delta (the general area of 'Stratopeda') has been found evidence of Greek settlement from throughout the sixth century and including the reign of Amasis. Two of these sites are fortified and make good candidates for the site of Herodotos' Greek garrisons. So the reign of Amasis had no archaeological impact on Naucratis, nor does it lead to the withdrawal of Greek mercenaries from any frontier posts found so far, and still less does it coincide with a lack of Greek imports more generally in Egypt.

Attempts may be made to reconcile archaeology and Herodotos: perhaps the 'Stratopeda' have not been found; perhaps the concession of Naucratis was merely legal or honorary; perhaps trade in Greek goods was in the hands not of Greeks but of another class of society who did not come under the edict of Amasis. Snodgrass argues that such strategies miss the more profound and theoretical point that archaeological and historical sources do not relate to the same social realities.

> The claim that Herodotos' account has been falsified by archaeology is a relapse into another variant of the 'positivist fallacy'. It assumes that archaeology and history are operating in essentially the same order of historical reality . . . In fact the overlap between the two is small.

This raises the question of what archaeology is about: what order of reality.

For many, as has been shown, archaeology is about art history. But what sort of art history? Attention to the character of artefact design is required here. Nor do archaeologists recover only material artefacts like pots and tools. Attention has been turning for a couple of decades now to animal husbandry, agriculture, diet, pathology, industrial techniques and the cultural landscape. This brings me to questions of the sort of reconstructions archaeologists may make of past society. But before turning to these, I wish to continue with some more points about archaeological sources.

IDEOLOGIES OF ARCHAEOLOGY

A message of previous chapters was that Classical archaeologists do not work in an intellectual vacuum. Projects are inseparable from interests, and these may be informed by metanarratives and ideologies such as Hellenism. The question must always be asked: What is on the agenda? After this reminder of the situated character of archaeological interpretation, let me move on.

COMMENTARY AND CRITIQUE: OBJECTS AND THE CHARACTER OF ARCHAEOLOGICAL INTERPRETATION

It might be assumed, as indicated above, that archaeological materials are produced by people and that therefore the task of social reconstruction is one of finding ways of moving from archaeological data to the people and society of which they are *expressions*. Material artefacts thus disappear, becoming quite insubstantial emanations of something considered more important. It will be argued that this is invalid as an assumption. The question tackled in this section is an ontological one: just what is the archaeological object? And what does this mean about archaeological interpretation?

The old pot found by an archaeologist is equivocal because it belongs both to the past and to the present. This is its history; it has survived. And the equivocality confers upon the pot an autonomy because it is not limited to the moment of its making or use, or to the intentions of the potter. It goes beyond. The archaeologist can look back with hindsight and see the pot in its context, so time reveals meanings that are accessible *without* a knowledge of the time and conditions of its making. The pot transcends. In this it has qualities which may be called timeless.

Here also *historicism* (explaining something by relating it to its historical context) must be denied, otherwise we would only be able to understand a Greek pot by reliving the reality of the potter, a reality which anyway was indeterminate and equivocal. We would be fooling ourselves in thinking that we were appreciating and understanding the art and works of other cultures.

Pots are often used as a means to an end by archaeologists. They are used for dating a context; they may be conceived as telling of the past in different ways. Historicist interpretation reduces the significance of a cultural work to voluntary or involuntary *expression*: the pot expresses the society, or the potter, or the date. This is quite legitimate. But there is also the pot itself, its equivocal materiality, its mystery and uncertainty, which open it to interpretation.

The pot does indeed preserve aspects of its time and it can be interpreted to reveal things about the past. So the integrity and independence of the pot does not mean that it does not refer outside of itself. It means that no interpretation or explanation of a pot can be attached to the pot forever, claiming to be integral or a necessary condition of experiencing that pot. The autonomy of the pot is the basis of opposition to totalising systematics: systems of explanation or understanding that would claim closure, completeness, a validity for all time. We must always turn back to the pot and its particularity. This autonomy brings a source of authority to interpretation, if it is respected.

The autonomy of the past is also the reason why archaeological method has no monopoly on the creation of knowledges and truths about the material past. Does a painting of a landscape by Dodwell reveal no truths of its object in comparison with archaeological treatment? Were there no truths about the material past before the formalisations of archaeological method from the late nineteenth century onwards?

There is a gap between the autonomy and dependency of the pot. If we were back in the workshop where the pot was made, we might have a good awareness of its meaning. If we were the one who actually made the pot, then it would very much be dependent upon us. But its materiality, equivocality, heterogeneity always withhold a complete understanding: the clay is always other than its maker; the pot is always more than its classification. People may interpret it in all sorts of different ways, according to their different interests and agendas. The material world provides food for thought, for negotiation of meaning.

There is another source of the tension between autonomy and dependency and one that is the basis of the archaeological. The pot was made long ago in Korinth and depended upon the potter taking clay and giving it form, relating it also to knowledges and structures which went beyond the potter. But the potter, Korinth, its people and buildings, the conditions wherein similar pots were made and used, are mostly gone. The pot remains. It is a fragment, part of a ruined past, and independent through its materiality, temporality, its duration. The pot is autonomous now because it is no longer the past due to the death, decay and loss which have occurred. So the tension within the pot between dependency and autonomy is a tension between its expressive (or significative) character and its materiality. It is a gap between, for example, an image (which has an autonomous existence) and its meanings. Or between the sound of a word and its meaning to which it cannot be reduced. To bridge these gaps requires effort, work, the time of interpretation. This work is one of detection, reconstruction and connection, putting back together the pieces which have been separated.

When a pot becomes part of the ruin of time, when a site decays into ruin, revealed is the essential character of a material artefact – its duality of autonomy and dependency. The ruined fragment invites us to reconstruct, to exercise the work of imagination, making connections within and beyond the remnants. In this way the post-history of a pot is as indispensable as its prehistory. And the task is not to revive the dead (they are rotten and gone) or the original conditions from whose decay the pot remained, but to understand the pot as ruined fragment. This is the fascination of archaeological interpretation.

The transcendence of a work from the past is a condition of its authority and contributes greatly to its fascination. It is a quality of the sacred; this authority once belonged with the sacred image. Consider an icon: the image, the physical painting, is more than the simple form that it represents, that of a saint or deity. Objects can have cult value. This is something that is clearly to do with the perceived character of Greek art. Benjamin relates this to a quality of *aura*. Many cultural works even today acquire a mystique which turns them into 'cult objects': from Harley Davidson motorbikes to Doctor Marten Boots to Leica Cameras. Many of these are 'collectables'. It is also clear that many are closely tied to sub-cultural identities. The concept of a 'designer' article also attempts to tap this cult value.

Here the artefact is reaching a condition of the inexpressive. The analogy of (material) culture as text is one that has taken a great hold in archaeology and the social sciences. Some antiquarian and philological versions of the analogy have been mentioned. The idea is that things form systems of communication which are like the systems and structures of language. If this analogy is followed in this context, we can say that the fascination held by cultural works involves aspects of language which cannot be reduced to communication. The sacred text may be held to be the word of God, more than what it communicates, and possessing an authority which forbids the posing of those normal questions which test the validity of communication by comparing it with experience (Did the person mean what they said? Perhaps they were mistaken?). Magical formulae and slogans also belong with this aspect of language which is not reducible to communication. Attention is shifted to the *texture* of language itself.

There is a fundamental point to be learned here. It is that things (or indeed words) are not simply signs. They only *become* signs, expressing and standing arbitrarily for something else, in certain circumstances. Language is more than a tool for communication; it has its own texture which is independent of our intentions. So too with objects: they are dependent on people, but also autonomous.

The tension within the (temporality of an) artefact between past and present, between autonomy and dependence upon its conditions of making, corresponds to the complementarity of critique and commentary. Commentary is interpretation which teases out the remnants of the time of the artefact, places it in historical context. Critique is interpretation which works on the autonomy of the artefact, building references that shift far beyond its time of making. It may be compared artistically with artefacts from other times and cultures in critical art history. Critique may consider different understandings of the artefact in our present. Critique may use the integrity of the artefact as a lever against totalising systems, undermining their claims to universality.

Both are necessary. Commentary without critique is empty and trivial information with no necessary relation to the present. Critique without commentary may be a baseless and self-indulgent appreciation of the aesthetic achievements of the past, or a dogmatic ideology, an unedifying emanation of present interests.

Commentary is made on the dependency of things upon their time of making, fleshing out information of times past. But the flesh needs to be brought to life, and this is the task of critique: revealing heterogeneity, yoking incongruity, showing the gaps in the neat orders of explanation, revealing the impossibility of any final account of things. This is a living reality because it is one of process rather than arrest. It is the ongoing dialogue that is reasoned interpretation.

Commentary is not enough. The archaeological past needs reconstructing now. Something edifying can be made of the most meagre things. Janet

Figure 5.2 Baron von Stackelberg. *Der Apollotempel zu Bassae in Arcadien.* Rome and Frankfurt am Main 1826. Plate 3. Temple interior

Spector develops so much from an artefact in her account of a native American society *What this Awl Means* (1992), just as an artist may make much of an ordinary still life, *nature morte*.

Given this character of archaeological sources, the task is not, I argue, to interpret as a means of getting back to the real past, understanding its motivations and interests, in its own terms. Interpretation organises, divides, arranges, composes connections, describes relations, but under no certainty of an origin. The archaeologist can only weave connections that establish insights and plausibilities and are as much about the present as the past.

THE NEED FOR A SOCIAL ARCHAEOLOGY OF CLASSICAL GREECE

I have followed a line of thought concerning the character of archaeological sources, attempting to encompass points from previous chapters about discourse, the construction of knowledges, and the relationship of past and present. Return is now made to a call, which has come from many archaeologists including Anthony Snodgrass and Kostas Kotsakis, for a social archaeology of Classical Greece. With an eye on the aims and methods of anthropological and prehistoric archaeology elsewhere, criticism has been made of the overly narrow horizons of a Classical archaeology content with systematisation of materials, art history and pseudo-historical narrative. The task is to use archaeological materials to generate insights into ancient society. How is this to be done? And how is the character of the sources to be respected?

APPROACHES TO SOCIAL ARCHAEOLOGY

Prehistoric archaeologists have long had an interest in reconstructing past societies. Earlier accounts, up to and indeed beyond the 1960s, used descriptive narrative of changing material cultures augmented with sketches of social life: outlines of everyday life; craft skills and workmanship; animals kept and plants grown. Inferences of social structure were drawn from diversity in the quality and apparent ownership of goods: rich burials meant a hierarchical society. The limits of inference were held to occur with evidences for religious and spiritual matters: there was no way to get to know what people believed. A popular example of such traditional social archaeology is Stuart Piggott's book *Ancient Europe* (1965).

Culture history is a particular body of theory relating archaeological materials to social change. Pottery style, for example, is carefully defined, classified and plotted in time and geography (chronological scheme and distribution map being two prominent graphical accompaniments to this typology). Different material culture items are grouped, on the basis of this typology and regular association in the archaeological record, into entities termed *cultures*. These are conceived to be the manifestation of a people, an ethnic group, who were usually named after an item of material culture (Beaker people) or after a typical site or region (Hallstatt). Understanding social change is a matter of connecting stylistic change to these peoples. Typical processes are invasion, the diffusion of an idea from one people to another, or migration, people spreading and taking their culture with them. For Gordon Childe, culture history 'aimed at distilling from archaeological remains a preliterate substitute for the conventional politico-military history with cultures, instead of statesmen, as actors, and migrations in place of battles'. This is the framework which lies behind Bernal's archaeology in *Black Athena*. It has been superseded.

Challenges to culture history came from anthropological archaeology in the 1960s. The 'New Archaeology' found fault with all its assumptions: the social reality of cultures; the supposed easy relationship between ethnicity and style; the use of migration as an explanation; the use of diffusion of ideas as an explanation. For some the development of an alternative body of theory to explain the archaeological record was a paradigm shift in the late 1960s and early 1970s to 'Processual archaeology'.

There are some good introductions to Processual archaeology, its aims and methods, and its critics, many of whom form another set of approaches under the name Postprocessual or Interpretive archaeology. Rather than provide a general outline of these archaeologies, and so duplicate, probably poorly, these introductions, I have chosen to consider how some Classical archaeologists have been developing a social archaeology, using it as a vehicle for raising the main issues involved in an approach to archaeological remains which aims to provide explanation in terms of social practices and social change.

POTTERY AND SOCIAL CONTEXT

To begin, let me pick up the case of pottery, used to illustrate points in previous chapters. In the last twenty years there have been several programmes to understand pottery in its social context. (References may be found for this section in the Bibliography.)

I have already mentioned the argument of Michael Vickers and David Gill that black and red figure Attic pottery is to be understood as belonging not with the 'artistic' aspirations of contemporary potters, but with social processes of *emulation*. This process had been introduced to archaeology by anthropologist Danny Miller. Pottery style, vessels designed for a class of social aspirants, was in imitation of more expensive metal vessels: 'Rather than being creative artists serving the upper echelons of Athenian society, potters and the decorators of pots had to follow fashions created for craftsmen working in a nobler and more costly medium than clay'. Ian Morris, Cathy Morgan and Todd Whitelaw have agreed that such a social phenomenon is an important process in understanding early Hellenic style.

Figure 5.3 A Korinthian vase painter

130

In an approach with closer ties to traditional art history, John Boardman has attempted to explain particular figurative and abstract elements of Geometric pottery from Argos as icons of the city and people that produced them. The idea is that pots were like advertisements for what Argos stood for. He notes references in literature to the horses and waters of Argos and relates these to pictures of horses, fish, water and fishing water birds upon the pots.

More generally, Anthony Snodgrass has interpreted the figured scenes on Attic late Geometric pottery as reflecting a social ethos which valued the heroic. This is something visible in other ways, particularly the 'hero cults' which develop from the eighth century – the placing of offerings in old Mycenaean tombs. Robin Osborne has given a wide-ranging historical account of changing social and ideological conceptions in eighth- and seventh-century Attika, concerning the growth of the polis and general structural characteristics of burial, religious activity, settlement pattern and artistic style. He has explained Geometric and Attic pottery in terms of the structure of their decoration and form reflecting deep and general social outlooks. From regularity, order without subordination, juxtaposition without connection, and a world taken for granted in the Geometric, there was a shift to questions posed (about life, death and myth), and challenges set by the style of Protoattic pottery.

I may also mention approaches to later Attic black and red figure which draw inspiration from Structuralist analysis, which developed in linguistics and anthropology, but has spread to many fields of cultural studies. Pot illustration is interpreted as the articulation of deep cultural dispositions and systems of values regarding, for example, sexuality, domestic life, the conceptual world of the city and its environs. An example of such interpretation will be given in the final chapter.

Nicholas Coldstream has applied the traditional archaeological concept of culture (relating clusters of similar artefacts to 'cultures' or peoples on the assumption that style reflects identity and interaction) to pottery decorated in the Geometric style. Variations in eighth-century Geometric he associates with the emergence of the city states, many developing their own version of the Geometric in asserting identity and unity.

Iconography has also been connected to politics. A set of theories has been developed about images of Heracles and Theseus on Athenian pottery of the sixth century. At this time the political scene was in some turmoil with the tyranny of Peisistratos and afterwards with the laying of the foundations of Athenian democracy. So, for example, the Exekias amphora in the Vatican Museum shows Ajax and Achilles playing dice. This has been interpreted as a reference to the tyranny of Peisistratos: when he entered Attica the Athenians, according to a story recorded by Herodotos, were either asleep or playing dice. Vickers and Gill find fault with this particular case and ask how this pot could convey such a political message to its viewers if it were buried alongside an Etruscan aristocrat in Italy; this would only be possible if it had a history of use before being sold on second-hand for an export market. But there seems to have been a very limited second-hand market in pots. However, if the pot were a copy of a bronze vessel decorated with silver figures, the matter would be different.

Further examples of approaches which consider pottery style in social context can be found in the next section.

THE SNODGRASS SCHOOL OF IRON AGE STUDIES

Processual archaeology developed a systematic body of theory to deal with society, or, in its terms social systems and social process. A major early application was in Aegean prehistory: Colin Renfrew, in his book *The Emergence of Civilisation* (1972), considered the development of social complexity in the Cyclades in the millennia preceding the famous Minoan and Mycenaean 'palace' societies. Another programme of social archaeology has been developed since the 1970s by Anthony Snodgrass and his students.

Anthony Snodgrass and the Greek city state: soft Processual archaeology

Snodgrass was a pupil of John Boardman, having taken a conventional route into Classical archaeology via public school and Oxford. His research topic was armour and weapons of the Dark Age, a conventional one in that it focused on a class of material culture, but, in dealing with iron, which has little 'aesthetic' appeal, Snodgrass moved into a marginal area avoided by art historians. It was relevant also to the historical question of hoplite reform; the field was also that of ancient history and military reform. And it was in social and economic ancient history that demands were being made for quantification and new approaches.

Snodgrass's innovation was to extend the traditional rigour of Classical archaeology to all artefact types and to concentrate on contexts of deposition. His work on weaponry led him to significant contributions to debates in ancient history. Generally Snodgrass has been successful in uniting ancient history and archaeology, drawing eclectically on historical, literary archaeological sources, making use of social and anthropological theory in social narratives of Dark Age and archaic Greece.

From his inaugural lecture as Lawrence Professor of Classical Archaeology in the University of Cambridge (1977), Snodgrass followed a project of developing a social archaeology of the rise of the Greek city state. This can be described as a descriptive and *systemic* model of social change. Greek society is conceived as a social system – an interrelated set of patterned behaviours influencing one another. Snodgrass plotted various 'system factors' and proposed a determining force or prime mover behind the development of the city state which ran through the social system in a series of 'multiplier effects' (positive feedback relationships where an increase in one factor reinforces, and is in turn reinforced by, another). Although he later decided in favour of multiple determining factors behind the polis, Snodgrass presented a powerful case, in his book *Archaic Greece* (1980), for demography being a prime mover to state formation in Greece. Using quantification of sites and graves, he plotted depopulation in the early Dark Ages with a population 'explosion' in the eighth century as the numbers of graves per generation increased sevenfold between 780 and 720 BC. His classic graphical representation of this extraordinary phenomenon is given in Figure 5.4.

The state was, for Snodgrass, an attempted solution to population increase as its effects ran through Greek society. Immediate consequences were on communication and the division of labour, with an increase in the pace of change: 'political change was mandatory'. Snodgrass notes that the polis was not a town so much as an idea. The new political form was a cluster of villages in its earliest times, as has been noted already for Korinth. Fortification came early at Smyrna, but nowhere else until later; urbanisation is not a good criterion of the early polis. He rejects continuity in Greece as an origin of the idea of the state and looks east instead, to Phoenicia.

Other system factors contributed to this process of social change. Dedications and temples attest to religious association as a factor in the early polis. Increases in metal production point to a higher-energy economy which fed into religion in the form of a considerable rise in dedications at

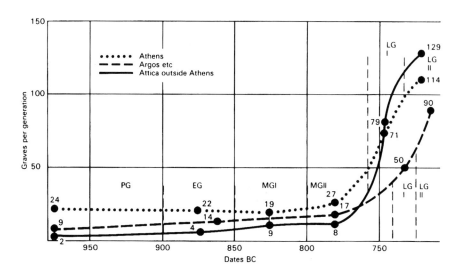

Figure 5.4 Total numbers of burials per thirty-year generation for Athens, Attika and Argos, 1050–700 BC. (*Source*: Anthony Snodgrass. *Archaic Greece: the Age of Experiment*. London: Dent, 1980. Figure 4)

sanctuaries in the eighth century. Snodgrass again uses quantification most effectively with tables of counts of artefacts at sanctuaries and compared with the investment of wealth in burial. Monumental temples were a new architecture: with early examples at Eretria, Samos (the Heraion), and Gortyn on Crete. The new cosmopolitan pan-Hellenic sanctuaries became media for interaction with their aristocratic gatherings. They were also a focus for a competitive agonistic ideology, with displays of physical prowess and the heroic ideal (so clear in Pindar's poetry). The ideology of religious legitimation is clear also in the status of Delphi as a centre of knowledge in the colonisation movement. The priesthood was a source of legitimation in political manoeuvrings; it was an instrument of persuasion, which gained a reputation as legal and political arbiter (the traditional role of the aristocrat). The development of a heroic ethos is connected by Snodgrass to the cults of local heroes (with evidences from the eighth century), as previously mentioned. With the emphasis on ancient links to the land, there seems to have been a consolidation of ownership of land. The development of the polis is thus connected to an economic revolution or change: from pastoral to arable farming. Reliance is here mainly on literature (Homer's is a pastoral world; Hesiod's is one of small arable farmers); the importance of ownership of land is very clear later. Population and a factor of land shortage (with the new emphasis on ownership) led to colonisation from 735 BC and the founding of Sicilian Naxos.

Craft technologies (e.g. tripod manufacture, metalwork and ceramics) can be related to religion (the major consumer of goods). Representational art seems a clear ideological interest in heroic ages which connects also with early epic poetry and thereby with new literacy, with its roots in a Phoenician alphabet – another connection with the east. Weaponry and imagery shows warfare close to the heart of the idea of the polis. Later (seventh century BC) changes seem to have involved a hoplite phalanx opened to wealthy non-aristocrats as part of a citizen militia. Political turmoil is known from historical sources and in many polities brought codifications of law which, being open and subject to scrutiny, established the arrival of a new public sphere. Wealth, political and social identity and new ideologies of popular heroism are thus combined in the field of battle, characterised in its early days by ritualistic convention. The basis of the polis was established as a settled population of prosperous soldier-citizen-farmers.

Mercenaries were travelling abroad from the seventh century. They were not the only export from Greece. An expansive economy with its new opportunities combined with colonisation and new political identities in the development, eventually, of a commercial sector and market. Central to this was slave labour, a material base of the city state economy.

Snodgrass listed the key changes as: citizenship taking primacy over kinship; the shift from a pastoral to an arable economy; slavery; the importance of tribal monarchy giving way to state institutions; the growth of the independent state – from 'useful aristocratic counterpiece' to an independent force; and commerce moving from prestige goods to partial mercantilism.

I have given some detail here to illustrate the power of Snodgrass's systemic account. It is a powerful integrating model combining many linkages between different parts of the social system (albeit mostly descriptive or circumstantial rather than rooted in interpretation of a social logic), between artefacts and social practices, and between different types of source material. Clearly displayed is the explanatory potential of quantification and statistical treatment of archaeological materials. Categories and assumptions are questioned (urbanisation associated with the state; the category of art, for example). The principle of understanding archaeological materials in terms of social process is shown to have a great future.

Quantitative Processual archaeology: Ian Morris and Attic burial practices

Snodgrass's systemic model upholds many of the precepts of Processual archaeology as developed in the United States, but absent is the emphasis on scientific explanation, the use of formal processes of inference, and explicit hypothesis testing through large-scale quantification and statistical analysis. It is also too *historical*.

In contrast with Snodgrass's more descriptive (circumstantial) and so 'soft' treatment, Ian Morris has presented a much more statistically rigorous explanation of the early city state, drawing heavily on anthropological approaches to mortuary analysis in what may be called a 'hard' processual model of social change.

Burial and Ancient Society (1987) is a confident sweep through the issues and literature that surround the rise of the Greek city state. Morris refines the theory and method of mortuary analysis developed in the 1970s by anthropological archaeologists Binford, Saxe and Tainter, and applies it to the graves from Attika. They developed a general cross-cultural theory of mortuary practices which Morris adapts to his purpose. Burial is conceived as a reflection of social structure (distinguished from social organisation, the actual things people do, in the classic way of structural-functionalist anthropology); burial is a 'mental template' of society. The difference between structure enacted in ritual ('ideal' society) and social organisation (what people may actually be doing) is, for Morris, the manifestation of ideology.

Given this cross-cultural setting, the task of Morris was one of finding a pattern in the cemeteries and reading social structures from it. Morris stresses the limitations and poor condition of the data and the inappropriateness of sophisticated statistical techniques, so often used by Processual archaeologists in mortuary analysis. But he skilfully used descriptive and analytical techniques, presented hierarchically, moving from simple observation to the more complex. Morris considered in turn the age structure of the cemeteries, demographic issues (population, grave plots, burying groups), the possibility of exclusion of part of the population from formal burial, the variability of the cemeteries, and grave goods as symbols of wealth.

The thesis is that from 1050–750 BC, and in Attika from 700–510 BC, small adult grave plots and cemeteries represent the *limited* burial of ranked groups. Around 750 BC occurred the emergence of the polis, ideas of the political community, and an ideology of denial of difference in status, hence the number and character of burials change. (Here is a direct challenge to the demographic model of Snodgrass.)

Behind this picture is a class struggle between aristocracy and serfdom, leading to a rejection of dependency of lower classes on aristocracy with the birth of the polis. Burial practices, for Morris, reveal an ideological merging of *agathoi* and *kakoi* in opposition to a new class of slaves. Athens of Solon and the Peisistratid tyranny is a special case of reversion to the old conflicts: 'Athens began to develop as a polis system, but then reverted to a pre-political relationship with the community after 700 BC.'

Morris approached the 1,400 burials with cross-cultural categories of society and structure; abstract measures of rank, variability and change; models of the polis, of social revolution; and general theoretical definitions of class, serfdom and slavery. He considered the basics of demography, but his view of the structure of society is a narrow one of rank displayed in burial.

Burial is held to represent social structure directly and Morris used componential analysis, pioneered in this context by Arthur Saxe, to discover the 'social personae' of society (a technical term referring to conventional characters and roles). Burials were classified without reference to their actual content, only their difference from others, and cemeteries according to the number and range of social personae, or rather different paths through the componential diagrams. Morris was able to compute a measure of variability (deviation from componential mode) and uses this to plot change in society. Consider, for example, the claim that a rise in variability score from 0.2425 to 0.2975 (the scale is 0–1) represents a rise from 'quite limited' variability to 'much more structure' of society. Morris provided qualification of this abstract and statistical description of society with simple description, but it is not clear what this abstract measure means in social terms. Nevertheless Morris made a case for considering social practices through *abstract* measures of change and variability.

For Morris, archaeological materials are only a set of formal relationships devoid of meaning. The formal patterning is there (hence the use of abstract and general models of structure and variability), but its meaning must come from *outside* of archaeology. Here Morris resorted to ethnographic analogy with other societies, but more importantly to literary sources, and in particular Aristotle's class analysis of ancient society. Material culture is thus epiphenomenal to society and the privileged access to meaning represented by the words of the ancients themselves.

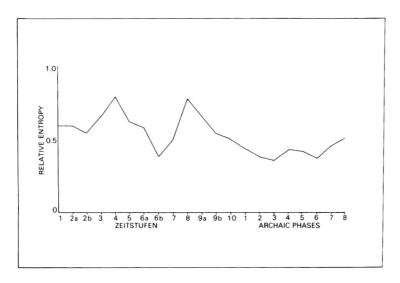

Figure 5.5 Relative entropy scores for the Kerameikos adult burials 1125–500 BC showing high entropy in egalitarian times. (*Source*: Ian Morris. *Burial and Ancient Society*. Cambridge: Cambridge University Press, 1987. Figure 50)

The abstractions of variability and change, and of classifying burial, carry, of course, the corollary that particularity, the form and meaning of material culture, is mysterious. Morris was not interested in why Athenians painted pots in the particular way they did. The particular mode of symbolising society becomes random; changes in particular modes of burial could be termed irrelevant, 'purely chronological process'. The significance is in the change. Such mystery is rooted in an old distinction between function and style, much discussed by archaeologists. Material culture functions to express social structure; the *style* of this functioning is inexplicable. As an abstract process function lacks particularity, and Morris took no account of the meaning of style, the reasons why burial may have taken the particular form that it did.

In spite of this issue of the relationship of general modelling and particular historical form, Morris has provided an approach to cemeteries, into which Classical archaeologists have delved for so long, which is as refreshing as it is enlightening. He has dealt with ideas, ideologies and concepts as major factors in social change, and with their archaeological visibility in an approach which makes the most of cross-cultural anthropological theory. In his sophisticated statistical analyses the strength of Processual social archaeology is again revealed to be its ability to summarise, to coordinate and draw into a coherent model of social change an enormous amount of empirical detail.

I will reserve further comment until after I have described two other archaeological interpretations of the early city state which further reveal the characteristics of Processual social archaeology.

Pottery and politics

In a sophisticated development of the idea that style relates to site of production, Cathy Morgan and Todd Whitelaw, in an article in the *American Journal of Archaeology* 1991, have investigated variability in the decoration of Geometric pottery produced in and around Argos. They have argued that pottery functions as a medium and index of interaction, and so reflects and takes part in changing relations of dominance by what came to be the main city state, Argos.

For Morgan and Whitelaw the style and use of pottery in the Argive plain from 1050–700 BC came to express social status; its iconography reflected status; style was an expression of community identity. Their main focus was on style as an 'index of interaction' between sites. Analysis of 947 pots coded on 16 variables according to 495 different elements of form and decoration aimed to establish a pattern to be correlated with relationships between the settlements around the city state of Argos.

The statistical analysis is again subtle, working from simple to more complex methods. A primary step was to identify diagnostic as opposed to random style: three variables were found to vary between sites in a way that 'deviated significantly from what could be expected due to chance factors alone'. These diagnostic variables concerned the form and placing of the main decorative design element. The three variables were then amalgamated into a summary measure of stylistic affinity which was used to map patterns of interaction: similarity between the ceramic assemblages of sites was compared with distance according to accepted chronological phasing. It was suggested that stylistic similarity at times represents political affiliation, that after experiment with earlier Geometric decoration, style was politicised in the ninth century BC, expressing social and political competition. This is related to what is known from historical references about the politics of the plain of Argos, and it was with this scenario that their paper began.

Morgan and Whitelaw homed in on an issue and region, developed a hypothesis, drew on general anthropological theory, that stylistic similarity is to do with relationships between communities, then carefully analysed relevant variables of a large data set, discarding what was considered irrelevant to the hypothesis. These are characteristics of Processual archaeology. They also related their findings to what is known historically of relationships between communities on the plain of Argos.

There is some reference to style as 'active', and used intentionally or purposefully, but that opposition remains built into the analysis between those aspects of style that are diagnostic and function to express society and interaction, and others that are creative or random, representing 'chance

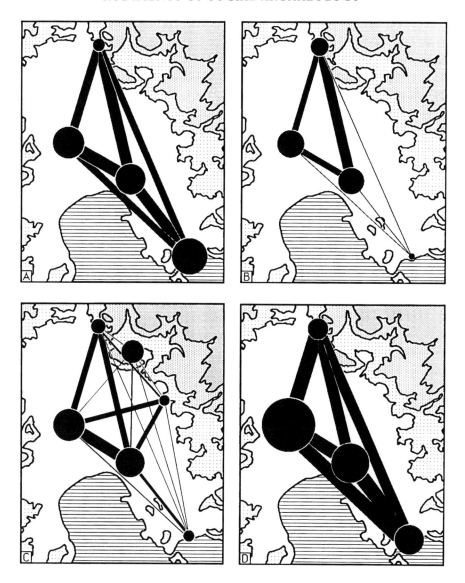

Figure 5.6 Stylistic similarity between sites on the plain of Argos, Greece, separated into periods. The size of the circle representing each site reflects the number of vessels included in the analysis. Width of lines represents the degree of stylistic similarity, wider representing greater similarity. Protogeometric (A); Early Geometric (B); Middle Geometric (C); Late Geometric (D). (*Source*: Todd Whitelaw and Cathy Morgan. 'Pots and politics: ceramic evidence for the rise of the Argive state', *American Journal of Archaeology* 95 (1991): 79–108)

factors'. 'Style was a political tool', claimed Morgan and Whitelaw. By this they meant that a particular combination of three elements of the design of pots seems to be non-randomly distributed between sites, given only this attribute index, distance, and an abstract notion of 'social interaction'. Their analysis was purposefully reductive: the style of pots, and all that this represents in terms of aesthetics, was reduced to a single measure, a summary attribute or number. Other aspects of design and manufacture were discarded as irrelevant to this analysis. The actual social practices of pottery design, as opposed to this abstract index, were also considered irrelevant to analysis. It was pointed out that there were problems with the variability of the samples, that often the quantification simply allowed recognition of sample size and did not provide an index of similarity. It may be suggested that the problem is of reducing a complex interplay of social practices and design strategies to one summary measure, an abstract notion of similarity.

The functions of artistic style

James Whitley's book *Style and Society in Dark Age Greece: the Changing Face of a Pre-literate Society* (1991) begins evocatively with two contrasting Athenian amphorae of the sixth and eighth centuries BC – one Geometric, the other black figure – and the problem of appreciating their difference. He does not eschew a humanist language of the appreciation of aesthetic quality, but his project is one wider than traditional art history. With admirable aims of reconciling art history, history and archaeology, Whitley's objective is to show that the ninth-century amphorae 'registers' Athenian society. In understanding the style of such an artefact, he claims reference must be made to its original social and historical context. Citing art historian Michael Baxandall, archaeologist Ian Hodder, and hermeneutic philosopher Hans-Georg Gadamer, Whitley describes his work as Contextual archaeology.

Most of the pots from 1100–700 BC, which Whitley chose to explain, were deposited with the dead. Consequently there is reflection also on the archaeological analysis of mortuary remains. And it is with concise critiques of art history, other approaches to style, and the processual archaeology of death, that the analysis begins. Under this contextual approach it is accepted that mortuary practices are 'an expression of the society that produced them', but 'the rules governing the transformation and self-representation of society at death are not universal, but culturally specific'. It is thus stressed that death and what people do with the dead are mediated by ideas, institutions and ideologies.

These Dark Age pots occur in graves; understanding comes from considering the social context of stylistic expression, it is claimed. So the bulk of Whitley's study, as presented in this book, has been to determine the patterning behind and of pots in cemeteries, and then to attribute meaning to this patterning in terms of social process or social structures. Computer-based factor analysis and a clustering program were used to find patterning, with each grave coded on over seventy variables. The intention was to reduce the complexity of the burying practices to a few dimensions, and to group the graves according to a general consideration of their form and contents (paying particular attention to the decoration of pots). The cluster and multi-variate analysis is accompanied by sometimes close (traditional) qualitative description of the burials, all done according to the chronology defined by traditional stylistic interpretation.

Whitley considers wealth an important factor in describing forms of burial, and devised a method of 'scoring' wealth according to the number and type of artefacts interred with a person. The search for patterning in the burials then became a search for correlation between 'style' and 'wealth'. Whitley claims to have found it; he refers to a process of 'social rationing'.

> A major social change occurred between the tenth and ninth centuries ... Athens underwent a transition from a relatively egalitarian to a more hierarchical society, whose organising principle was the social rationing of valued tokens, exotic artefacts, certain decorative features, and the right of formal burial.

So the development of style is to be intimately linked with social change: in the ninth century being buried in a particular way with some types of pot was a privilege of a social elite.

This picture is fleshed out towards the end of the book as Whitley moves from attributing meaning to social typing and ethnographic analogy. Reflecting on the social origins of the city state, Whitley suggests an analogy between Dark Age Greek society and Melanesian 'big man' societies. But for Athens, he follows historian Oswyn Murray in looking to Nuristan, with its social rationing, as an ethnographic parallel. In this society there is a direct link between style and status: 'art and decoration have a direct and unambiguous meaning, referring to social rank'.

For many art-historian Classicists, Whitley's narrative, indeed the style of his book, littered with dendrograms and factor scores, must be very provocative, especially with its thesis of art as the manifestation of status competition. And in addition to presenting this primary thesis, Whitley performs a useful service of synthesising previous observations on Attic burial practices. Some of these are very interesting and suggestive: for example, the clear differences in treatment according to gender, and the considerable variability of practices within Attika and between Attika and other regions of Greece. In this way too Whitley presents an interdisciplinary study. Coordination of large amounts of data via summarising statistics and the definition of patterning to be related to social structure is again shown to be a powerful feature of Processual archaeology. Ethnographic analogy and cross-cultural anthropological theory is used, with a particular stress upon the function of artistic style to express social status.

Consider some other features of Whitley's book. The link between material culture (the style of pots and burial) and society is described in various ways. Sometimes society is 'expressed' in material culture, sometimes 'registered', 'reflected', 'realised', 'symbolised', or 'defined'. What, it might be asked, is this 'society' which is so registered, etc.? Whitley writes of 'social personae' and 'social identities': these are the roles of rank and status that people play. It does appear that there are two levels of reality: hard social relationships, and then their representation or expression, here in material culture. In what ways material culture might, in this way, be less real than 'society' is not indicated. The problems of such a splitting of social reality are not considered.

Whitley does make the point that the link between society and material culture is one that is mediated; it is not direct, something comes between. This is a process of 'social rationing' and there are thus four elements in Whitley's argument: burial, the style of pottery, social rationing, and society. Society finds its expression, via social rationing, in what people did with their pots and the dead. This is a reasonable argument: rich people have posh things which others are not allowed to use or have. But Processual archaeology can make society seem quite one-dimensional.

Whitley's argument reduces so much variability to a basic relationship of expression of society conceived mainly in terms of rank and status. Is this all there is to the structure of society? Another question always seems to remain: Why express society in this way? Why with Geometric amphorae? Why express it at all? Because this is art? Because burial is 'ritual' enactment of society? To keep society going? Style itself is treated by Whitley as simply the presence or absence of particular decorative 'stylistic' motifs and traits without considering the processes of design and manufacture, the structures of style. This is the one-dimensional picture.

A great strength of anthropological archaeology and particularly Processual archaeology is the use of statistical techniques, some computer-based, to find patterning in complicated data sets, to make complexity simple. Indeed, Whitley's argument depends on a claimed discovery, via cluster and multivariate analysis, of the emergence of a pattern of social rationing: that there were times when everyone had equal access to all types and styles of goods. Whatever the quality and success of the quantification and statistical analysis, it is designed to play a main part in explanation and dominates the style of processual texts such as those of Whitley, Morgan and Whitelaw, and Morris. This is the *rhetoric* of these archaeologies: not the definitive catalogue or classification (though these are certainly referenced), but the technical display of control over detail through its encompassment in numerical summary.

For early eighth-century cemeteries, Whitley uses factor analysis to group graves and not, as would be usual, to analyse and simplify dimensions of variability. With graves held to be the expression of a social persona, he seems to treat individual factors as social identities. Society is read from a factor list. Cluster analysis is certainly used to locate social identities. A group of clustered graves represents 'a socially recognised type of person'; and much space in Whitley's book is taken to present and discuss dendrograms, the graphical display of the results of cluster analysis.

Whitley professed the laudable aim of reconciling art history and archaeology. But where, it might be asked, is the humanism, the aesthetic appreciation in the perusal of pages of factor attribute lists, factor scores given to five decimal places? A re-education of the reader's sensibilities may be required, for what is there to prevent a mathematical figure being appreciated in its beauty? But, in fact, the aesthetic becomes what Whitley admits he cannot explain. Or rather, the aesthetic of Geometric pottery needs no explaining. Decorative change is 'autonomous, aesthetic and technical'; that is, decoration which cannot be correlated with the clustering agents. And with style defined as decorative attribute, just where is Whitley's reconciliation of art history and archaeology? If style does not function, for Whitley it is simply to be appreciated in its aesthetic autonomy from the rest of society. The autonomy of the aesthetic is, as has been shown, the defining assumption of traditional Classical art history.

PROCESSUAL CLASSICAL ARCHAEOLOGY: SOME SUMMARY POINTS

Archaeological theory, anthropological and sociological dealings with material culture, make it clear that style relates to communication between people; it is about interaction, and involves reference to social position and power. Style is to be understood in context, and it is the great value of these three works to have argued this with conviction and, in places, with great skill. The strengths of Processual archaeology in outlining major vectors of change are apparent. Above all, perhaps, is shown how ideas of social system and function can work to coordinate into neat models of social change the considerable amount of empirical detail remaining from these times. The control of the empirical afforded by quantification and theoretical awareness is one that should be taken very seriously.

Some more particular features are as follows.

- The social context, which is conceived as explaining what is archaeologically visible, is given a very narrow definition: it is rank or status, interaction, and the parameters of population and residence.
- In a research strategy of discovering pattern in the archaeological record, which is then held to represent the pattern of society, privilege is given to *abstract* descriptive measures.
- In the use of such abstract variables, analysis is purposefully reductive. There is clearly a case to be made for the 'analytical', that is cutting through the mass of the whole data set to reveal basic constituent

processes – seeing through the mass of detail to what is really going on. Morris makes a case for being interested in the *structure* of the archaeological record, as opposed to its *empirical content*. But the loss of detail is the price of methodological rigour. Neither Morgan and Whitelaw nor Whitley give account of what to many must be the most distinctive aspect of the design of the pottery they study – it is decorated with geometric figures. Morris gives no account of why people in Attika actually did what they did with their dead. Snodgrass avoids being overly reductive by sacrificing methodological rigour in an impressionistic account of interconnectivity and humanistic narrative, but explanatory emphasis was still placed on a single prime mover: demographic change. The challenge remains of reconciling the detail and particularity of traditional descriptive approaches with methodological rigour and theoretical awareness.

- This is connected with a reliance upon *functionalist* explanation, and a conception of material culture as *representative*. The style of pottery and style of burial are held to reflect or represent society. The primary term in this relationship, given this social archaeology, is *society*. Material culture functions in expressing society, but the question of the *form* of the representation, expression or function is not asked.

- There is a different rhetoric being used by these authors. Snodgrass opts for humanistic narrative with a simple but powerful motor of change. Compare also the dendrograms and factor scores of Whitley's analysis; the lorenz scores and variability measures of Morris's burial and Attic society; the regression lines and similarity measures of the 'politics of Argive Geometric' with the notion of the definitive multi-referencing catalogue; or humanist art history and the careful illustrative elaboration of traditional Classical archaeological narrative.

What is clear is that these sophisticated social archaeologies do not seem to be attending to all dimensions of the character of their sources, as considered above. How might it be possible to build on the insights represented here?

THE CATEGORY OF THE DECORATIVE: ON MEANING AND MATERIAL CULTURE

In some Processual archaeology, style may have a social function; otherwise its meaning must be sought, if at all, in regions that have nothing to do with social archaeology. Just as those archaeologies discussed above give primacy to the expression of society in material culture, discarding other matters, so conventional Classical archaeology focuses upon iconographic expression in material culture. Meaning is hereby limited to the illustrative, and particularly that of myth or religious significance (subjects of iconology). It has already been discussed in Chapter 2 how a distinction is made between that which carries (iconic) meaning, and that which does not. The latter is usually called the 'decorative'.

So, for example, the sphinx appears many times painted upon Korinthian pottery. Bosana-Kourou, in her doctoral dissertation of 1979 at Oxford University, undertook a large survey of the sphinx in early Archaic art, and concluded that, for the most part, the sphinx is a purely decorative motif:

> There are only a few representations showing sphinxes in scenes involving human beings. At first sight these scenes can easily be taken as mythological, but closer analysis proves them to be of a purely decorative character and usually an unconventional imitation of some oriental model, and without any awareness of the model's original meaning.

Meaning and myth are separated from lack of meaning and the decorative. The argument is also that the oriental borrowing is selective, or alters the 'original', therefore seems to bring no meaning, therefore the motif is decorative. It is clear that Bosana-Kourou considers the presence of human figures as the key to meaning, because they may allow the identification of a scene from myth. Animal art is thereby allocated to the decorative; and much Korinthian pottery depicts merely animals. The decorative is not wholly without meaning, but the meaning is an (art) historical one: the diffusion and copying of designs can be traced. For example, Bosana-Kourou writes: 'Protocorinthian art of the early seventh century is under strong Syrian influence, and we find Syrian motifs copied without reference to their original meaning.' Here also is reference to the idea of *original* meaning: that the graphic of a sphinx has a meaning which is somehow attached, or inheres. This equation of graphic and meaning omits many other possible levels of meaning. It is a restriction to the iconic, omitting particularly the significative and symbolic: sphinxes may have little to do with particular myths, but symbolise things in their relationships with other creatures. In his study of Klazomenaian sarcophagi (1981), Robert Cook also refers to this distinction between meaning and the decorative. He adds another twist, by rejecting 'esoteric' meanings as inappropriate to simple craftsmen.

So the decorative is a general category for all those elements of design that cannot easily be explained by function and iconic meaning. For example, Whitley claims adherence to an approach he terms, after Michael Baxandall, iconographic minimalism: 'there is no need to add layers of meaning in order to appreciate Geometric art. So, recent attempts at rich readings of the decoration and iconography of Geometric and Protoattic vases must be regarded as misguided.' As detailed above, he found no patterning in much of Geometric decoration with which he could correlate social structure or process (the function of style) and consequently attributed this sort of decoration to the aesthetic. Much of the decorative is that which is to be 'appreciated' in its ineffable humanism by aesthetics. The drawing of a

145

sphinx may be enjoyed, and this is its significance – it is purely decorative. Dietrich von Bothmer, in his article on connoisseurship referenced for the section on Beazley in Chapter 2, refers similarly to overinterpretation of vases beginning in the nineteenth century with such works as C.A. Boettiger's *Griechische Vasengemälde* (three volumes, Weimar and Magdeburg 1797–1800). German connoisseurship emphasised systematisation according to fabric, chronology and shape. For von Bothmer the defining feature of pottery study is attribution.

Some studies have blurred the distinction between figurative meaning and decorative design. Himmelmann-Wildschutz, in two classic studies published in the 1960s, has proposed that many 'decorative' elements of Geometric art are not abstractly decorative (subject only of aesthetic appreciation), nor iconic, but represent concepts or values. Others have stuck more clearly with the distinction between icon and decoration, but have turned the decorative into the iconic. In her survey of Attic Geometric funeral scenes (*Prothesis and Ekphora* 1971), Gudrun Ahlberg claims that some 'filling ornament' has 'substantial and/or symbolic function': some Geometric devices such as triangles and circular motifs provide an environment, architectural and landscape, for the scenes of prothesis and ekphora. Boardman too has interpreted apparently abstract decorative devices upon Argive Geometric as representing a set of themes to do with the city of Argos (see above). There may be an overlap between the meaningful and the decorative, but the distinction remains.

What does it mean to describe a frieze painted upon a pot as decorative? To decorate is usually taken to mean the addition of ornament, texture and colour, etc. to make more attractive: there is a sense of addition and of taste. The category of the decorative places primary emphasis upon appearance, order, formal rather than substantive content, an aesthetic. A decorative choice is therefore one that is based upon an aesthetic sense, upon taste: some things look good together, others do not. The question then becomes one of the source of this taste, and there may be discussion of form and beauty, the sense of the aesthetic.

The decorative may refer to something of a sense of cliché – that certain scenes became meaningless (and perhaps 'aesthetic' or 'tasteful') through repetition. The passage from Bosana-Kourou cited above mentions oriental *models* for sphinxes, copied without reference to their original meaning, therefore 'decorative'. The decorative here is the use of 'stock' scenes, formulae, traditional or otherwise, which have lost their original meaning through use and transmission. In this claim by Bosana-Kourou, the use of stock scenes is equated with the decorative, which in turn is taken to indicate an absence of meaning. So sphinxes are often found in pairs throughout near eastern and early Hellenic art. Other creatures are also found in such 'heraldic' pairs. Lion hunts and lions leaping upon animals are other subjects frequently found elsewhere. The animal frieze itself is not an invention of Korinthian potters.

146

Elements of figured scenes in Orientalising design may well be observed elsewhere, before and after, but this does not explain their appearance, which may or may not have to do with the scenes being generic. The key question remains: why paint the scenes, stock and generic or otherwise? This is partly answered by arguments such as that of Carter (in an article in the *Annual of the British School at Athens*, 1972), who made much of the borrowing by Greek artists of generic and traditional scenes from eastern art for the eventual purpose of depicting narrative. He proposes an interest in depicting action and narrative as the reason for the adoption of eastern convention. Hurwitt (in 1985) has referred to cultural anxiety upon contact with the east, and a conscious decision to be influenced. But why Geometric 'decorative' devices and not others? But why these borrowings, not others? And a historical question – whence the interest in eastern art?

To write that the painting upon a Korinthian pot is decorative means one of two things: that the painted designs are an (aesthetic) ornament, and/or that the painted designs are the choice of convention or tradition. The first allows the painter the choice of taste; the second implies the painter is applying or following a taste established elsewhere. Both imply that meaning and signification are subordinate to form or convention. So, the decorative finds its meaning in that division of the aesthetic into art and craft, fine and applied art:

decorative	meaningful
formulaic	purposive
tradition	beauty
craft	art
application	decision
ornament	form
artisan	artist

The distinction is an old one, belonging with a valuation of the genius of the individual artist, whose identity lies in creativity, over the technical skill of the artisan, whose identity lies in labour. The anonymity of the traditional skills of the artisan is subordinated to the individual ego of the artist. Both art and craft share the realm of the aesthetic, of perception and the production of things, but craft remains less than art. The cultural field to which this distinction belongs is vast. A parallel is at the root of the capitalist division of labour into management, reason and decision, over workers, operations and execution of tasks. Hence the origins of the Arts and Crafts Movement of the late nineteenth and early twentieth centuries.

The discourse to which this distinction belongs allows two routes to understanding the decorative: through an abstract aesthetics of beauty and form, appreciating how some decorative devices are better or more 'beautiful' than others; or through tracing the 'life of forms', the creation, use and transmission of graphical conventions, devices and schemata. Both tend to idealism (argument over the nature and appreciation of 'beauty') and/or a detachment of design from production and its social origins, as described above.

It may be held that to decorate is to add a surface of adornment or aesthetic enhancement. The dualism of the category extends also to a distinction between some essential form to which is added decoration. Something is created, then decorated. In this way, decoration is a supplement both to the pot and to the potter-painter creating a functional vessel and expressing meaning. The decorative is surface finish. But everything has a surface or outside; and every surface has a finish of some sort. Finishes may vary: some may be described as more or less elaborated; the potter-painter may choose to invest more or less time and interest towards the end of the production process. But finish is not supplemental; it is the dimension that supplies form. The term decorative may be used for an artefact that displays more concern with elaboration and labour investment in the final stages of production. But a simple textured surface could be described as decorative. The initial choice of material, such as fine Korinthian earthenware, may well imply (or *intend*) a certain finish; the process of production (black-figure firing, for example) also. A process of production is not often an accidental amalgam of separable activities: black-figure surface and painting requires a set of practices from clay extraction to brush manufacture. In this way the finish is *internally related* to production. So I argue that the term 'decorative' has no specific field of reference, because everything can be described as decorative or decorated. The decorative is simply the appearance of the form of an artefact.

The corollary is that the aesthetic is not an abstracted and separate field of meaning or activity (as in Art, 'beauty' or 'taste'). The aesthetic is that which pertains to perception; it is an adjectival concept, not substantive.

In the decorative, meaning is subordinated to form and tradition. But can there ever be a limit case of a purely decorative or formal surface empty of meaning? I would argue that there cannot, because a graphic or design always implies at least the conditions of its production. The decorative must always be the outcome of a set of relations of (artistic) production, and these can never be without meaning, purely 'technical' or functional. A pair of miniature sphinxes upon a Korinthian pot implies the fine brush and slip, the manufacture of both, the acquisition of the skills necessary to paint them, knowledge of the firing process, the belief that such a design will enhance the surface and help the sale of the pot, and much more. All this can hardly be called meaningless.

I have already also commented how meaning has a most narrow reference in Classical art history and iconography or iconology. It is restricted to the iconic or representational (see, for example the monumental volumes of *Lexicon Iconographicum Mythologiae Classicae*). But there are many levels of reference and meaning to be found in cultural production. This has been a major contention of anthropology and the social sciences at least since Freud and Marx. A key concept is that of structure, or of a system of relations lying beneath or beyond the surface appearance of things and in which their significance or meaning can be found. So what seems to be required is a shift of attention away from the individual artist as transcendent creator of culture and meaning, away from the evolutions of abstract artistic style. This is happening in approaches to be described in the next two chapters.

In summary, the term decorative (or decorated) needs to be carefully qualified.

- The term usually belongs to an unhelpful division of production: culture and the aesthetic, a division that is rooted historically in a view of the individual as autonomous, the artist as transcendent creator of culture. The category of the decorative exists as a supplement to this idea of the artistic expressive ego; the decorative is what is left over when the artistic ego is removed.
- Use of the term has tended towards an idealism of the aesthetic, or of traditions of style: decoration is assessed either according to formal principles of taste, or according to the transmission and use of 'stock' scenes and designs.
- When used in the sense of a supplement (of finish or adornment), the term decorative or decorated has no specific field of reference; everything can be called decorative. The term is thereby meaningless or redundant.
- The discourse to which these uses of the term belongs is one that has too restricted a notion of meaning, no concept of structure.

In this section I have tried to build on the insights of Processual archaeology by considering an aspect of material culture – the investment of meaning in design. A purpose was to show how important it is to consider carefully the character of archaeological sources, and the different contexts which may help in their understanding. Those Processual archaeologies dealt with above may have discarded a little too much from their analyses.

JOHN BERGER, PETER FULLER AND LESSONS OF IDEALIST ART HISTORY

To what extent is a work of art independent of society? Is material culture design to be wholly explained in terms of the conditions of its social production? These questions have appeared several times. Marxist aesthetics, particularly after such popular works as *Ways of Seeing* by John Berger and others (1972), has seen art as social production, and responses to art conditioned by social circumstances. Art is to be explained by its social context. But other traditions, and some in Classical archaeology have been outlined above, hold that sociological explanations miss a key feature of art – its relative autonomy. This is something I have tried to deal with in the outline of the character of material culture as source at the beginning of the chapter. Some items of material culture, let them be called art, seem to maintain an aesthetic appeal. What may be made of this?

On 5 April 1928 the SS *Lotus* left Marseilles and cruised around the Mediterranean taking members of the Hellenic Travellers' Club to some of the sites of Greece, Crete and Sicily. On board, Dr T.R. Glover, Fellow and Lecturer of St John's College, Cambridge, and Public Orator in the University, delivered a lecture on 'The Influence of Greece on Human Life'. He began: 'Suppose that the sturdiest of all opponents of Greek studies . . . had been standing by when the Venus di Milo, or whatever the archaeologists would have us call her, was discovered in Melos in 1820, would he have wished her to be buried again?' Glover picked on one of the most famous artefacts of antiquity to make his point. 'Here is a thing in itself, which, without associations – with never a Greek word to add to it or subtract from it – untouched by history – yet by its unexpected and inherent beauty, has in modern times made life a fuller and a happier thing.'

A goodness untouched by history: thus did Peter Fuller, the art critic, consider the Venus de Milo, the armless statue of a woman now on prominent display in the Louvre, in relation to ideas of art, continuity and history. His essay, in the book *Art and Psychoanalysis* (1980), reveals many issues central to the history of Classical art in the last century and a half. Fuller begins with the story of the discovery of the statue on the island of Melos in 1820 and its extraction from the Ottoman Empire. There seems to have been a fight on the beach of Melos between French and Turks over the statue which was damaged, possibly quite severely. A later French writer Aicard was convinced that what had originally been found was a statue of a woman with an apple in her hand and that the arm was broken off in the battle on the beach. But the statue immediately answered a demand in France for antiquities, brought on after the forced return of 5,000 works of art looted by Napoleon and stored in the Louvre. And upon its arrival in Paris arguments began over attribution.

Quatremère de Quincy, Permanent Secretary of the Académie Royale des Beaux Arts reckoned, on a 'spiritual' estimation of its qualities of truth and beauty, grace and nobility (a method discredited by Morelli), that it was by Praxiteles. This went down well with King Louis XVIII who wanted a famous and great sculptor's work in France's possession. A problem was the inscribed plinth which said that a sculptor called (Ages)andros made the work (and with epigraphy later dated by Fürtwangler as anywhere between 200 BC and the Christian era and hence too late for Praxiteles). The inscribed plinth was argued away in various ways (as incidental restoration, for example); then it was lost (conveniently?). Argument continued over its date and attribution.

The Venus became one of the sights of Paris. Various authors and artists enthused over it, proclaiming Romantic rapture:

Salut! a ton aspect le coeur se précipite.
Un flot marmoréen inonde tes pieds blancs;
Tu marches, fière et nue, et le monde palpite,
Et le monde est à toi, Déese aux larges flancs! . . .

(Leconte de Lisle, *La Vénus de Milo*)

In the Victorian High-Renaissance of the 1870s and 1880s the statue became a model of excellence. 'For the insipid idealising fantasists of British Classicism, the Venus was not so much an object which excited passions as an unsurpassable ideal', and Fuller notes many specific and general references to the work in, for example, the work of Leighton and Alma-Tadema. He also remarks on a tension in the work and its reception between Naturalism and its idealisation, its fragmentation and its supposed formal perfection, between its energy and formal stasis (particularly naked upper and draped lower halves).

Romantic and Classical attitudes were accompanied by various desires for restoration and repair expressed up to the 1890s. The Venus de Milo was seen to have been part of a group such as the Judgement of Paris, or to have been linked to an Eros. Some had the statue holding a spear. Another had the Venus defending herself against the unwanted attentions of a man. She was envisaged holding a shield; dealing in various ways with Ares; arranging her hair. The distinguished Classical archaeologist Fürtwangler took a close look at the statue and some associated fragments (particularly of the arm perhaps broken off on the beach on Melos) in the 1890s and decided that the Venus originally had been positioned in a niche in the Gymnasion on Melos, and was the combination of a Venus of traditional type and a goddess of Good Luck (Tyche). Her left arm, holding an apple, he restored resting on a pillar while her right arm reached across to support the drapery above her knee. He admitted however that 'the two arms thus restored lend neither unity nor harmony to the composition; in short, their loss is one less to be deplored than might at first appear'. Regarding date, he put the statue in a late second century BC renascence of High Classicism, part of a reaction against Hellenistic excesses; hence it looked older than it was. Fürtwangler's study marked the end of the prevalent types of speculation about the statue.

We do not now follow the nineteenth-century attitude of reverence and interest in the sculpture. Fuller refers to changes of taste with reference to the Apollo Belvedere, revered from Raphael to Winckelmann and, as judges Kenneth Clark, one of the two most famous works of art in the 1820s. This has been relegated to relative obscurity. But the Venus de Milo has been transformed into a symbol of another kind. Look now not for poems about the statue and artistic reconstructions, but to posters, advertisements, slimming foods, beauty products.

As the Fine Art tradition, and its related literary and critical activities, began to appear perilously historically specific, the Venus slid right out

151

of it into the new, emergent Mega-Visual tradition. . . . The floor of the Louvre still wears away disproportionately in front of her every year, and who knows how many soap-stone maquettes find their way into living-rooms and greenhouses everywhere.

Fuller is dealing here with questions of the reception of a work categorised as art. He asks the question of how we are to understand the work. What are we to make of all this? He proposes that the Venus is not one physical thing, but countless images and ideas, each of which has a history of its own – the reconstructions, advertisements, attributions, and tourist souvenirs – different things in different historical circumstances. So the social and historical context makes the artefact what it is, at that time. The artefact becomes transient, though it has a material substratum which may bear witness to its times (wear and chipped surfaces). The Venus is not just an image; it is three-dimensional. Fuller argues that changes in the surrounding space constitute a change in the original artefact itself. It is displayed in isolation, within an inlaid circle and upon its pedestal in the Louvre, exposed on all sides. But it was originally designed for a niche, something very evident from the less finely worked back. The Venus is now a mutilated fragment, not the original. He criticises attitudes that refuse to take account of these changes and instead see in the work some eternal, unchanging verities to do with craftsmanship and expression of the human form. Instead he points out that the Greeks would not hold such views of the work now, because of where it is and because it is broken and worn.

Fuller ascribes the success and fascination of the work to social and cultural conditions in the nineteenth century. Specifically he draws attention to the statue being a fragment from the earth. The cult of the fragment was central to Romanticism which had superseded the neo-Classicism of the French bougeoisie, and its embodiment of universal, true and eternal ideals in the new republic. The monster and the ruin came to prominence, for example, in the sentimental humanism and scientism of Mary Shelley's Frankenstein: a creature of fragments joined through the application of reason (just as were the efforts to restore the Venus). Fuller brings in the development of archaeology and dispute over the antiquity of the human species centred upon fragments drawn from the earth. With respect to the emergence of what he calls the mega-visual tradition, Fuller points to the ambiguity of the statue as a signifier. With no arms and drapery appearing as if it were about to fall, the Venus is on the point of exposure. This sense of timing and view of women he relates to the development of the photographic pin-up, the helpless available woman. The Venus was transferred to this idiom and achieved further success.

For Fuller such contexts help explain the Venus de Milo and its place in the nineteenth and twentieth centuries. It is a relativist posture which attempts to account for the continuity in a response to an artefact by emphasising the variability of both signifier and signified. (The signified is the message or idea contained within a sign and the signifier is vehicle of that message: so the word statue is signifier while the signified is the concept of a human form worked in a durable material.)

But it is not enough, he claims. The concrete statue is dissolved, he thinks, into a series of *disembodied* relations, to do with ideas in the nineteenth century and such. Fuller has argued elsewhere that to reduce a work of art, or any artefact, to its conditions of manufacture and to contexts of reception and consumption cannot explain why some works of art are more aesthetically successful than others. Sociological context is not enough to explain why some works continue to fascinate people.

Here Fuller makes an argument which I connect with some ideas that are coming into human geography and indeed into archaeology; they are commonly called phenomenological approaches. Some have been arguing that to understand people's relationships to landscape and architecture, we need to appreciate the characteristics and experiences of the human physical condition. This is something that has a basis that has been constant since the human species emerged tens of thousands of years ago. We all have bodies which age, which have certain physical characteristics and attributes, and these help condition our responses to natural and cultural environments. Buildings have different scales and ambiences; landscapes and cityscapes are structured with respect to our movements through them and experiences of others within them. The social and historical construction of things is shot through with the biological. There are sculptural elements of the Venus de Milo which transcend class and history, according to Fuller, who follows the view of many art historians. These pertain to areas of the experience of reality which are common to all those who have human bodies. So the Venus de Milo as an artefact communicates to us not just as a museum piece, but because we share a common human condition with its maker. He quotes Della Volpe: 'Sculpture is the expression of values or ideas by means of a figurative language of non-metaphorical volumes and surfaces leading into depth. It is a language of free three-dimensional visual forms.' This language is rooted in common physical conditions of human existence such as being in space, subjection to gravity, etc. Hence it is possible to see the Venus not just as a product of nineteenth- and twentieth-century ideologies but also as an aesthetic working with the human form which is more or less successful on aesthetic and formal grounds. We might appreciate here Fürtwangler's comment that the statue is better fragmented than whole, when it would not have worked aesthetically as well. This brings me again to the point that the statue is an archaeological fragment. If Fürtwangler is right, the statue is a complex composition involving a modification of traditional images of Venus according to a cult of Tyche, associated also with a symbol of Melos, the apple, and applied to Greek athletic practices. Its style is a reference to contemporary taste, which criticises its archaism. We may also note the gender factors in the positioning of the statue in the Gymnasion, focus of masculine gender definitions. This is all mostly gone. We have very little left of the ideological and social context of its making. The statue has become more of a floating signifier, and its fragmentary character directs attention to those elements of its composition that are relatively constant, the biological. So too, many other archaeological remains, stripped of context and as worn traces or relics, fascinate according to their attestation to mortality, frailty and perhaps creativity. The presence of the person in the past who made the pot now broken and worn, signified in the marks upon the surface of the sherd, allows us to touch what seems intangible.

Fuller relates these biological constants to psychoanalytical constants to be found in the physical and psychical development of the human child and he picks up the ideas of Melanie Klein. Whether or not we follow this line, he has posed some questions of sociological and aesthetic understanding (that is, rooted in the formal characteristics of a work), which have considerable relevance to Classical archaeology. Different contexts form the basis of understanding. Of course, Fuller is not dealing with the conditions of design and consumption of the Venus de Milo in the last few centuries BC, but all that he decides about its reception can be applied also to its design, if the contextual information were available. The interesting comment here is that on the reincarnations of the Venus de Milo, which makes us think of the life-cycles of material and archaeological artefacts, those (ruptured) continuities from design and manufacture through consumption and deposition, loss or discard, through to recovery by contemporary archaeological interest and the different receptions thereafter.

UNDERSTANDING THE ARCHAEOLOGICAL AND A PREHISTORY OF THE CLASSICAL PAST

The central concept of this chapter has been context. Different contexts combine with different interests, and questions are raised regarding the object of social archaeology – its purpose and what it is that may be reconstructed using archaeological materials.

Two major themes identified in Processual social modelling are conceptual shifts (the relationship of ideas to social practices and their archaeological outcome) and social power. Snodgrass and Morris in particular stressed the importance of ideological factors in understanding the social changes of the city state. Archaeology is not just about material forms, but also about how these relate to structures of meaning. Their topic was the early state. Central to the formation of the state is a reorganisation of class and power. There is thus an institutional focus on social systems. Meanwhile Vickers and Gill have brought the study of Greek ceramics down from lofty aesthetic heights to the accoutrement of everyday life. This is a quotidian focus which has been stressed by many prehistoric archaeologists, such as John Barrett, who argue that material culture is the location of the everyday construction of those institutional structures considered by the likes of Snodgrass and Morris. The issue is one that has been implicit in this book so far: the relationship of the individual and their creative powers and talents to the societies and histories they inhabit. The material reality of the early state could thus be argued to be the everyday environments of those living then: the 'city of images', in the words of a fascinating work of French Classical archaeology. New phenomenologies in Prehistoric archaeology attend to everyday experience as the locale of people's agency, their creative power, investigating how people relate to architectures, landscapes, in all their lifeworld. I am thinking of the work of Richard Bradley, Ian Hodder, Chris Tilley and John Barrett. Some Classical archaeologists are making much of what they term viewer-centred art histories, and that French book just mentioned can be classed as such. These approaches, and more will be said of them in the next chapter, mark a significant meeting of viewpoint between Classical and Prehistoric archaeologies.

This, however, is not the place to describe recent developments in Prehistoric archaeology and debates about social theory. But what can be concluded perhaps is the possibility of a 'prehistory' of Classical Greece that comes before the interpretive complexities of written sources: a prehistory that recognises a fundamental difference and mystery to the remains of the past, and which is not modelled on a notion of transparent textual communication of what the ancients were thinking when they were writing. In all there is expressed a need to theorise the object of archaeological interest, its location in social practices past and present. The result cannot be a homogeneous account of the Classical past.

6

SOME TOPICS AND ISSUES IN A SOCIAL ARCHAEOLOGY OF CLASSICAL GREECE

Chapter 5 presented some reflections on the character of archaeological sources, then considered some approaches which have taken the view that the social context of artefactual remains of the past is central to interpretation, referred these back to characterisations of art, and then took a short look outside of Classical archaeology at other social archaeologies. The chapter as a whole viewed a constellation of issues around the essential multiplicity of material culture: its temporality and constituting relationships with contexts of design, exchange, consumption and deposition.

This chapter is an outline of several fields of interest in the project of a social archaeology. Care needs to be taken here to avoid the problems noted especially in Chapter 3. Essentialism is a term that encapsulates much of what was criticised: this holds that history and society have underlying essences or principles which lie behind their particular expressions. It was shown, for example, how Hellenism assumes an underlying character to the Greek, a Greek 'spirit' expressed in artefacts and indeed in history. Metanarratives too may take the form of an essentialism, defining the character of history prior to its experience in empirical sources. Searches for ultimate origins, of Europe and the west for example, can severely attenuate understanding, linked as they may be to ideological systems. Chapter 5 articulated several questions, without providing essentialist answers, about the character of Greek art and its relationship to the category of material culture. An attempt was made to deal with high cultural bias in conceptions of art.

Given these provisions, this chapter will consider chronology and tempo-rality, economics and social archaeology, social change, social connections, style, religion and ritual, space and landscape. The purpose is not to go into great detail with comprehensive coverage, but to provide some flavours and a framework within which current work in social archaeology may be placed.

CHRONOLOGY AND TIME

For most of the period covered by Classical archaeologies of Greece and Rome, from about 700 BC to AD 600, changes in the style of finer ceramics have been used to establish a chronological framework. The scheme has been tested by new finds in historically dated contexts and by stratigraphy which, in providing sequence, is the basis of relative chronologies.

One problem with the framework concerns the fact that fine wares cover only a fraction of contemporary production, are geographically uneven, and are not consecutive. Another relates to the fixed historical dates. Here is to be reiterated the point made by Snodgrass that archaeological and historical (written) sources are hard to bring together because they represent different facets of historical reality. I will follow his treatment of this issue.

Fixing dated points in archaeological time is to do with connecting a secure archaeological context (a layer or feature of a site) with an event whose date can be established using historical sources. The most secure (chronologically) archaeological context is when it is stratigraphically undisturbed or sealed. An example is the closing of a tomb or the destruction and abandonment of a site. But the association of a sealed context with a historical and dated event is relatively rare. Then there is the question of what material is to be associated with the sealing event (which objects in the layer of settlement debris, which artefacts in the tomb?). So, for example, what stage in the pottery sequence was reached when Knossos was destroyed? Was it Late Minoan II or IIIA1 or IIIA2? What was the pottery phase when Thera was destroyed by the volcanic eruption? These are typical questions which have concerned, sometimes obsessed, Aegean prehistorians, and they are not alone. Clearly much depends also upon typological identification, and the arguments over its finer details are probably without resolution.

Historical dates are often derived from artefacts imported from Egypt, datable to the reigns of Pharaohs. Here is presented the problem of the contemporaneity of the import. It may have been traded over long distances; it may have been in circulation for a long time before deposition with later local goods. Then there are arguments about the chronology of the Egyptian Pharaohs and dynasties. Another source of historical points for a chronological scheme is dated burials, for example communal graves associated with battles (Marathon (490), Delion (424), Chaeronea (338)). These are not common. Payne's book *Necrocorinthia* (1931), mentioned several times already, presented a chronological scheme for the early Archaic Greece and the Mediterranean which has stood for several decades with relatively minor modification. Its utility is directly related to the prevalence of exports of Korinthian pottery around the Mediterranean. The fixed points are supplied by dates of the foundation of Greek colonies: Thucydides provides 728 and 628 BC for the foundation, respectively, of Megara Hyblaea and Selinus. The question is how these dates are to be related to the archaeological remains of the colonies. It depends on what is considered to be the earliest remains of the settlement. But, of course, further examination may at any time reveal earlier deposits than those upon which have been based chronological calculations.

CLASSICAL ARCHAEOLOGY OF GREECE

These and other related problems have led some to challenge the orthodoxy of the chronological systems established for Mediterranean protohistory. A notable example here is the book *Centuries of Darkness: a Challenge to the Conventional Chronology of Old World Archaeology* by P. James, I.J. Thorpe, and N. Kokkinos (1991). One approach to the problems has been resort to chronometric dating. But radiometric methods (such as that based on Carbon 14) have their own set of problems to do with their precision; nor is dendrochronology a panacea, especially with its restricted applicability.

Only little account is taken of social processes that condition the design, consumption and deposition of artefacts. Some of these have already been mentioned. There is emulation, where people may desire artefacts in a style associated with social classes of a higher rank. There is inevitably a temporal delay in adopting the style, which may thereby acquire a temporal drift away from any clear and narrow chronological locale. Heirlooms are subject to curation, and the relevance of trade to chronology has been mentioned: degrees of circulation of items before deposition are vital considerations, and these are social questions.

Precise dating may not matter so much in the new social archaeologies, which are not so concerned to produce those 'counterfeit history books': chronological schemes for the sake of an interest in the control of detail. Morris, Whitley, Morgan and Whitelaw all used traditional chronological schemes, but it was not necessary to adopt the precision they sometimes claim. Fine-grained chronologies are not so relevant to broader social sketching. Snodgrass certainly managed to produce his account without having it depend upon a detailed, typologically based chronological scheme.

Criticisms have been made of the particular character of time valued in these chronological schemes. Criticism has been levelled at the narrow association of time with date and change. That time is a measurable abstract dimension and analogous to spatial coordinates has been shown to be intimately related to our contemporary Modernist appreciation of temporality. This poses serious questions for the supposed neutrality of typological schemes of ordering. It is important to consider social contexts and practices, which actually constitute time.

The biggest issue is that no account is taken of the character of archaeological time, which has been the topic of several discussions in previous chapters. A simple example will reiterate the point: if I consider the room in which I am writing, there is no one answer to the question of its date. The floor is very old, the walls have been modified several times, there is a continuity, while the machines on the desk are part of the project of mine taking that continuity forward. If it is objected that projects are not part of date, how otherwise would the room and its contents have come into being? These events and processes, these projects construct the temporality of this room which is far more than a collection of dates.

ECONOMIC PREHISTORY/ARCHAEOLOGY

A major development in prehistoric archaeology over the last forty years has been the attention given to subsistence practices and evidences about economic organisation. Grahame Clark's book *Prehistoric Europe: the Economic Basis* (1952) was a landmark, but the major impetus came with anthropological archaeology emphasising the importance of society–environmental relationships. The logic is one of cross-cultural generalisation and a body of evolutionary theory holding that cultural change is centred upon subsistence practices, the material basis of society.

The influence of such ideas upon some of the social archaeologies already discussed should be clear: the emphasis in Snodgrass upon demography, for example. The ancient historian Tom Gallant has considered peasant economies in ancient Greece through a wide range of historical, ethno-historical, archaeological and anthropological sources in his book *Risk and Survival in Ancient Greece: Reconstructing the Rural Economy* (1991). Another influence here is economic ancient history, which will be considered more below, under trade. Interest in classes of archaeological sources other than material culture (environmental data, faunal and floral remains) is growing, particularly in Aegean prehistory. The character of the ancient economy must be a central concern of social archaeology, and certainly the development of area surveys of sites and regions, considered below, is so informed.

Concerning more mundane but enlightening economic matters, Vickers and Gill have used gold weights and values to establish comparisons between ancient and modern monetary scales. The point outlined in Chapter 3 is that pottery prices were so low as to make trade in ceramics commercially unviable. Ideas of Athenian and Korinthian potting industries in commercial competition, so often the feature of historical accounts, are in consequence likely to be severely misguided.

Scales of pottery production have been estimated. Robert Cook estimated the rate of survival of Attic Panathenaic amphorae, a pottery form produced in fixed and known quantities for the games, as one quarter of 1 per cent. Accordingly, he suggests 500 workers were involved in the Attic pottery industry in the fifth century BC, and half that number at Korinth when production there was at its height. This is evidence again against those who adhere to Snodgrass's positivist fallacy: the considerable numbers and importance of pots in the archaeological record do not represent an equivalent importance in the ancient world.

SOCIAL CONNECTIONS

A beginning will be made with trade. Understanding the movement of goods still often suffers from ideas of Greek commerce. A simple descriptive account of trade allied with a common-sense understanding of its economic working (traders taking goods from point of surplus to point of demand) is still evident in many conventional archaeologies and ancient histories of ancient Greece. A trend in approaches to the Greek economy which has developed in ancient history has brought a more anthropologically sophisticated understanding which questions the easy application to early Greece of concepts and models of economy and trade drawn from study of more modern economic systems of medieval Europe and after. Theoretical impetus has come from Marxian analysis and social history (notably in the work of Moses Finley). Many issues crystallised in the long-running debate between formalist or modernising accounts of the ancient economy. The former use general and formal concepts which are not necessarily related to the substantive field of reference, to the particular society studied. Accounts which may be described as *substantivist* or *primitivist* make use of concepts that take account of the character of the particular society studied (premodern or 'primitive'). The basic point is that there is no general category of the 'economic', but that it is embedded in wider society and varies according to society type.

The picture of the ancient economy presented in a primitivist model is of the self-sufficiency of relatively small and cellular social and economic units (from farms to towns), based on agriculture and depending little on inter-regional trade. High overland transport costs meant that no region could undercut another in the production of cheap essentials, and export was dominated by prestige or special items. Many now adhere to a minimalist model of ancient trade before later Classical times, considering the archaeological evidences of scale of production and its predominantly local character and lack of merchant ships.

The movement of goods, in the absence of a developed market economy, thus becomes more of an anthropological question. Sally Humphreys, in her *Anthropology and the Greeks* (1978), has made a case for the embeddedness of the archaic Greek economy in wider social institutions. This interconnectivity has been noted as a feature of Processual modelling. Trade becomes part of a wider set of experiences. War, seafaring, raiding, and perhaps attendance at the sanctuary games were opportunities to establish personal alliances, to display prowess, to dispose of and acquire goods. Fighting, travel and seafaring were the main political outlets for young men who had not yet received their inheritance or who may have had little or no land to inherit. Travelling and joining a colony was also a means of acquiring land which had become unavailable at home. The illegitimate and therefore landless poet Archilochos led the life of seafarer and mercenary before settling as hoplite and landowner in the colony of Thasos. Carrying a few fine pots was merely a sideline.

The major advance offered by anthropological archaeology generally concerns the heterogeneity of the distribution of goods. Models of simple inter-societal links, understood through common-sense and ethnocentric categories of 'trade', have given way to heterogeneity and social embeddedness.

Traditional archaeological equations of material culture and political relations, such as colonisation and political control (represented by stylistic change), have gained a new currency in the work of Bernal, but have been transformed by work such as that of Morgan and Whitelaw, as it is realised that there is much to the workings of style and its relationship to social links.

Classical Greece was composed of many independent city states as well as *ethnoi* who did not adopt the polis form. Links between these polities (as opposed to types of society) have been foregrounded in the concept of peer polity interaction. The argument is that understanding the social changes of Classical Greece cannot remain at the level of the individual state, but city states are to be considered in their particular and historical relations with other polities. Competition and rivalry (over temple building for example), and tensions between state interests and those of aristocracies and other sections of society who moved in circles beyond the individual polity, are important.

A particular model of inter-societal (as opposed to peer-polity) linkage has been extensively referenced in explaining the 'margins' of the Graeco-Roman world; this is the theory of core and periphery associated frequently with world systems analysis.

Core–periphery modelling began as part of development theory in politics and geography, exploring the relationships between different parts of the world capitalist economy, with core and peripheral elements related to an international division of labour (the separation of raw material extraction, manufacture and consumption across different societies and states) and multiple cultural systems. For the first millennium BC, central Europe has been seen as a periphery to the city states of the Mediterranean. A demand in the Greek city states for raw materials and slaves was answered by central European societies in exchange for prestige goods. The latter fed into their own social structures as key elements in the maintenance of power relations between chiefs and their dependants. The often cited example is that of late Hallstatt society up the Rhône Valley in south-west Germany, eastern France and Switzerland, with its 'princely burials' containing rich goods imported from the Mediterranean.

Such core–periphery models are effective in explaining the movement of artefacts and raw materials. They answer the need for social modelling rather than reliance upon simple models of trade, being therefore models that are effective at integrating data while supplying a social process. But in spite of the sophistication of the disciplinary sources, many inter-regional relations within and beyond the Mediterranean have come to be described simply in terms of economic supply and demand. So for Barry Cunliffe, for example in his *Greeks, Romans and Barbarians* (1988), the Classical and barbarian worlds were inextricably bound together in a network of economic inter-dependence, with a core of Mediterranean consumer states and a dependent barbarian periphery supplying raw materials.

161

But in this simple caricature, variations in production, modes of exchange and the role of different categories of material culture are glossed over. The simple question of why Hallstatt chiefs should find these particular goods desirable raises a set of questions about material values and aesthetics, attitudes to design and symbolics. Core–periphery modelling has also, for many, come to depend on drawing boundaries. It is difficult to envisage a core, 'the Greek world', because of the lack of political and economic integration in Greece, where there is indeed no typical state form. Integration in Greece was more symbolic than economic, and variability seems as important.

In spite of the faults found with simple models of trade and commercial traffic and core–periphery linkages, fine Korinthian and Attic wares did move, but the significance of the movement does not fit easily within common-sense sociological categories (such as economics or politics). Emphasis upon consumption brings further variability: as Korinthian pots left Korinth they became part of the experience of travel, part of the material culture of those carrying the goods, and when they were deposited in graves in a colony's cemetery, they were part of a different context of bereavement and mortuary practices.

Core–periphery models are part of a world systems perspective. Developed by Immanuel Wallerstein, world systems analysis works with this fact that the boundaries of a society are frequently artificial constructions, because very rarely do societies exist separately from others. There are always material and conceptual flows which require sociological understanding to be of networks of relationships rather than discrete entities which go under the name of a society or polity.

Susan and Andrew Sherratt (article listed in Bibliography) have presented a modernising economic model (in the sense defined above) of the Mediterranean in the first millennium BC which owes much to world systems analysis. They propose the development of an independent commercial sector uniting the Mediterranean and the east. With the erosion of direct political control of the economy (as in the bronze-using polities of the second millennium), there developed trading systems rooted in the Phoenician need to answer the demands of the Assyrian Empire. As they put it: 'the increasing scale of the near-eastern economy was a powerful motor of growth through-out the contemporary world system'. So earlier ideas of the diffusion of civilisation from the east (and associated phenomena such as Orientalising art) are seen to be about the active intervention and response of merchant enterprise. An input of capital from the east was the motivating force, with maritime expertise and capital concentration in Phoenicia. So again there are proposed patterns of commercial competition (including Korinth and Athens).

The merchant enterprise of the Sherratts may be interpreted as another metanarrative of the origins of capitalism, but they do address those archae-ological connections upon some of which Bernal has also turned his attention.

162

Goods, people and ideas were moving and conventional ideas of separate ethnic and social units do not adequately explain the linkages. World systems are a way forward.

UNDERSTANDING STYLE

The style of material culture has featured prominently so far. Here I introduce an example of those approaches in French Classical archaeology that treat imagery as signs to be read of deep structures of meaning lying within Greek culture.

François Lissarague, in *Aesthetics of the Greek Banquet* (English translation 1990), has made an exploration of the Greek imagination through the images upon those pots whose forms are associated with the aristocratic drinking party, the symposion. He follows a field of metaphors relating to drink and the social gatherings. The symposion involved the shared pleasure of gathering with drinks, perfumes, songs, dancing, games, sex and conversation. They were held in rooms which seem never to have been very big, and they were associated with cult as at the sanctuary of Artemis at Brauron in Attica. The symposion was thus an enclosed space of guests who formed a self-sufficient community of peers, and it was a social ritual with strictly codified acts.

Wine was considered an ambiguous drink and this is expressed in the play about meanings and allusions. Many of the games have wine as their point of departure (it is not just a drink) in addition to the vases which become toys or bodies that are handled and in turn manipulate the drinker. Cups are made with body parts or as sculpted forms; there is a class of trick vases which seem magically to fill themselves, playing with hydraulics; others spill over the tricked drinker. Metaphorical links are made with metal-working, with pictures of forges. Flute and bellows could take the same name – *aulos*; wine was compared with fire.

Wine and the symposion appear as a realm of otherness, with men pictured dressed as Scythians or as women. The mixing bowl was focus (wine was not drunk neat). Symbol of hospitality, the word *krater* can mean symposion. It was a special artefact, an *agalma* (candidate for a gift to the gods). Play is made upon the wine-dark sea (*oinops pontos*), with wine, navigation, sea and symposion united. Pottery vessels may indeed be sea vessels. Herakles the master drinker is pictured upon one pot in a *dinos*. One of his labours was to go beyond the ocean to the island of Erythia to steal the cattle of Geryon, triple-bodied giant. On the way he shot at the sun because of its heat and in admiration of this audacity he was given a golden vase in which to cross the ocean.

It is not possible to do justice here to the richness of Lissarague's revelations. His interpretation opens up understanding of the symposion as a locus for metaphor and illusion, both poetic and visual, defamiliarising the stock

Figure 6.1 Herakles at sea in a *dinos*. Attic red figure cup, early fifth century BC

images of the Classical banquet in a Hollywood epic. This richness of every-day textures connects with new views of the symposion as social institution. Some ancient historians, among them Oswyn Murray, have come to see the symposion as a major focus of male political and social association, a struc-turing feature of Classical society. Here again definitions of gender identity may be interpreted as vital components in understanding the Greeks.

Whereas conventional connoisseurship and art history deals with artefacts in terms of artist and overarching stylistic change, work such as that of a Structuralist pedigree, represented by the work of Lissarague in this section, has shifted attention to the consumer of the artefacts and images. Hence there are increasing calls for viewer-centred readings of ancient artefacts. The (mixed) metaphor refers to the artefact as text to be read or interpreted. Contexts are here again so vital (the symposion for Lissarague's images).

Many Attic pots turn up in Etruscan tombs, with their designs complementing the aristocratic tastes of the deceased. The image and the viewer may be taken as the important matters; the painter and the potter, focus of the interest of connoisseur, can be argued to be almost irrelevant. Etruscan tombs were not galleries of artists but of images relating to experiences of death.

RELIGION AND RITUAL

The apparent remains of what today is classed as religious form a major category of evidence for the Classical archaeologist. The great excavations of sanctuaries were informed by very different interests to those of contemporary social archaeology. Cemeteries have been a major source of artefacts, but their analysis in archaeology has come a long way in the last two decades. Colin Renfrew pioneered new Processual approaches with a study of the cist tombs of the early Bronze Age in the Cyclades. The work of Ian Morris was considered in some detail in the last chapter. In stressing social context, such studies have contributed to the anthropological truism of the embeddedness of religion and ritual. Here may be mentioned a classic study by the Marxist anthropologist Maurice Godelier, which showed how religion could function as part of the economic structure of society (*Marxist Perspectives in Anthropology*, English translation 1977), and not simply be concerned with spiritual matters. The importance of religion to the ancient economy has been much stressed, with great justification, by Snodgrass. It is no longer possible legitimately to separate out from wider social analysis religious and ritual matters.

SPACE, SURVEY AND LANDSCAPE

François de Polignac argued for a tight connection between sanctuaries and the spatial organisation of the early Greek city state, indeed its very origins. This brings me to the long-standing interest in the Greek landscape which goes back to early travellers such as Choiseul-Gouffier and William Martin Leake.

In a conventional but effective study, Adamasteanu has used air photographs to access the archaic land apportionment in the territory of the Greek colony of Metapontum. But what I want to concentrate on in this section is the recent development of geographical survey in Classical archaeology, which puts the discipline at a forefront of methodological innovation. As well as drawing on the tradition of topographical interest, survey in Greece is as much an effect of the importance given to survey and the systematic study of regions in New and Processual archaeology.

These survey projects use intensive field walking to record systematically the traces of all human activity in a given region. This supplies data relevant to demography, and integrates information about environmental changes, agriculture, landholdings, communications and infrastructures. The bias of documentary sources is on the urban elite. Survey, in contrast, justifies itself simply in that it focuses attention on the rural base of Classical antiquity. It is cheaper than excavation and 'non-invasive', but has required many years of groundwork and is only now beginning to supply new insights into the workings of ancient society. The low profile of survey projects has been ascribed to the lack of application of the method to traditional problems in archaeology and history. Debate within the field has also been a little inward-looking, focused mainly on methodological issues.

The consensus among its practitioners is for intensive survey with quantified observations and controlled artefact collection. What this means is line-walking by team members no more than 15 to 20 metres apart, with the generation of artefact samples as large as an excavation. The results are 100 times as many sites located than in earlier, less intensive surveys. For example, the Nemea Valley Archaeological Project dealt with 5,000 tracts, each of 1 or 2 hectares. For each were recorded data on visibility, environment and contemporary land use and information about several categories of artefact for each 100 metre section of the traverses covered by fieldworkers. The result was a considerable amount of data necessitating computer manipulation.

The sorts of features encountered in surveys of this sort include terraces, roads, bridges, quarries and mines, caves (used for cult, burial or habitation), pottery and lime kilns, cisterns, wells, graves, oil and wine presses, chipping floors used in tool manufacture, isolated towers, animal folds, agricultural storage sheds, farmhouses and rural sanctuaries. It seems clear that landscapes were full of features in Classical times and sometimes may have approached dangerously high population densities.

The plotting of densities of artefacts has shown that the definiton of a site is an interpretive matter. The threshold for a scatter of artefacts to be classed as a site is generally taken to be 30–50 sherds per 100 square metres, but there is great variation from region to region and from period to period. Nor are artefacts distributed in neat areas corresponding to ancient sites: there is considerable spread or 'haloes'.

Clear also are off-site artefact scatters. These are taken by the main protagonists of intensive survey (John Cherry, Anthony Snodgrass, Sue Alcock, Jack Davis and John Bintliff to name some) to be not just surface garbage or background noise, but valuable evidence for agricultural practices. So the question of the origin and character of these scatters has come to be a question of manuring - deliberate fertilisation of the cultivated landscape using animal manure and household rubbish incorporating pottery – hence the archaeological visibility.

Manuring is an issue of real importance related to intensity of land use, methods of cultivation, and systems of land tenure. It has been questioned whether manuring can account for the artefact scatters on its own, and

Figure 6.2 Intensively surveyed block of land to the west of the Tretos Pass, Nemea Valley, Greece.
(*Source*: Susan E. Alcock, John F. Cherry and Jack L. Davis. 'Intensive survey, agricultural practice and the classical landscape of Greece', in *Classical Greece: Ancient Histories and Modern Archaeologies*, ed. Ian Morris. Cambridge: Cambridge University Press, 1994)

impressive calculations have been made involving amounts of rubbish, likely rates of manuring, periods of cultivation, and ploughing techniques. Whatever the disagreements, the result is changing views of Classical and early Hellenistic cultivation. The standard model, extrapolated from early modern and present-day Greek agriculture, is of nucleated residence at a distance from fields. Regular fallowing accompanied fragmented landholdings with long-distance seasonal transhumant pastoralism, because animals could not be kept on small dispersed parcels of land and because the adoption of fallow precluded fodder crops. There is thus a fundamental divorce of arable farming from stock husbandry.

In this extensive system, manuring could only be light, but this does not fit with the findings of field survey. A new model proposes intensive agriculture and a close association of arable farming and stock. Cereal and pulse rotation, rather than biennial fallow, produced fodder crops, which in turn enabled animals to be kept in sufficient quantity and close to the arable land to produce fertilising manure. Landholdings were of moderate size. The implications of this agricultural model for the type of stock which could be kept is significant. Horses become an expensive luxury, and draught animals are of less importance than in an extensive system. There are connections here with that association of horses with wealthy aristocracies.

With its impressive calculations of household faecal wastes and manuring rates, such economic modelling is far removed, it might seem, from the aesthetics of art style. We are firmly within the everyday, and we do well to remember the importance of the landed citizen to the early Greek city state: without them there would have been no 'Greek miracle'.

CONCLUDING REMARKS

Interpenetrations of everyday life and broader social modelling reveal both the need for anthropological understanding and awareness of difference or variability. Social archaeologies may better conceive their object not as 'societies' but social networks which do not respect the political and geographical divisions of today and which may have deep resonances through the cultural imaginary of the ancient Greeks.

7

ARCHAEOLOGY, CLASSICS AND CONTEMPORARY CULTURE

But while all this trouble's brewing
what's the Prussian monarch doing?
We read in his own writing,
how, while all Europe geared for fighting,
England, Belgium, France, Russia
but not of course his peaceful Prussia,
what was Kaiser Wilhelm II
up to? Excavating on Corfu,
the scholar Kaiser on the scent
of long lost temple pediment
not filling trenches, excavating
the trenches where the Gorgon's waiting
there in the trenches to supervise
the unearthing of the Gorgon's eyes.
This isn't how warmongers are
this professor in a panama
stooping as the spades laid bare
the first glimpses of her snaky hair.

The excavator with his find
a new art treasure for mankind.
                    (Tony Harrison, *The Gaze of the Gorgon*)

At the turn of the century the German Kaiser bought a retreat on the island of Corfu which had belonged to Elizabeth, Empress of Austria prior to her assassination in 1899. She had brought with her a statue of Heinrich Heine, German Romantic poet and dissident Jew, rejected by his fatherland. The Kaiser evicted the statue again, not liking what it stood for (subversive radical democratic Jew) and, while Europe prepared for war, claimed he was excavating the pediment of a Greek temple (of the seventh century and dedicated to Artemis) which featured a giant Gorgon sculpted in stone. In the poem-film *The Gaze of the Gorgon*, Tony Harrison traces the fortunes of the statue of Heine transplanted through Europe, to its resting place in

Toulon, France. At the same time he sets off a series of metaphors centred on the Gorgon, monstrous female whose gaze turns men to stone, unleashed now upon the twentieth century by the excavating scholar Kaiser.

> The Gorgon worshippers unroll
> the barbed wire gulags round the soul.
> The Gorgon's henchmen try to force
> History on a straighter course
> with Gorgonisms that impose
> fixities on all that flows,
> with Führer fix and crucifix
> and freedom-freezing politics.

Harrison makes pointed use of the panoptic and petrifying gaze of this Gorgon, made to represent the beginnings of the High Art, High Culture of the Greeks, the 'so-called "Eternal Being" the Gorgon gulls us into seeing'. European connections are spun, national boundaries transcended in the journeys of the statue of Heine, and transcended because of anti-semitic and right-wing bigotry, with references to the transnational cultures so associated with the Classical and with Classically educated elites. The Gorgon comes to be systems of fixed and supposedly eternal values imposed upon history; intolerance and inflexibility distilled in deathly gazes; and war from Flanders to the Gulf. Themes of identity and belonging are here (the transient statue of Heine), and systems of thought in twentieth-century Modernity. Systems of petrification are contrasted with forms of vitality. In excavating monuments, attentions are focused upon the stones, forgetting that monuments are invitations to remember (*monimenta* in Latin), to make acts of recalling the past into the present.

Tony Harrison turns round the Greek, opposing Hellenism, reworking, translating the Greek according to its special qualities – the rich networks of metaphor and cultural association threaded through the centuries. These are surely the roots of the fascination with the Greek. His translation is into a radical cultural and political relevance to the present. Harrison has translated the fifth-century tragedian Aeschylus. These rich reworkings (hardly accurate petrifications), championing English regional dialect and vernacular imaging, are performed in, among other places, ancient theatres, Delphi and Epidauros.

The new hypermarket in a town nearby to where I live in rural Wales has a Doric forecourt. Its roof is sloped and is fitted with ceramic pantiles. Its predecessor was a system-built warehouse. All over the western world Postmodern pastiche announces a new return of neo-Classicism. The international style of clean glass-sided rectangles, primary colours, simple lines and lack of ornament is giving way, with interests in expressing more local and human scales. Charles Windsor, Prince of Wales, in another line of the

German aristocracy, has precipitated something of a debate in popular circles, with his television programmes and books, illustrated with water-colours, arguing that Modernist architectures, nasty carbuncles on the modern city, must give way to new vernaculars. He is (I believe plans have gone ahead) building the late twentieth-century equivalent of a Laird's village, replete with picturesque mock-Georgian Classicism, on his estates in the west country. Questions of taste, style, regional and transnational identity continue to be raised.

The relation between Classicism, Modernism and Postmodernism is an indeterminate one: there is no easy categorisation or periodisation, except in books. Just as Hellenism went with Romanticism, Modern forms can be quite Classical in their simplicity of line and avoidance of excessive ornament. Adolf Loos, arch-Modernist author of *Ornament and Crime* (1908) considered that 'Greek vases are as beautiful as a machine, as beautiful as a bicycle'. But the International Movement has indeed been challenged by a renewed interest in old and Classical forms in the production of what some call Disneyland, toytown architectures.

I will continue this diversion into Classical studies more generally to consider the relationship of the Classical to the late twentieth century, posing the question of the agenda of a Classical archaeology critically aware of its constituting metanarratives.

Figure 7.1 Robert Sayer. *Ruins of Athens.* London 1759. Plate 5

171

The relevance of Classics is a question which has been on educational agendas on both sides of the Atlantic. Should study of the Classics continue to hold the prestigious position in educational curricula that it has held for nearly two centuries? A crisis in Classics was introduced in Chapter 4 as part of Morris's interpretation of contemporary Classical archaeology. Some deny the problem. Some are taking a broader view, as has been shown, in the adoption of new methods for dealing with Classical materials. Some assert the continuing relevance of ancient Greece into the 1990s. An anecdote is in order here. I recently delivered a conference paper on Korinthian ceramics which juxtaposed its iconography with that of a contemporary movie. The conference was being held at a university in England which has become well known for developing new course materials for the teaching of Classical Languages. Its professor has lobbied parliament for the inclusion of Classics in the National Curriculum of England and Wales, arguing its continuing relevance to modern Britain. I had expected a sympathetic reception, but, from some quarters of the audience, it was one of the most hostile reactions I have ever received, and would certainly contradict any notion that academic conferences are dry and lifeless occasions. I had not realised the agenda. It is to find new ways of delivering the *same* message about Classical Greeks. Some others, like Morris, want a refigured discipline facing up to the task of 'problematising' its assumptions and practices.

Generally, interest in the Classics continues; it is a popular subject in universities, though the language component (for nineteenth-century Hellenists the key to an authentic communion with the ancient Greeks) has become less emphasised. This is not the place to get into the questions of educational policy, the National Curriculum in Britain, and supposed falling standards on both sides of the Atlantic. There is a set of wider issues. In Classical archaeology Morris sets Modern against Postmodern. In archaeology too there are debates about the true character of the discipline and its future, which are often conducted as if there were two armed and opposing camps: scientists and humanists, anthropological and historical archaeologists, Processualists and Postmodernists.

John Bintliff and Colin Renfrew, two archaeologists working in Greece, but also interested in general matters of archaeological theory, have made several attacks on developments in archaeology, criticising those who maintain, as does this book, that archaeology is as much about the present as about the past (articles cited in Bibliography). They make a stand for a scientific discipline which develops knowledges of the past and which involves eliminating the present as far as is possible. Bintliff sees his opposition as Postmodernists, in that they call for local knowledges, pluralist views of the past from different present interests, the complexity and ambiguity of cultural fragments, archaeology as an open construction of the present directed to the future rather than the past-the-way-it-was. Behind their criticisms seems to be the idea of a dispossessed Humanities (dispossessed by the success of science) in search of a new empire; an imaginary world of the interpreter's creation which will flatter low and popular (democratic?) tastes. A response of theirs is to put people in their place, archaeologists in the present and in respective theoretical camps, the past quite separate, and upon which archaeologists should focus.

How can this apparent impasse be avoided? Let us consider Nietzsche.

NIETZSCHE AND THE CLASSICS

Harrison prefaces his poem with Nietzsche, from *The Birth of Tragedy*. 'Art forces us to gaze into the horror of existence, yet without being turned to stone by the vision'.

Friedrich Nietzsche denied the existence of a divine sanction for morality and, being strongly opposed to a distinction between spirit and matter, rejected Platonic notions of abstractions like absolute good or truth. Instead, he upheld a relativist ethics based upon a realist psychology. His impetus to philosophy derived from his study of the ancient world and not only of its philosophy but still more of the religious and intellectual climate in which those systems of ideas developed.

German Classicism, with people such as Friedrich August Wolf at Göttingen, was not so much an academic as a literary movement. It was mentioned in Chapter 3 that Winckelmann was as much concerned with art itself as with art history. Goethe and Lessing were familiar with the ancient world, but for the sake of literature and art rather than scholarship. The link between the two worlds was Wilhelm von Humboldt, scholar and statesman, prominent among the founders of the University of Berlin – the model of modern education. Its nineteenth-century success, as we have seen, was *Altertumswissenschaft*, dominated by the historical outlook.

The link between Romanticism and the new growth of a historical sense (historicity) involved new historical writing, rich in cultural and social detail, and owing much to Romantic novels of the like of Sir Walter Scott. But with *Altertumswissenschaft* literature and the arts became separated from scholarship. Nietzsche opposed what he saw as the dullness and dryness of professional scholarship seduced into the fantasies of a concrete and positive science, a systematised and specialised historicism despising the unsophisticted Classicism of Goethe. He attacked philologists for being unable to teach art and culture. Similar arguments, in one of his *Untimely Meditations*, were directed at historians. His criticism was that prevailing materialism was driving scholars to emulate the positive and concrete achievements of natural sciences (this is positivism) in mechanised collection of facts.

Nietzsche's essay 'We Philologists' (to be another *Untimely Meditation*) related what above was termed Hellenism to an ignorance of antiquity, a false idealisation of the Greeks, who were less humane than Indians and Chinese. He ascribes it to the arrogance of schoolmasters, to the tradition of an admiration of Greeks inherited from Rome, to prejudice for or against Christianity,

Figure 7.2 National Tourist Board of Greece. Advertisement of 1992

and to the belief that where people had dug for so long there must be gold. Hellenism was about professional interest and escapism. He considered that if people could grasp the real nature of Classical antiquity they would turn from it in horror. For Nietzsche, horror is difference and heterogeneity.

The *Birth of Tragedy* is a reassessment of Greek culture, life and thought which was bitterly attacked in its day. Its thesis is that Greek tragedy was not Aristotelian katharsis, a purifying purging or discharging of feelings, but a synthesis of the Apollonian and Dionysian elements of Greek culture. Its purity of form contained also an affirmation of life represented by delight in destruction and annihilation – Dionysos. This was an explicit criticism of old Romantic Classicism. Behind the calm and dignity praised by Winckelmann was, for Nietzsche, a struggle to achieve a balance, since terrible and irrational forces were not repressed but used for their own purpose. This is a process of sublimation. In tragedy, ancient gods stood for the fearful realities of a universe in which people had no special privileges. This is the horror.

Nietzsche's primary objection was to the separation of scholarship from understanding: 'the most important thing and the hardest is to enter into the life of antiquity and feel the difference'. This emphasis on the experiential and affective accounts for the great importance assigned to music (a Wagnerian influence).

Nietzsche combines fascination for the Greek with critique, something which is encapsulated in his attitude to Socrates. Clever Socrates used pure reasoning in dialectics, exposing contradiction and irrationality in an opponent's argument through making assumption and lines of argument explicit, destroying, from inside, the opponent. It has been upheld as the philosopher's method, the triumph of reason in pure searches for truth. But Nietzsche argued that this method is socially offensive and is, in fact, easily ignored. The dialectician uses pure reasoning, ignoring other rhetorical devices of persuasion (see the section of discourse in Chapter 4). 'One chooses dialectics only when one has no other expedient. One knows that dialectics inspire mistrust, that they are not very convincing . . . Dialectics can be only a *last-ditch weapon* in the hands of those who have no other weapon left.' This is Nietzsche's realism, and it can appear somewhat outrageous: Socrates was ugly and a social misfit, so he developed his skill of dialectics.

> From scenting out 'beautiful souls' [a reference to Goethe], 'golden means' and other perfections in the Greeks, from admiring them in such things as their repose in grandeur, their ideal disposition, their sublime simplicity – from this 'sublime simplicity', a *niaiserie allemande* [German stupidity] when all is said and done, I was preserved by the psychologist in me. I saw in their strongest instinct the will to power.

Oliver Taplin, in *Greek Fire*, pits Allan Bloom and I.F. 'Izzy' Stone against each other in an assessment of Socrates, democratic ideals and the relevance of ancient Greece to the contemporary west. But the argument, as he points

175

Figure 7.3 Socrates

out, is long-standing and not restricted to two best-selling authors in the United States of the late 1980s.

Bloom's exemplar is Socrates the great philosopher. With many others on both the right and the left, he complains of spineless Postmodern relativism, indeterminacy, and lack of scholarship. He also voices those general complaints about the 1960s and academic left-wingers. Many, like him, call for a return to established values, to established truths and procedures, whether they be conservative and based on high culture or Marxist. Socrates so also complains about the sophists who put rhetoric before truth and he stands for the constants of truth achieved through pure reasoning. Here is a desire to get back to rational universal and scientific method. Classics in its high cultural variants, as representative of traditional standards and precepts, as *Altertumswissenschaft*, is easily associated with this social and political programme.

Socrates was put on trial and executed by the Athenian state. Nietzsche has a case against this Socrates and what Classics had come to stand for. Stone in *The Trial of Socrates* (1988) argues that the Athenians had a case against Socrates, because he was undermining democracy by claiming he had some special access to higher truths, absolutes and certainties which come before the opinions of ordinary mortals – the mob with their incessant bickering.

But this should not be taken as a false polarisation. Nietzsche's case against Socrates is not based on the grounds of relative values or of no values, a position which holds that anything may be done to pursue any desired ends. Nietzsche complains about Socrates' *etiquette*, that he is unsociable and rude. The point is that truths are shared and that they are historical. They are not something that we develop individually by some mystical communion with the real world and its underlying character and then communicate to the rest of humanity. Truths, whether about beauty and goodness, or what happened in the past, are real, made, shared and historical. This is Nietzsche's argument, and one that was articulated in a different form in Chapter 4.

NIETZSCHE AND EFFECTIVE HISTORY

Michel Foucault finds in Nietzsche (one of his *Untimely Meditations*) a case for effective history or a historical sense. This aims to avoid synthetic philosophies of history which impose transcendent meanings upon history (including what I have termed metanarratives such as European identity). Foucault and Nietzsche oppose three uses of history: the monumental, devoted to the veneration of the past and great deeds; the antiquarian, dedicated to the preservation of the past as the continuity of identity in tradition; and the critical, which condemns the past on the grounds of present truth (truth thus removed from history and defined universally). Instead the historical sense or effective history is parodic, opposing the theme of history as memory (a record of times past) or as recognition of something great. Such history is dissociative, finding heterogeneity insted of easy identities and continuities (such as the Greek spirit). It is sacrificial – directed against absolute truths used to measure history. It proposes no absolute foundations but problems. As Mitchell Dean, in his book *Critical and Effective Histories* (1994), expresses it:

> Let us call history 'effective' to the extent that it upsets the colonisation of historical knowledge by the schemas of a transcendental and synthetic philosophy of history, and 'critical' in proportion to its capacity to engage in the tireless interrogation of what is held to be given, necessary, natural, or neutral.

Consider sexuality. Scholars have long been aware of the prevalence in the

Greek imagination of homosexual love, but it was not until Kenneth Dover's book *Greek Homosexuality* that a serious attempt was made to understand this. Central to his project were more than 500 vase paintings, and the role of material culture and iconography in understanding the everyday has been mentioned. But the point is a greater one. Dover warns us that the modern tendency to consider the world as divided into homosexuals and hetero-sexuals is a local accident. Students of Classics such as David Halperin, in his *One Hundred Years of Homosexuality* (1990), have been developing an effective history of the sort just described, presenting a genealogy of things taken to be constants, such as sexuality, tracing the changes in their very nature through history.

ARCHAEOLOGICAL ROLES: VITAL *HISTORIES* FOR THE PRESENT

Nietzsche preferred the philosopher Herakleitos to Socrates. One of his aphorisms goes: 'The Lord whose oracle is at Delphi (the god Apollo and source of wisdom and truth) neither declares nor conceals but gives a sign'. The condition of knowing is not one of revelation of meaning, but of con-structing knowledges from signs: the semiotics of tracking down the truth.

Taplin, in *Greek Fire* (1989), makes an apparently reasonable claim:

Rather as Freud said that childhood must be studied in order to under-stand the adult, so we look to 'the childhood of man', as Marx called Greece, in an attempt to clarify the present. So the ancient Greek message – its original stone long since fragmented – has meant different things to different ages; and many interpretations have been 'right' for different times and places. It is monumental and eternal, yet broken up and open to reformations.

Here is a good point about the interpreted character of history. He writes approvingly of an ironic Postmodern revisiting of the past:

A new return to ancient Greece is all part of this. Instead of trying to reconstruct or imitate Greece as a whole, the new return recognises the vast differences between now and then, in tension with the similarities, and the fragmentariness of the evidence and of our knowledge; and recognises how any picture of ancient Greece must be selective, preju-diced, not innocent. It not only asks what is timelessly 'right', it also seeks what can be made of Greece now.

Here is an idea of the ancient Greek message being one of the interpretability of history; but the relation of ancient Greece to the present is conceived as part of that metanarrative of European origins discussed in Chapter 3 – Greek universality and individual appropriations or versions. What is needed is a recognition that this relationship with Greece is *not* a unique and European

178

one. All cultures exist in this anthropological paradox. We are prejudiced and prejudging, but in establishing common ground, in translating and addressing carefully the 'other' in local and particular ways, according to our interests, we may learn. Such a hermeneutic dialogue of understanding is the permanence and necessity of interpretation. To bypass this universality–ancestor dualism, history and archaeology need defamiliarising and to be made problematical. This process of making problematic is about realising that it is not possible definitively to eradicate ethnocentrism: escapes into insight are always provisional. Contextualisation and bias can be critically acknowledged in holding that knowledges are always constructed.

Herzfeld, as discussed in Chapter 3, treats the anthropology of Greece as a practice, comparable, as a mode of cultural production, to what it observes. Anthropology and constructions of Greece in the eighteenth and nineteenth centuries are also historically derived in part from some of the same sources (colonialism and nationalistic imperialism). Anthropology (and here can be included Classical and Prehistoric archaeology) becomes another mode of expressing identity, 'which trivialises its own significance by ignoring this condition of its existence'. The argument can be extended to hold that past and present, just as anthropologist and subject of interest, are symmetrical. This is a critique of exoticism (of the past and of other cultures) and the power relations so entailed between observer and observed, subject and object of knowledge. A principle of symmetry denies that anthropology, archaeology and Classical archaeology have any necessary and a priori privileged status in the relationships that constitute knowledge.

Hard and fast notions of identity (of what the past really is, or of Europe or archaeology), hard and fast categories of analysis and understanding are thus to be avoided. An effective history of Greece follows the trajectory of historical forms of truth and knowledge, without origin or end, disturbing easy narratives of progress (from ancient to modern Europe), seeking to remain open to change – the multiplicity of the things with which archaeologists deal. The attitude is one of perpetual vigilance and scepticism towards the claims of various histories which are, in fact, philosophies of history because they claim to know the meaning of history. This may be described as a Postmodern attitude – turning what is given to us into a problem, not providing an analytic of truth, but an investigation of the ontology of the present.

ACTUALITY: THE TIME OF ARCHAEOLOGY

The time or temporality of such an archaeology conceived as effective history is *actuality* – a return of what is no longer the same. Actuality is the non-arbitrary conjunction of presents: the past's present; the time of excavation and working upon the past; and the time of reading what has been produced.

Compare archaeology with memory. Memories live on with us, as does the material past, and as we reinterpret memories and incorporate them into new stories of our life, so the past may be conceived to change: what was once a temple becomes tourist attraction or archaeological source. Memories sometimes seem to escape time in that they stay with us. We may feel too that archaeological remains sometimes witness that which escapes time, the timeless. The timeless here is not an unbounded infinity, but is convoluted or folded time, a folding or recycling of past moments. As conjuncture between the temporality of person remembering and past event, memory crosses time, just as the archaeological fragment witnesses lost instants in time past.

Memory is in fact the *act* of memorising. The past as memory does not just exist as it was. The past has to be recalled: memory is the act of recalling from the viewpoint of a subsequent time. So too archaeological remains are meaningless unless lent a past and a future, given a place in history. This is done by the contextualisation that takes place in interpretation: we read the signs, make connections and follow tracks.

We may add also the idea of *rapturous* temporality: memory holds on to the past, just as archaeology arrests decay, the past potentially missed, ruined away. In memory time stands still: there are no clocks. In the world remembered there is no bottom line, no horizon, no past-as-it-was, no ordained chronology. There are instead but enfoldings: the art and science of making contextual links. A naturalistic archaeological reconstruction may require chronicle: dates and linear chronology. A realistic memory (or archaeology) may need flashbacks, long-term backgrounds, and reflexive reinterpretations of past events.

To point out the affinities between memory and archaeology, and to emphasise the temporality of actuality is not a call for 'relevance', to recognise simply that archaeology happens in the present, that this matters above all else and so we should ensure the relevance of archaeology to present interests. Such an argument corresponds (as opposite or negation) to a historicism which denies the present in a self-effacing posture emphasising that what happened in the past is the measure of all archaeology. Instead we should retain the ambiguity and tension which is actuality; actuality is the *primacy*, but not the *superiority*, of the present over the past. This is simply to acknowledge that the soluble present is the medium of knowing the past.

So archaeology has a multiple temporality involving the past, its decay, and the encounter with remains in our future-orientated projects.

Archaeology presents us with inventories of mortality, quoting fragments, creating juxtapositions potentially as strange as a vase, quernstone and ox scapula which may be found together in an archetypal archaeological report. archaeology turns the now (remains) into the past, or more grandly, into history, depending upon the rhetoric. Reality is turned antique. Documented triviality is made memorable.

CLASSICAL HERITAGE AND CONSUMING
INTERESTS

Classical archaeology provides so many materials for contemporary heritage interests: European heritage, Greek heritage, world heritage, indeed the heritage of archaeology, given the role of Classical antiquities in the history of the discipline. Here is a major cultural field which, according to the arguments of this book, needs to be addressed and a stand taken.

Heritage interests take the past and use it in the present. Criticism is often made that this may simply be consumerism, an expansion of the market to include the past which is bought and sold without attention to scholarship and without respecting what actually happened then.

But the heritage industry continues to expand. It is popular and gains considerable political and commercial support. Why? The power of heritage is that it is a symbolic exchange of past for present which takes the form of an apparent sacrifice of the past for the present. The significance of things from the past is what they mean to the present, and this is mostly to do with contemporary senses of identity. Heritage attends to this vital interest with active mobilisation of the past. And heritage does not just tell a boring academic story of the past. Heritage is an affective field of *experience*: the multidimensional experience, for example, of visiting the past and all that it has come to stand for in a walk up Akrokorinthos. Through the category of experience I argue that archaeology and heritage are comparable and commensurable because they are both active mobilisations of people and things from the past. Heritage projects are concerned with work done on the past for the present; as projects they look forward too (to expansion, more visitors, conservation and such). Archaeologists, visitors, things, times, feelings, perceptions, images, books, places are related. Heritage and archaeology deal both with perceptions and experiences of the times of things and with how these are connected with knowledges of who we are, have been and want to be.

A significant difference is that heritage often explicitly focuses upon the place of the past in the present. This is foregrounded, not least, because heritage attends to those who will be visiting or who want to relate to the past. The difficulty of giving a precise definition of heritage, and the dangers of treating as a unity such a disparate and heterogeneous assemblage (exceptions and anecdotes contrary to any particular argument can usually be found) attests to the dispersal of heritage through indeterminate fields of feeling, sentiment, culture, knowledge and experience – many of which are not consciously or discursively formulated. Courses in Cultural Resource or Archaeological Heritage Management are academic attempts to colonise, to service the heritage 'industry'. For most academic and professional archaeology these are concerns separable from producing knowledge of the past. The conventional main task, I suggest, is seen to be ensuring that heritage and all it represents does not stop archaeologists from doing what they want to do.

181

Many arguments have been aimed at the dangers of an uncritical and romantic appropriation of the past. So too in the heritage industry easy sentiment, spectacle and melodrama may be preferred in the place of work done upon the past. Cliché, stereotype, stock metanarratives or myths may take the place of careful empirical attention to the past as 'other', as an agent reciprocal in our self-definition. There are many such 'consumerist' experiences where gratification comes from the act of consumption: abstract consumption where the item consumed is of no importance or is assimilated with no effort, without reflection or critique. A consuming interest is one which is self-gratifying, introverted and erosive, returning nothing.

But there is nothing wrong with consuming the past, if, by this, is not meant consumerism as just defined, but rather consumption as taking something 'other' within the self. Consumption of the past may be seen as an exchange: the past renovated, reincarnated, as it is taken within the self, providing material for personal and cultural construction. This reciprocality is the potential power of heritage – the past developed for the present. The active involvement of the past in the present's self-definition is a source of critique. Attention to the independence and character of archaeological sources is the basis of a challenge to present complacencies and a realisation of the heterogeneity of both past and present. I hope it is clear from materials presented in this book that Classical archaeology holds so much potential for such a project.

SELECT BIBLIOGRAPHY
AND SUGGESTED FURTHER
READING

A full bibliography would have been of considerable length and would have perhaps confused rather than clarified routes into the discipline. What follows is a listing, according to the main subjects of each chapter, of recommended, standard or summarising/synoptic works. The reader is advised to consult this bibliography of suggested further reading after completing a chapter. Discussion of the texts mentioned and full bibliographies can be easily found in the recommended items.

Generally recommended:
Books to which I have constantly referred or which I admire include the following:
La Cité des Images. Paris: Nathan, 1984. Now translated by Deborah Lyons with the title *A City of Images: Iconography and Society in Ancient Greece.* Princeton, NJ: Princeton University Press, 1989.
Morris, Ian (ed.). *Classical Greece: Ancient Histories and Modern Archaeologies.* Cambridge: Cambridge University Press, 1994.
Schnapp, Alain. *La Conquête du passé: aux origines de l'archéologie.* Paris: Carré, 1993.
Snodgrass, Anthony. *An Archaeology of Greece: the Present State and Future Scope of a Discipline.* Berkeley: University of California Press, 1987.
Vernant, Jean-Pierre. *Mortals and Immortals: Collected Essays.* Various translators. Princeton, NJ: Princeton University Press, 1991.

On a Constructivist philosophy:
Latour, Bruno. *Science in Action: How to Follow Scientists and Engineers Through Society.* Milton Keynes: Open University Press, 1987.

For a most interesting approach to history and appreciation of the character of material sources:
Benjamin, Walter. *Illuminations.* Various translators. London: Jonathan Cape, 1970.
Benjamin, Walter. *Paris: capital du XIXe siècle: le livre des passages.* Translated by J. Lacoste. Paris: Cerf, 1989.
Eagleton, Terry. *Walter Benjamin: Or Towards a Revolutionary Criticism.* London: Verso, 1981.

For his translations of Greek drama:
Harrison, Tony. *Dramatic Verse 1973–1985.* Newcastle-upon-Tyne: Bloodaxe, 1985.

See also:
Vidal, Gore. *Creation*. London: Heinemann, 1981.

Note:
The main journals are the quickest route into the discipline. In English: *Annual of the British School of Archaeology at Athens*; *American Journal of Archaeology*; *Journal of Hellenic Studies*. The periodical *L'Année Philologique* is a bibliographic listing which gives an idea of the international discipline and the topics which are the focus of publication.

AN INTRODUCTION

The study of Korinthian and early Greek art:
Shanks, Michael. *Art and the Early Greek City State: an Interpretive Archaeology*. Cambridge: Cambridge University Press, forthcoming.

Standard introductions to Classical archaeology and the ancient history of Greece include:
Biers, William R. *The Archaeology of Greece: an Introduction*. Ithaca, NY: Cornell University Press, 1980.
Hurwitt, J.M. *The Art and Culture of Early Greece 1100–480 BC*. Ithaca, NY: Cornell University Press, 1985.
Levi, Peter. *Atlas of the Greek World*. Oxford: Phaidon, 1980.
Murray, Oswyn. *Early Greece* (2nd edn). London: Fontana, 1993.
Osborne, Robin. *Greece in the Making: 1200–479 BC*. London: Routledge, 1996.

On the general archaeological background to the book, which also covers relationships between archaeology and history:
Hodder, Ian, Michael Shanks, Alexandra Alexandri, Victor Buchli, John Carman, Jonathan Last and Gavin Lucas (eds). *Interpreting Archaeology: Finding Meaning in the Past*. London: Routledge, 1995.

For the debate around anthropological and Classical archaeology:
Courbin, Paul. *What is Archaeology? An Essay on the Nature of Archaeological Knowledge*. Translated by Paul Bahn. Chicago: Chicago University Press, 1988.
Dyson, Stephen L. 'From New to New-Age archaeology: archaeological theory and Classical archaeology – a 1990s perspective', *American Journal of Archaeology* 97 (1993): 195–206.

For general changes in archaeological thought up to the 1980s:
Trigger, Bruce. *A History of Archaeological Thought*. Cambridge: Cambridge University Press, 1989.

French Classical Studies:
A City of Images and the work of Vernant, cited above.

Constructivist philosophy:
Latour, cited above.

A convenient up-to-date introduction to Constructivist philosophy with full bibliography is:
Schwandt, Thomas. 'Constructivist, interpretivist approaches to human inquiry', in *Handbook of Qualitative Research*, ed. Norman K. Denzin and Yvonna S. Lincoln. London: Sage, 1994.

For critical historical archaeology in the United States:
McGuire, Randall and Robert Paynter (eds). *The Archaeology of Inequality*. Oxford: Blackwell, 1991.

A fine example of a critical archaeological project is reported by:
Leone, M.P., P.R. Mullins, M.C. Creveling, L. Hurst, B. Jackson-Nash, L.D. Jones, H.J. Kaiser, G.C. Logan and M.S. Warner. 'Can an African-American historical archaeology be an alternative voice?', in *Interpreting Archaeology: Finding Meaning in the Past*, ed. Ian Hodder, Michael Shanks, Alexandra Alexandri, Victor Buchli, John Carman, Jonathan Last and Gavin Lucas. London: Routledge, 1995.

1   A SEARCH FOR SOURCES

For Korinth:
Salmon, J. *Wealthy Corinth: a History of the City to 338 BC*. Oxford: Clarendon Press, 1984.

On the British School:
ANASKAPHES: a Celebration of the Centenary of the British School at Athens 1886–1986. London: Camberwell School of Arts and Crafts, 1992.
Waterhouse, Helen. *The British School at Athens: the First Hundred Years*. London: Thames and Hudson, 1986.

The project on Korinthian pottery:
Shanks, cited above.

2   CITIES AND SANCTUARIES, ART AND ARCHAEOLOGY

The history of pottery studies:
Cook, Robert. *Greek Painted Pottery*. London: Routledge, 1996 (3rd edn). This also serves as an excellent standard handbook.
Rasmussen, Tom and Nigel Spivey (eds). *Looking at Greek Vases*. Cambridge: Cambridge University Press, 1991.
Sparkes, Brian A. *The Red and the Black: Studies in Greek Pottery*. London: Routledge, 1996.

For extensive bibliographies on Korinthian pottery see:
Shanks, Michael. 'Style and the design of a perfume jar from an archaic Greek city state', *Journal of European Archaeology* 1 (1992): 77–106.
Shanks, Michael. 'Art and an archaeology of embodiment: some aspects of archaic Greece', *Cambridge Archaeological Journal* (1995).
Shanks, Michael. *Art and the Early Greek City State: an Interpretive Archaeology*. Cambridge: Cambridge University Press, forthcoming.

German art history:
Podro, M. *The Critical Historians of Art*. New Haven: Yale University Press, 1982.
Whitley, James. 'Art history, archaeology and idealism: the German tradition', in *Archaeology as Long Term History*, ed. Ian Hodder. Cambridge: Cambridge University Press, 1987.

On Beazley:
Kurtz, D.C. 'Beazley and the connoisseurship of Greek vases', in *Greek Vases in the J. Paul Getty Museum*. Malibu: J. Paul Getty Museum, 1985.
Von Bothmer, Dietrich. 'Greek vase painting: 200 years of connoisseurship', in *Papers on the Amasis Painter and his World*. London: Thames and Hudson, 1987.
Whitley, James. 'Beazley as theorist', *Antiquity* 71 (1997): 40–7.

On individuals:
Shanks, Michael and Christopher Tilley. *Social Theory and Archaeology*. Cambridge: Blackwell Polity, 1987.

On Sherlock Holmes, Morelli and abduction:
Eco, Umberto and Thomas Sebeok (eds). *The Sign of Three: Dupin, Holmes, Peirce*. Bloomington: Indiana University Press, 1983.
Ginzburg, Carlo. *Clues, Myths and the Historical Method*. Translated by John and Anne C. Tedeschi. Baltimore: Johns Hopkins University Press, 1989.

Iconography:
Different approaches and extensive bibliographies can be found in:
Moon, W.G. (ed.). *Ancient Greek Art and Iconography*. Madison: University of Wisconsin Press, 1983.

History of collection and excavation:
Items listed for Chapter 3.

American School of Classical Studies and the Agora excavations:
Lord, L.E. *A History of the American School of Classical Studies in Athens: 1882–1942*. Cambridge, MA: Harvard University Press, 1947.

3 ROOTS IN THE PAST: GREEK MYTHS AND METANARRATIVES

Collectors and antiquarians:
Etienne, R. and F. Etienne. *La Grèce antique: archéologie d'une découverte*. Paris: Gallimard, 1990.
Schnapp, Alain. *La Conquête du passé: aux origines de l'archéologie*. Paris: Carré, 1993.
Stoneman, R. *Land of Lost Gods: the Search for Classical Greece*. London: Hutchinson, 1987.

On the travellers:
Constantine, D. *Early Greek Travellers and the Hellenic Ideal*. Cambridge: Cambridge University Press, 1984.
Eisner, R. *Travellers to an Antique Land: the History and Literature of Travel to Greece*. Ann Arbor: University of Michigan Press, 1991.
Tsigakou, Fanny-Maria. *The Rediscovery of Greece: Travellers and the Painters of the Romantic Era*. London: Thames and Hudson, 1981.

Winckelmann:
Potts, Alex. *Flesh and the Ideal: Winckelmann and the Origins of Art History*. New Haven: Yale University Press, 1994.

Vickers and Gill have gathered their ideas and researches in:
Vickers, Michael and David Gill. *Artful Crafts: Ancient Greek Silverware and Pottery*. Oxford: Clarendon Press, 1994.

Lord Elgin:
Cook, B.F. *The Elgin Marbles*. London: British Museum, 1983.
St Clair, W. *Lord Elgin and the Marbles*. Oxford: Oxford University Press, 1967.

German scholarship:
Bruford, W.H. *Culture and Society in Classical Weimar: 1775–1806*. Cambridge: Cambridge University Press, 1962.

Bruford, W.H. *The German Tradition of Self-Cultivation: 'Bildung' from Humboldt to Thomas Mann*. Cambridge: Cambridge University Press, 1975.

Diehl, C. *Americans and German Scholarship: 1770–1870*. New Haven: Yale University Press, 1977.

Classicism:

Greenhalgh, M. *The Classical Tradition in Art*. London: Duckworth, 1978.

Haskell, F. and N. Penny. *Taste and the Antique: the Lure of Classical Sculpture 1500–1900*. New Haven: Yale University Press, 1981.

Neo-Classicism and Romanticism:

The literature is extensive. I have found the following useful:

Clay, J. *Romanticism*. London: Phaidon, 1981.

Furst, L. (ed.). *European Romanticism: Self Definition*. London: Methuen, 1980.

The Age of Neo-Classicism. 14th Exhibition of the Council of Europe at the Royal Academy and Victoria and Albert Museum. London: Arts Council, 1972.

The Victorians and ancient Greece:

Jenkyns, R. *The Victorians and Ancient Greece*. Oxford: Blackwell, 1980.

Turner, F.M. *The Greek Heritage in Victorian Britain*. New Haven: Yale University Press, 1981.

Tourism and culture:

Bourdieu, Pierre. *Distinction: a Social Critique of the Judgement of Taste*. London: Routledge and Kegan Paul, 1984.

Horne, Donald. *The Great Museum: the Re-presentation of History*. London: Pluto Press, 1984.

Urry, John. *The Tourist Gaze*. London: Sage, 1991.

Hellenism:

Bernal, Martin. *Black Athena: The Afro-Asiatic Roots of Classical Civilisation. Volume 1: The Fabrication of Ancient Greece*. London: Free Association, 1987.

Bernal, Martin. *Black Athena: The Afro-Asiatic Roots of Classical Civilisation. Volume 2: The Archaeological and Documentary Evidence*. London: Free Association, 1991.

Kotsakis, Kostas. 'The powerful past: theoretical trends in Greek archaeology', in *Archaeological Theory in Europe: the Last Three Decades*, ed. Ian Hodder. London: Routledge, 1992.

Morris, Ian. 'Archaeologies of Greece', in *Classical Greece: Ancient Histories and Modern Archaeologies*, ed. Ian Morris. Cambridge: Cambridge University Press, 1994.

Trigger, Bruce. 'Alternative archaeologies: nationalist, colonialist, imperialist', *Man* 19 (1984): 355–70.

On the city of Athens:

Travlos, J. 'Athens after the Liberation: planning the new city and exploring the old', *Hesperia* 50 (1981): 391–407.

Anthropology and European origins:

Herzfeld, Michael. *Anthropology through the Looking Glass: Critical Ethnography in the Margins of Europe*. Cambridge: Cambridge University Press, 1987.

Rowlands, Mike. 'Repetition and exteriorisation in narratives of historical origins', *Critique of Anthropology* 8 (1989): 43–62.

Bernal and Orientalism:

'The challenge of "Black Athena"', *Arethusa (Special Issue)* (1989).

Said, Edward. *Orientalism*. London: Routledge and Kegan Paul, 1978. Reviews also in *Journal of Mediterranean Archaeology* 3 (1990).

4 SCHOLARSHIP AND DISCOURSE

On photography and the image:

Shanks, Michael. 'Photography and the archaeological image', in *Visual Archaeology and the Shape of Meaning*, ed. Brian Molyneaux. London: Routledge, 1995.

Histories of the discipline:

Donohue, A.A. 'One hundred years of the *American Journal of Archaeology*: an archival history', *American Journal of Archaeology* 89 (1985): 3–30.

Dyson, S.L. 'The role of ideology and institutions in shaping classical archaeology in the 19th and 20th centuries', in *Tracing Archaeology's Past: the Historiography of Archaeology*, ed. A.L. Christenson. Carbondale: University of Southern Illinois Press, 1989.

Morris, Ian. 'Archaeologies of Greece', in *Classical Greece: Ancient Histories and Modern Archaeologies*, ed. Ian Morris. Cambridge: Cambridge University Press, 1994.

Sheftel, P.S. 'The Archaeological Institute of America', *American Journal of Archaeology* 83 (1979): 3–17.

On Schliemann:

Calder, W.M. and D.A. Traill (eds). *Myth, Scandal and History: the H. Schliemann Controversy and a First Edition*. Detroit: Wayne State University Press, 1986.

Traill, David. *Schliemann of Troy: Treasure and Deceit*. London: John Murray, 1995.

Discourse:

Foucault, Michel. *The Archaeology of Knowledge*. London: Tavistock, 1972.

Foucault, Michel. 'The order of discourse', in *Untying the Text*, ed. R. Young. London: Routledge and Kegan Paul, 1981.

Latour, Bruno. *Science in Action: How to Follow Scientists and Engineers Through Society*. Milton Keynes: Open University Press, 1987.

Latour, Bruno. 'Clothing the naked truth', in *Dismantling Truth: Reality in the Postmodern World*, ed. Hilary Lawson and Lisa Appignanesi. New York: St Martin's Press, 1989.

Latour, Bruno. 'Drawing things together', in *Representation in Scientific Practice*, ed. Steve Woolgar and Michael Lynch. Cambridge, MA: MIT Press, 1990.

Macdonnell, D. *Theories of Discourse: an Introduction*. Oxford: Blackwell, 1986.

Tilley, Christopher. 'Michel Foucault: towards an archaeology of archaeology', in *Reading Material Culture: Structuralism, Hermeneutics and Poststructuralism*, ed. Christopher Tilley. Oxford: Blackwell, 1990.

Discourse analysis in archaeology:

Clarke, David. 'Archaeology: the loss of innocence', *Antiquity* 47 (1973): 6–18.

Hodder, Ian. 'Writing archaeology: site reports in context', *Antiquity* 62 (1989): 268–74.

Tilley, Christopher. 'Discourse and power: the genre of the Cambridge inaugural lecture', in *Domination and Resistance*, ed. Daniel Miller, Michael Rowlands and Christopher Tilley. London: Unwin Hyman, 1989.

Tilley, Christopher. 'On modernity and archaeological discourse', in *Archaeology after Structuralism*, ed. Ian Bapty and Timothy Yates. London: Routledge, 1990.

Rhetoric:
Gross, A.G. *The Rhetoric of Science.* Cambridge, MA: Harvard University Press, 1990.
Whately, R. *Elements of Rhetoric* (7th edn). London: Parker, Son and Bourn, 1863.
Winterowd, W.R. *Rhetoric: a Synthesis.* New York: Holt, Rinehart and Winston, 1968.

Postmodernity:
Bauman, Zygmunt. *Postmodern Ethics.* Oxford: Blackwell, 1993.
Harvey, David. *The Condition of Postmodernity.* Oxford: Blackwell, 1989.
Jameson, Fredric. *Postmodernism: or, the Cultural Logic of Late Capitalism.* London: Verso, 1990.
Lawson, Hilary and Lisa Appignanesi (eds). *Dismantling Truth: Reality in the Postmodern World.* New York: St Martin's Press, 1989.
Lyotard, J.-F. *The Postmodern Condition: a Report on Knowledge.* Minneapolis: University of Minnesota Press, 1984.

History and narrative:
Last, Jonathan. 'The nature of history', in *Interpreting Archaeology: Finding Meaning in the Past,* ed. Ian Hodder, Michael Shanks, Alexandra Alexandri, Victor Buchli, John Carman, Jonathan Last and Gavin Lucas. London: Routledge, 1995.
Ricoeur, Paul. *Time and Narrative: Three Volumes.* Translated by K. McLaughlin and D. Pellauer. Chicago: University of Chicago Press, 1984–8.
White, Hayden. *Metahistory.* Baltimore: Johns Hopkins University Press, 1973.
White, Hayden. *The Content of the Form: Narrative Discourse and Historical Representation.* Baltimore: Johns Hopkins University Press, 1987.

5 RUDIMENTS OF A SOCIAL ARCHAEOLOGY

Archaeological sources:
Snodgrass, Anthony. 'Archaeology', in *Sources for Ancient History,* ed. Michael Crawford. Cambridge: Cambridge University Press, 1983.
Snodgrass, Anthony. *An Archaeology of Greece: the Present State and Future Scope of a Discipline.* Berkeley: University of California Press, 1987.

The double hermeneutic:
Shanks, Michael and Christopher Tilley. *ReConstructing Archaeology: Theory and Practice* (2nd edn). London: Routledge, 1992.
Shanks, Michael and Ian Hodder. 'Interpreting archaeologies', in *Interpreting Archaeology: Finding Meaning in the Past,* ed. Ian Hodder, Michael Shanks, Alexandra Alexandri, Victor Buchli, John Carman, Jonathan Last and Gavin Lucas. London: Routledge, 1995.

Literary sources:
Donohue, A.A. *Xoana and the Origins of Greek Sculpture.* Atlanta: Scholars Press, 1988.
Thomas, Rosalind. *Oral Tradition and Written Record.* Cambridge: Cambridge University Press, 1991.
See also:
Dougherty, Carol. *The Poetics of Colonization: From City to Text in Archaic Greece.* Oxford: Oxford University Press, 1993.
McGlew, James F. *Tyranny and Political Culture in Ancient Greece.* Ithaca: Cornell University Press, 1993.

Social archaeology, Processual and Postprocessual:

Hodder, Ian. *Reading the Past: Current Approaches to Interpretation in Archaeology* (2nd edn). Cambridge: Cambridge University Press, 1991.

Renfrew, Colin and Steven Shennan (eds). *Ranking, Resource and Exchange.* Cambridge: Cambridge University Press, 1982.

Renfrew, Colin and Paul Bahn. *Archaeology: Theories, Methods, Practice.* London: Thames and Hudson, 1991.

Shanks, Michael and Christopher Tilley. *Social Theory and Archaeology.* Cambridge: Blackwell Polity, 1987.

Trigger, Bruce. *A History of Archaeological Thought.* Cambridge: Cambridge University Press, 1989.

Pottery in context:

Boardman, John. 'Symbol and story in Geometric art', in *Ancient Greek Art and Iconography*, ed. W.G. Moon. Madison: University of Wisconsin Press, 1983.

Coldstream, J.N. 'The meaning of the regional styles in the eighth century BC', in *The Greek Renaissance of the Eighth Century BC: Tradition and Innovation*, ed. R. Hägg. Stockholm: 1983.

Osborne, Robin. 'A crisis in archaeological history? The seventh century BC in Attica', *Annual of the British School at Athens* 84 (1989): 297–322.

Snodgrass, Anthony. 'Towards the interpretation of the Geometric figure scenes', *Mitteilungen des deutschen Archäologischen Instituts, Athenische Abteilung* 95 (1980): 51–8.

Snodgrass, Anthony. *An Archaeology of Greece: the Present State and Future Scope of a Discipline.* Berkeley: University of California Press, 1987.

The Snodgrass 'school':

Morgan, Cathy and Todd Whitelaw. 'Pots and politics: ceramic evidence for the rise of the Argive state', *American Journal of Archaeology* 95 (1991): 79–108.

Morris, Ian. *Burial and Ancient Society: the Rise of the Greek City State.* Cambridge: Cambridge University Press, 1987.

Snodgrass, Anthony. *Archaeology and the Rise of the Greek State. An Inaugural Lecture.* Cambridge: Cambridge University Press, 1977.

Snodgrass, Anthony. *Archaic Greece: the Age of Experiment.* London: Dent, 1980.

Whitley, James. *Style and Society in Dark Age Greece: the Changing Face of a Pre-literate Society.* Cambridge: Cambridge University Press, 1991.

A critique of Processual archaeology:

Hodder, Ian. 'Theoretical archaeology: a reactionary view', in *Symbolic and Structural Archaeology*, ed. Ian Hodder. Cambridge: Cambridge University Press, 1982.

Fuller: the essay on the Venus de Milo is in:

Fuller, Peter. *Art and Psychoanalysis.* London: Writers and Readers, 1980.

Some Postprocessual narratives:

Barrett, John. *Fragments from Antiquity: An Archaeology of Social Life in Britain, 2900–1200 BC.* Oxford: Blackwell, 1994.

Bradley, Richard. *Altering the Earth: The Origins of Monuments in Britain and Continental Europe.* Edinburgh: Society of Antiquaries of Scotland, 1993.

Hodder, Ian. *The Domestication of Europe.* Oxford: Blackwell, 1990.

Tilley, Christopher. *A Phenomenology of Landscape: Places, Paths and Monuments.* Oxford: Berg, 1994.

6 SOME TOPICS AND ISSUES

Chronology and time:

Biers, W. *Art, Artefacts and Chronology in Classical Archaeology.* London: Routledge, 1992.

Shanks, Michael and Christopher Tilley. *Social Theory and Archaeology.* Cambridge: Blackwell Polity, 1987.

Snodgrass, Anthony. 'Archaeology', in *Sources for Ancient History,* ed. Michael Crawford. Cambridge: Cambridge University Press, 1983.

Economics and trade:

Cook, R. 'Die Bedeutung der bemalten keramik für den griechischen Handel', *Jahrbuch des deutschen archäologischen Instituts* 74 (1959): 114–23.

Finley, Moses. *The Ancient Economy.* London: Chatto and Windus, 1973.

Garnsey, P., K. Hopkins and C.R. Whittaker (eds). *Trade in the Ancient Economy.* London: Chatto and Windus, 1983.

Humphreys, Sally C. *Anthropology and the Greeks.* London: Routledge and Kegan Paul, 1978.

Renfrew, Colin and Steven Shennan (eds). *Ranking, Resource and Exchange.* Cambridge: Cambridge University Press, 1982.

Peer polity interaction and world systems:

Arafat, Karim and Catherine Morgan. 'Athens, Etruria and the Heuneburg: mutual misconceptions in the study of Greek–barbarian relations', in *Classical Greece: Ancient Histories and Modern Archaeologies,* ed. Ian Morris. Cambridge: Cambridge University Press, 1994.

Champion, Tim (ed.) *Centre and Periphery: Comparative Studies in Archaeology.* London: Unwin Hyman, 1987.

Cunliffe, Barry. *Greeks, Romans and Barbarians: Spheres of Interaction.* London: Batsford, 1988.

Purcell, Nicholas. 'Mobility and the polis', in *The Greek City from Homer to Alexander,* ed. O. Murray and S. Price. Oxford: Clarendon Press, 1990.

Renfrew, Colin and John Cherry (eds). *Peer–Polity Interaction and Sociopolitical Change.* Cambridge: Cambridge University Press, 1986.

Rowlands, M., M. Larsen, and K. Kristiansen (eds). *Centre and Periphery in the Ancient World.* Cambridge: Cambridge University Press, 1987.

Sherratt, S. and A. Sherratt. 'The growth of the Mediterranean economy in the early first millennium BC', *World Archaeology* 24 (1993): 361–78.

Wallerstein, Immanuel. 'A world system perspective on the social sciences', *British Journal of Sociology* 27 (1976): 343–52.

Style and viewer-centred art histories:

Henderson, John. '*Timeo Danaos*: Amazons in early Greek art and pottery', in *Art and Text in Ancient Greek Culture,* ed. Simon Goldhill and Robin Osborne. Cambridge: Cambridge University Press, 1994. Other articles too in the same book.

Hoffmann, Herbert. '*Dulce et decorum est pro patria mori*: the imagery of heroic immortality on Athenian painted vases', in *Art and Text in Ancient Greek Culture,* ed. Simon Goldhill and Robin Osborne. Cambridge: Cambridge University Press, 1994.

Lissarague, François. *The Aesthetics of the Greek Banquet: Images of Wine and Ritual.* Translated by A. Szegedy-Maszak. Princeton, NJ: Princeton University Press, 1990.

Osborne, Robin. 'Looking on — Greek style. Does the sculpted girl speak to women too?', in *Classical Greece: Ancient Histories and Modern Archaeologies*, ed. Ian Morris. Cambridge: Cambridge University Press, 1994.

On the symposion see also:
Murray, Oswyn (ed.). *Sympotica: a Symposium on the Symposion.* Oxford: Clarendon Press, 1990.

Cemeteries:
Morris, I. *Death Ritual and Social Structure in Classical Antiquity.* Cambridge: Cambridge University Press, 1992.
Morris, Ian. 'Poetics of power: the interpretation of ritual action in Archaic Greece', in *Cultural Poetics in Archaic Greece: Cult, Performance, Politics*, ed. Carol Dougherty and Leslie Kurke. Cambridge: Cambridge University Press, 1993.

Space and survey:
Alcock, Susan E., John F. Cherry and Jack L. Davis. 'Intensive survey, agricultural practice and the classical landscape of Greece', in *Classical Greece: Ancient Histories and Modern Archaeologies*, ed. Ian Morris. Cambridge: Cambridge University Press, 1994. With full bibliography.
Alcock, Susan E. and Robin Osborne (eds). *Placing the Gods: Sanctuaries and Sacred Space in Ancient Greece.* Oxford: Clarendon Press, 1994.
de Polignac, F. *La Naissance de la Cité Grecque.* Paris: Editions La Découverte, 1984.

For a critique of metanarratives:
Fotiadis, Michael. 'Modernity and the past-still-present: politics of time in the birth of regional archaeological projects in Greece', *American Journal of Archaeology* 99 (1995): 59–78.

7 ARCHAEOLOGY, CLASSICS AND CONTEMPORARY CULTURE

Arrowsmith, William. 'Nietzsche on Classics and Classicists', *Arion* 2.1 (1963): 5–18, 2.2 (1963): 5–27.
Dean, Mitchell. *Critical and Effective Histories: Foucault's Methods and Historical Sociology.* London: Routledge, 1994.
Dover, K.J. *Greek Homosexuality.* London: Duckworth, 1978.
Foucault, Michel. 'Nietzsche, genealogy, history', in *The Foucault Reader*, ed. Paul Rabinow. Harmondsworth: Penguin, 1986.
Halperin, David. *One Hundred Years of Homosexuality.* London: Routledge, 1990.
Harrison, Tony. *The Gaze of the Gorgon.* Newcastle-upon-Tyne: Bloodaxe, 1992.
Nietzsche, Friedrich. *The Birth of Tragedy out of the Spirit of Music.* Translated by Shaun Whiteside. Harmondsworth: Penguin, 1993.
Nietzsche, Friedrich. *Twilight of the Idols and The Anti-Christ.* Translated by R.J. Hollingdale. Harmondsworth: Penguin, 1968.
Nietzsche, Friedrich. *Untimely Meditations.* Translated by R.J. Hollingdale. Cambridge: Cambridge University Press, 1983.
Taplin, Oliver. *Greek Fire.* London: Jonathan Cape, 1989.

Two archaeologists on Postmodernism:
Bintliff, John. 'Why Indiana Jones is smarter than the Postprocessualists', *Norwegian Archaeological Review* 26 (1993): 91–100.
Renfrew, Colin. 'Comments on "Archaeology into the 1990s"', *Norwegian Archaeological Review* 22 (1989): 33–41.

On heritage interests:

Shanks, Michael. *Experiencing the Past: On the Character of Archaeology.* London: Routledge, 1992.

Walsh, Kevin. *The Representation of the Past: Museums and Heritage in the Postmodern World.* London: Routledge, 1992.

INDEX

interests and desires (leading people to
the past) 1, 3, 4, 5, 7, 25, 48, 51,
72, 91, 92, 96, 97, 108, 119, 120,
123, 180, 181
interpretation 4, 16, 19–21, 38–9, 42,
43, 59, 92, 110–11, 117, 121,
123–6, 156, 178, 179; *see also*
interpretive archaeology,
hermeneutics

Jefferson, T. 56
Johansen, K.F. 22, 24, 41

Keats, J. 114
Klenze, L. 44, 46, 74, 79
Korinth 1, 3, 9, 11, 12, 14, 15, 17,
20–1, 50, 122, 133; Akrokorinthos
10, 11, 18, 20, 181; American
excavations 9, 14, 27, 47; archaic
Korinth 9–15, 19–20, 24, 25, 52;
Korinthian pottery and style 22–4,
25, 26, 30, 31–3, 35, 41, 97, 145,
146, 157, 159, 162, 172; 'Potters
Quarter' 9–10, 14, 27, 97
Kossinna, G. 90
Kotsakis, K. 79, 80, 81, 128
Kuhn, T. 103, 108; *see also* sociology
of knowledge

Las Vegas 12, 109
Leake, W.M. 20, 72, 165
Leighton, Lord 151
LeRoy, D. 69
Lévi-Strauss, C. 83
Lexicon Iconographicum Mythologiae
Classicae 42, 148
Lissarague, F. 163–4
Loos, A. 171
Lorrain, C. 72
Louis XIV 53
Ludwig of Bavaria 44, 58, 65, 72, 74, 79

Magna Graecia 13, 22, 24
Mani (Peloponnese), 16–17
Marxism 52, 149, 160, 165, 176
material culture studies and design 3,
5, 19, 89–90, 123–8, 129–32,
136–7, 138–54, 156, 158, 163–4
Mausoleum (Bodrum) 44–5
metanarratives 2, 7, 21, 58, 82–7,
89–91, 97, 104, 109, 117, 119, 123,
156, 162, 171, 178; *see also* ideology
and ideologies

modernism 106, 110–11, 158, 170–1
modernity 7, 17, 41, 78, 81, 108,
110–11, 170–1, 172
Montelius, O. 86
Montfaucon, B. 54, 71
Morelli, G. 37–8, 58, 64, 150
Morgan, C. 48–9, 138–40, 142, 144,
158, 161
Morris, I. 14–15, 36, 58, 81, 96, 97,
99, 108, 110, 111, 135–7, 142, 144,
154–5, 158, 165, 172
multiple pasts and pluralism 5, 7, 104,
111–16, 117, 121, 126, 152–3,
172–3, 176
museums, collecting and collections 7,
9, 12, 15, 17, 21, 25, 26, 43–4, 52,
53, 54, 59, 60, 64, 76, 94, 96, 121,
125, 150, 152
myth and legend 9, 19, 20, 21, 24,
26–7, 32, 42–3, 50, 88, 96, 101,
145, 163, 169–70

narrative, in art, archaeology and
history 1, 6, 24, 25, 30, 42, 52, 95,
96, 106, 116–17, 128, 144, 147,
179
nationalism 80, 81, 82–5, 87, 91, 117,
179
native American issue 5
neo-classicism 57, 58, 60, 66, 68,
73–5, 76, 79, 152, 170
Newton, C.T. 44–5, 99, 100
Nietzsche, F. 41, 173, 175–8
Norton, C.E. 64, 98

objectivity 5, 111–16, 119; *see also*
science and archaeology,
constructivism
Olympia 12, 14, 46–7, 49, 51, 74, 76,
95, 96, 101
orientalising design 9, 12, 19, 24–5,
27, 30, 86, 87, 88, 145, 146–7, 162
orientalism 85, 86–7
Otto of Bavaria 46, 79

Parthenon and its marbles, the 44, 46,
51, 55–6, 58, 65, 74, 79
Pauly-Wissowa 92
Pausanias 12, 49–50, 51, 72, 102
Payne, H. 12, 16, 24, 25, 30, 41
Peirce, C. 38
Pendlebury, J.D.S. 16
Penrose, F. 15